NEW PARADIGMS FOR
FINANCIAL REGULATION

New Paradigms for Financial Regulation

Emerging Market Perspectives

MASAHIRO KAWAI

ESWAR S. PRASAD

editors

ASIAN DEVELOPMENT BANK INSTITUTE
Tokyo

BROOKINGS INSTITUTION PRESS
Washington, D.C.

Library of Congress Cataloging-in-Publication data
New paradigms for financial regulation : emerging market perspectives / edited by Masahiro
Kawai and Eswar Prasad.
    p.   cm.
Includes bibliographical references and index.
ISBN 978-0-8157-2264-9 (pbk. : alk. paper)
 1. International finance—Government policy. 2. International finance—Law and legislation.
I. Kawai, Masahiro, 1947– II. Prasad, Eswar.
HG3881.N4135 2012
332'.042—dc23   2012038318

9 8 7 6 5 4 3 2 1

Printed on acid-free paper

Typeset in Adobe Garamond

Composition by Circle Graphics
Columbia, Maryland

Printed by R. R. Donnelley
Harrisonburg, Virginia

Contents

Preface

The global financial crisis has necessitated a sweeping re-evaluation of frameworks for financial market regulation and macroeconomic policies. Some progress has been made on strengthening these frameworks, both at the national and international levels, but there are still numerous challenges in developing an analytical framework to guide these changes in a manner that promotes financial stability.

A conference held at the Asian Development Bank Institute's headquarters in Tokyo, Japan, in October 2011 brought together leading academics as well as senior central banking officials on the frontlines of policymaking for an intensive discussion of these issues. This volume contains selected papers from the proceedings of that conference.

This book provides some refreshing new perspectives on the desired contours of financial sector and macroeconomic policies as well as the interactions between these policies. It also provides some practical ideas on how to resolve the apparent tensions between financial stability on the one hand and, on the other, development and broadening of access to the financial system.

This is a joint project of the Asian Development Bank Institute, the Brookings Institution, and Cornell University. We are grateful to Peter Morgan for managing this project and providing guidance at various stages. We also thank Quynh Tonnu for excellent administrative support and Janet Walker and Larry Converse for coordinating the editing and production of this book.

1

Introduction and Overview

MASAHIRO KAWAI AND ESWAR S. PRASAD

The global financial crisis has led to a sweeping reevaluation of frameworks for financial market regulation and macroeconomic policies. Some progress has been made on strengthening these frameworks, both at the national and international levels, but numerous challenges lie ahead in terms of developing an analytical framework to guide these changes in a manner that promotes financial stability. This book provides a stock-taking exercise for these issues and evaluates recent developments from an emerging markets perspective.

The main objective of this book is to develop analytical frameworks and policy prescriptions for emerging markets for balancing the goals of financial development and broader financial inclusion, with the imperative of strengthening macroeconomic and financial stability in these economies. The book starts with two chapters that provide an overview of the global regulatory landscape and discusses these from the perspective of Asian emerging markets. The next set of chapters discusses how to promote financial development and inclusion in these emerging markets in a manner that takes account of regulatory concerns and constraints. The third set of chapters evaluates different approaches to strengthening macroeconomic frameworks in a manner that promotes financial stability. Finally, the book turns to issues related to cross-border regulatory coordination, which are becoming increasingly important as financial institutions operate freely across national borders and as capital flows serve as a channel for the rapid international transmission of financial shocks.

Part I. The Evolving Global Regulatory Landscape: Implications for Emerging Markets

Chapter 2, by Viral Acharya, is titled "The Dodd-Frank Act and Basel III: Intentions, Unintended Consequences, and Lessons for Emerging Markets." This chapter attempts to explain the changes to financial sector reforms under the Dodd-Frank Act in the United States and Basel III requirements globally, their unintended consequences, and the risks to fast-growing nations such as India from the adjustment by the global financial sector to these changes. The chapter also provides some broader lessons for India concerning financial sector reforms, government involvement in the financial sector, possible macroprudential safeguards against spillover risks from the global economy, and finally, management of government debt and fiscal conditions.

Acharya argues that the Dodd-Frank Act has a number of shortcomings. These include lack of adequate attention to the distortive role played by government guarantees to the financial sector, an ill-conceived resolution authority that is likely to contribute to substantial uncertainty at the time of the next crisis, and inadequate regulation of shadow banking. Turning to Basel III, Acharya argues that, like its predecessors, it is fundamentally flawed as a way of designing macroprudential regulation of the financial sector. He argues that the Basel capital requirements employ static risk weights, fail to recognize that risk weights alter the incentives of the financial sector exposed to different asset classes, ignore correlated or concentrated exposures of the financial sector to apparently safe asset classes, and do not employ direct firm-level or asset-level leverage restrictions. He acknowledges that Dodd-Frank has several redeeming features, including requirements of stress-test-based macroprudential regulation and explicit investigation of systemic risk in designating some financial firms as systemically important.

Acharya contends that emerging markets like India should resist the call for a blind adherence to Basel III and persist with the approach adopted by the Reserve Bank of India, including asset-level leverage restrictions and a dynamic sector risk-weight adjustment approach. Indeed, these asset-level and dynamic approaches, which are popular in India and some other Asian countries, would be useful for the Basel Committee and other Western regulators to consider in future financial reforms. The author makes the case for the following financial sector reforms in India:

—Institute a fee for government guarantees to the banking sector (especially the explicitly guaranteed, state-owned sector).

—Undertake a fully macroprudential view of its financial sector regulation (covering not just banks but also shadow banks).

—Strive for a consensus among fast-growing emerging markets as well as in the G-20 for principles guiding systemic risk containment in the financial sector, which in turn can limit global spillover risks (such as the eurozone debt crisis).

—Manage the government debt level and fiscal deficit in a countercyclical manner, while also deepening credit and fixed-income markets.

The chapter by Yoshinori Shimizu, titled "Global Financial Regulations and the Asian Financial System: Lessons from the Financial Crisis," draws three lessons from the global financial crisis and proposes some directions for global regulatory reform. The three lessons identified in the chapter are as follows. First, the regulatory system that existed at the time of the crisis was hopelessly outdated, with weak capital requirements, lack of transparency, and an unregulated shadow banking system. Second, liquidity assurance is the key to avoiding financial crises. Adequate liquidity is difficult to measure using standard metrics, especially as the concept of adequacy hinges on the relative importance of different funding sources for the banking system, which is specific to each country. Third, global regulations will need more freedom and flexibility to deal with complex financial institutions that operate in different segments of the financial system and also across national borders.

The chapter notes that previous capital regulations created incentives for regulatory arbitrage that resulted in the financial crisis. The new regulations proposed under Basel III will not by themselves prevent a recurrence of financial crises. The chapter proposes the use of a "market-valued capital ratio" as a better measure of a bank's soundness, a ratio that should be carefully monitored by supervisory authorities. This ratio, which is easily observable, is given by the total market valuation of a bank divided by its total assets.

The chapter offers three proposals for regulatory improvements in the context of Asian emerging markets. These would achieve both financial stability and stable economic growth through regulations that reflect the unique characteristics of individual countries. The emphasis would be on macroprudential regulation and supervision suited to the circumstances of the financial markets of individual jurisdictions. Regulations should be reviewed and reassessed periodically to better address the procyclicality problem.

Part II. Promoting Financial Development and Inclusion

The next set of chapters focuses on the financial development agenda for Asian emerging markets and attempts to come to grips with the difficult balance between maintaining financial stability and allowing innovation and development in financial markets.

Cyn-Young Park's chapter, titled "The Asian Financial System: Development and Challenges," reviews the development agenda for Asian financial systems in the face of a rapidly changing global financial landscape in the aftermath of the financial crisis and the worldwide recession that ensued. The chapter goes on to explain the salient features of the region's financial sector developments, discusses the sector's challenges for balanced and inclusive growth in Asia, examines approaches to financial development for diversity and stability, and concludes with some policy implications.

The author contends that there are two important reform priorities across the Asian region that provide a framework within which financial sector policies need to be determined. The first is an overriding interest of economic growth and development in the context of financial stability. The second is the drive to create inclusive growth to support social stability and equity. The chapter argues that special attention needs to be paid to not only the balance between growth and stability but also the balance between financial innovation and regulation.

The author then makes the case that the experience of the global financial crisis underscores an unfinished financial sector reform agenda. Following the crisis, and the G-20 responses to it, significant reforms have been put in place aimed at building a stronger, more globally consistent, supervisory and regulatory framework for the financial sector. Despite the critical nature of these reforms for the future of the global financial landscape, their focus has been rather exclusively on strengthening global regulatory guidelines such as the Basel III standards, filling regulatory gaps, and broadening the regulatory perimeter.

There is an urgent need to establish effective and collaborative implementation mechanisms at the national level, reinforcing global efforts at revamping the financial architecture to avoid a repeat of the crisis. However, such reform efforts should not overlook the enormous development challenges faced by the region's low- and middle-income countries and the different conditions that they face in terms of financial sector and market development, regulatory capacity, availability and flow of information, and financial openness.

The chapter by Francisco Ceballos, Tatiana Didier, and Sergio L. Schmukler, titled "Financial Globalization in Emerging Countries: Diversification versus Offshoring," presents some basic stylized facts on where emerging economies, and Latin America in particular, stand on financial development. It documents the major trends since the early 1990s comparing Asia, Eastern Europe, and Latin America among themselves and with advanced countries and shows that the financial systems of emerging economies have become more complex and more diversified.

According to the author, domestic financial systems in emerging market economies are becoming less bank based, with equity and bond markets playing a more important role. Moreover, institutional investors are gaining ground in channeling domestic savings, thus increasing the availability of funds for investment in capital markets. Several emerging market economies have also started to reduce currency and maturity mismatches. Despite these developments, many emerging countries still lag behind the progress attained by advanced economies, and there is no convergence between the financial systems of these two groups of economies. Furthermore, in many emerging markets a few large financial institutions continue to capture most of the domestic savings. In the case of Latin America, despite the many efforts on reforming the macroeconomic and financial sectors, financial development has not taken place as fast as previously envisioned, trailing behind several emerging economies, most notably those in Asia. The expectation of a broad market-based financial system with dispersed ownership has yet to materialize.

Despite all the improvements, he argues that many emerging economies are financially still relatively underdeveloped. In fact, the countries that have developed the most in recent years are the advanced economies. Therefore, the gap between developed and developing economies regarding financial development has, if anything, widened. This disparity has increased in most parts of the financial system. As a result, the financial sectors of emerging economies are expected to continue to expand in the years to come. Eventually, emerging economies will need to catch up, develop their financial systems, and take more risk, in the process of becoming more like developed nations. The challenge is in doing so without undermining financial stability. Clarity about the rules that policymakers are adopting will help in this regard. Macroprudential policies that limit expansions constitute a clear example. It will be difficult to distinguish between potentially dangerous financial booms and innovation-fueled expansions in financial markets, for the same reasons that it has been difficult to spot bubbles in the financial systems of many developed countries.

Part III. Strengthening Macroeconomic Frameworks

The three chapters in this part, written by prominent central bank officials who have been at the front lines of both practical policymaking and intellectual discussions about central banking, review how emerging markets can make their macroeconomic frameworks more resilient to external shocks and provide a strong foundation for financial stability.

Subir Gokarn's chapter, titled "Strengthening Macroeconomic Frameworks: The Indian Experience," seeks to explain how developing countries in Asia as a whole proved to be quite resilient to the global economic slowdown in the wake of the recent financial crisis that started in the United States. The author illustrates his points using India as an example. He contends that the impact of the crisis on the Indian economy came mainly through three channels: trade, finance, and confidence, which in turn affected both the financial and the real sectors directly and indirectly, reflecting the interdependence and integration of the two sectors. The chapter notes the robust policy responses that kept India relatively protected from the aftershocks of the crisis.

The chapter goes on to discuss the emerging new consensus about monetary and regulatory frameworks, especially how monetary and financial stability policies can no longer be easily disentangled. The chapter discusses three areas in which a suitable balance will have to be struck. The first is financial stability versus innovation—how to maintain room for innovation and flexibility in financial markets without this threatening regulatory control and financial stability. The second is global versus domestic—how to strike a balance between policy responses to global and domestic shocks, which might sometimes call for different settings of policy instruments. The third is aggregate versus composite—how to adjust and calibrate different policies so that the right mix can be obtained—that for instance balances considerations of growth with price and financial stability. Getting the combination of monetary and fiscal policies right is another difficult but important challenge, particularly for an emerging market economy like India, with a high level of public debt and a monetary policy whose effectiveness is hindered by lack of fiscal discipline.

Kiyohiko G. Nishimura's chapter is titled "The Macroprudential Policy Framework from an Asian Perspective." This chapter takes up several key issues relating to macroeconomic policy frameworks, explicitly taking account of financial markets, or macroprudential policies, especially from an Asian perspective. It asks the following two questions: What methods should regulators and the central bank employ to detect an intolerable accumulation of risks in the financial system? And how should regulators maintain financial stability in the short run, while improving efficiency in credit intermediation functions to support long-term economic growth? The author seeks practical, best-practice answers to these questions, rather than optimum solutions based on a particular theory. One guiding principle is the need to effectively coordinate monetary and macroprudential policies. Another principle is ensuring that macroprudential policies don't create a false sense of security about the dangers posed by tail risks in the financial system.

Before attempting to answer some of these questions, the chapter reviews the evolution of the current financial crisis in the United States and Europe and of that in Japan two decades ago. Although much attention has been focused on financial excess as typified by excessive leveraging in financial institutions, the author emphasizes the importance of underlying changes in fundamentals, especially demographic factors such as population aging. The latter has particularly important implications for the future in Asia. The basic message of the chapter is that many of Asia's growing economies may face problems in the near future similar to those of developed countries, and it is thus of the utmost importance to implement appropriate macroprudential policies without delay.

Mehmet Yörükoğlu's chapter is titled "Emergence in the Postcrisis World: Widening Asymmetries between Advanced and Emerging Economies." According to the author, globalization, the rising openness of emerging market economies, and rapid technological changes will impact the global economic landscape even more strongly after the financial crisis. This has important effects and implications on macroeconomic policymaking in emerging economies. Increasing growth and inflation differentials between advanced and emerging economies under an environment of abundant liquidity and savings glut make inflation targeting insufficient to maintain price stability and financial stability together.

To achieve the job of maintaining price stability without accumulating financial instability risks, the inflation targeting framework should be supported by strong macroprudential and more disciplined fiscal policies. Many emerging economies, including Turkey, have started to use macroprudential tools more actively after the global financial crisis. This chapter discusses what macroeconomic policies are appropriate for emerging economies in the post-financial-crisis world, as globalization and emergence processes continue at an even faster pace, and offers some perspectives from the Turkish experience.

Part IV. Developing a Sound Global Regulatory Architecture

Rising financial integration through cross-border capital flows and banks that operate in multiple jurisdictions are creating new challenges for financial regulation and, ultimately, for financial stability. The two chapters in this part critically evaluate recent proposals for revamping the global regulatory architecture and offer some prescriptions for steps to cope with the challenges posed by rising financial globalization.

In a chapter titled "The Impact of Changes in the Global Financial Regulatory Landscape on Emerging Markets," Tarisa Watanagase notes that large and complex financial institutions have become increasingly prominent and global in their operations. A framework for cross-border resolution needs global cooperation and consistent legal frameworks. She warns of a potential moral hazard problem if the resolution plan is not credible and argues that these institutions should be reduced in size to better serve the real economy.

The chapter notes that the supervisory capacity and approach, not just regulation, also need improvement and that risk-focused supervision is more important than just regulation. The chapter also warns of the risk of moral hazard due to a bad incentive structure if remuneration in the financial sector remains linked to short-term profitability. It stresses the use of macroprudential tools for financial stability purposes, which also contributes to individual bank soundness and the reduction of systemic risk: loan-to-value ratio, sectoral risk weight, and credit card holder requirements.

Many new requirements under Basel III, such as capital buffers for concentration risk and liquidity risk, do indeed help promote stability but cannot by themselves ensure financial stability. The chapter argues for the need to strengthen regional safety nets in Asia, which could include increasing the size of the Chiang Mai Initiative, expediting the process for liquidity support, and developing the ASEAN+3 network, which would reduce the need for individual countries to accumulate reserves. The chapter concludes that it is important to ensure resilience by using the right mix of monetary policies, fiscal policies, and macroprudential measures to guard against financial imbalances and maintain policy space.

Duncan Alford's chapter is titled "International Financial Reforms: Capital Standards, Resolution Regimes, and Supervisory Colleges and Their Effect on Emerging Markets." Since the fall of 2008—when the G-20 met in Washington, D.C., at the beginning of the financial crisis—the heads of state of the G-20 have proposed a flurry of reforms to the international financial system. This chapter focuses on three proposed reforms: the improved capital requirements intended to reduce the risk of bank failure (Basel III), the improved recovery and resolution regimes for global banks, and the development of supervisory colleges of cross-border financial institutions to improve supervisory cooperation and convergence.

The chapter then addresses the implications of these regulatory reforms for Asian emerging markets, arguing that a new concordat between home and host countries with respect to crisis management is needed. Supplanting the Basel Concordat that focuses on home-host supervisory coordination, this new concordat would set standards allowing for the resolution of cross-border banks. Under the new concordat, financial institutions would be able to enter a market only if effective resolution arrangements existed in both the home and host countries.

The chapter concludes that an international regime for the orderly winding up of insolvent banks is a necessary component for truly effective international regulation and supervisory coordination. Without such a regime, policymakers are left with two stark choices: failure of the financial institution, with the resulting economic disruption; or using taxpayer funds to recapitalize the financial institution.

Conclusion

The major message of the volume can be summarized in the following way: Financial systems in emerging economies have developed and deepened over recent decades, but they still lag behind those of developed economies. In general, they have yet to reduce the presence of the state in financial markets (such as state-owned banks), create money markets that function well (including derivatives instruments), or diversify the modes of financial intermediation (for example by strengthening local-currency bond markets). Emerging economies need to encourage further financial opening and innovations to allow them to achieve convergence with developed economies. Thus, emerging economy financial systems can continue to develop and deepen so they resemble those in developed economies. At the same time, their policymakers need to enhance their financial market supervisory and regulatory capacity to avoid a buildup of financial imbalances—such as asset price bubbles—given that their economic growth will remain high and their financial sectors will expand rapidly.

Emerging economies must pursue a balancing act. They need to develop and deepen their financial sectors (which is vital for economic growth) while at the same time maintaining financial stability (which is needed to sustain growth and social stability). They must try to promote financial opening and innovations (which are needed for dynamic growth) and encourage financial inclusion (which is vital for inclusive growth) while improving policy and institutional frameworks to supervise and regulate financial systems in an increasingly market-based and globalizing environment.

In this context, the central bank of a country needs to balance the objectives of supporting growth, price stability, and financial stability. This is a considerable challenge particularly when it does not have macroprudential policy tools. In this case, the central bank needs to work closely with supervisory and regulatory authorities who are in charge of macroprudential policies, in order to achieve macroeconomic and financial stability.

Emerging economies often face additional challenges of maintaining fiscal and debt sustainability and managing international capital flows. In the short term, an appropriate mix of monetary, fiscal, macroprudential policies, and, to the extent necessary, capital flow management measures is needed to maintain stable growth and price and financial stability. In the longer term, structural reforms are needed to strengthen market infrastructure for financial systems and improve corporate governance of both banks and bank borrowers so as to make the financial market more resilient to domestic and external shocks.

Emerging economies can be victims of volatile behavior by global large complex financial institutions (LCFIs). The international community needs to develop an international agreement on supervisory and resolution frameworks for LCFIs. Clearly defined coordination between home and host supervisory authorities will help to protect the financial stability of emerging economies that could be adversely affected by the failures of LCFIs operating in their jurisdictions. An agreement on resolving the problems caused by failed LCFIs would benefit all the economies concerned, particularly emerging economies.

Finally, at the regional level, there is a strong case for greater financial cooperation to promote regional financial stability. For example, the ASEAN+3 framework in Asia for regional macroeconomic and financial surveillance and financial safety nets can be further strengthened.

PART I

The Evolving Global Regulatory Landscape: Implications for Emerging Markets

2

The Dodd-Frank Act and Basel III: Intentions, Unintended Consequences, and Lessons for Emerging Markets

VIRAL V. ACHARYA

This chapter is an attempt to explain the changes to financial sector reforms under the Dodd-Frank Act in the United States and, globally, under the Basel III requirements; their unintended consequences; and lessons for currently fast-growing emerging markets. The following are also addressed: government involvement in the financial sector, possible macroprudential safeguards against spillover risks from the global economy, and the management of government debt and fiscal conditions. I start with a summary of reforms under the Dodd-Frank Act and highlight four of its primary shortcomings:

—Lack of any attention to the distortive roles played by government guarantees to the financial sector;

—A somewhat ill-conceived resolution authority that will likely contribute to substantial uncertainty at the time of the next crisis;

—Regulating by form rather than function with the several restrictions imposed on the Federal Reserve's lender-of-last-resort role; and

—Not adequately dealing with shadow banking, especially with collections of individual small contracts and markets such as repurchase financing and money market funds that are, collectively, systemically important.

I then focus on the new capital and liquidity requirements under the Basel III reforms. I argue that Basel III, like its predecessors, is fundamentally flawed as a way of designing macroprudential regulation of the financial sector: Basel requirements employ *static* risk weights on asset classes and fail to capture any time variation in relative risks of assets; they fail to recognize that risk weights alter incentives of the financial sector to be exposed to different asset classes; they ignore as a result any correlated or concentrated exposure of the financial sector to an asset class that has looked historically stable; and they do not employ more direct firm-level or asset-level leverage restrictions.

In contrast, Dodd-Frank has several redeeming features, including requirements of stress-test-based, macroprudential regulation and explicit investigation of systemic risk in designating some financial firms as systemically important. These overall limitations and some benefits of Dodd-Frank and Basel III are also brought out in a "back to the future" exercise that asks what difference, if any, these reforms would have made had they been in place during 2003–08. I argue that India should resist the call for a blind adherence to Basel III and persist with the Reserve Bank of India's asset-level leverage restrictions and *dynamic* sector risk-weight-adjustment approach. Indeed, these asset-level and dynamic approaches, which are popular in India and some other Asian countries, are useful for the Basel Committee and other Western regulators to consider in future financial reforms.

I conclude with some important lessons for the regulation of the financial sector in emerging markets based on the crisis and on the proposed reforms:

—Charge for government guarantees to the banking sector (especially the explicitly guaranteed, state-owned sector) and plan for a graceful exit to obtain a level playing field in financial risk taking;

—Undertake a fully macroprudential view of a country's financial sector regulation (covering not just banks but also "shadow banks"), so that the perimeter of leverage restrictions retains its sanctity;

—Strive for a consensus among fast-growing emerging markets as well as among the G-20 for principles guiding systemic-risk containment in the financial sector, which in turn can limit global spillover risks (such as the eurozone debt crisis);

—Manage government debt capacity and fiscal deficits in a countercyclical manner (relative to risks to rest of the economy), while also creating a depth of institutions in credit and fixed-income markets to withstand economywide shocks and dampen the blow of equity market volatility induced by portfolio flows exposed to global risks.

Lead-Up to the Dodd-Frank Act

The Dodd-Frank Wall Street Reform and Consumer Protection Act of 2010, enacted by the Obama administration, is perhaps the most ambitious and far-reaching overhaul of financial regulation since the 1930s. The backdrop for the act is now well understood, but it is worth an encore.

When a large part of the financial sector is funded with fragile, short-term debt and is hit by a common shock to its long-term assets, there can be en masse failures of financial firms and disruption of intermediation to households and corporations. Being aware of such financial panics from the 1850s until the Great Depression, Senator Carter Glass and Representative Henry Steagall pushed through the so-called Glass-Steagall provisions of the Banking Act of 1933. They put in place the Federal Deposit Insurance Corporation (FDIC) to prevent retail bank runs and to provide an orderly resolution of troubled depository institutions—"banks"—before they failed. To guard against the risk that banks might speculate at the expense of the FDIC, they ring-fenced their permissible activities to commercial lending and trading in government bonds and general-obligation municipals, requiring the activities of the riskier capital markets to be spun off into investment banks.

At the time it was legislated, and for several decades thereafter, the Banking Act of 1933 reflected in some measure a sound economic approach to regulation. It would *identify market failure,* that is, why the collective outcome of individual economic agents and institutions does not lead to socially efficient outcomes, which in this case reflected the financial fragility induced by depositor runs. It would *address market failure through government intervention* by insuring retail depositors against losses. And it would *recognize and contain the direct costs of intervention, as well as the indirect costs due to moral hazard arising from the intervention,* by charging banks up-front premiums for deposit insurance. These three activities restricted banks from risky, cyclical investment. Through subsequent enhancements—requiring that troubled banks face a "prompt corrective action"—an orderly resolution would be achieved in an early stage of distress.

Over time, however, the banking industry nibbled at the perimeter of this regulatory design, the net effect of which was to keep the government guarantees in place but to largely do away with any defenses the system had against banks' exploiting the guarantees to undertake excessive risks. What was perhaps an even more ominous development was that the light-touch era of regulation of the financial sector starting in the 1970s allowed a parallel (shadow) banking system, consisting of money market funds, investment banks, derivatives and securitization markets, and so on, to evolve. The parallel banking sector that was both opaque and highly leveraged reflected regulatory arbitrage, that is, the opportunity and the propensity of the financial sector to adopt organizational forms and financial innovations that would circumvent the regulatory apparatus designed to contain bank risk taking. Over time, the Banking Act began to be largely compromised.

Fast forward to 2004, which many argue was the year when a perfect storm began to develop that would eventually snare the global economy. Global banks were seeking massive capital flows into the United States and the United Kingdom by engaging in short-term borrowing, increasingly through uninsured deposits and interbank liabilities, financed at historically low interest rates. They began to manufacture huge quantities of tail risk, that is, risk (even though small) of catastrophic outcomes. A leading example was the so-called safe assets (such as the relatively senior—AAA-rated—tranches of subprime-backed mortgages) that would fail only if there was a secular collapse in the housing markets. As the large and complex financial institutions (LCFIs) were willing to pick up loans from originating mortgage lenders and pass them around or hold them on their own books after repackaging them, a credit boom was fueled in these economies. As table 2-1 shows, 20 percent of U.S. mortgage-backed exposure was guaranteed by nonagencies, that is, by the private sector. However, unlike traditional securitization—in which the AAA tranches would get placed with the pension fund of the proverbial Norwegian village—these were to a significant extent originated *and* retained by banks, thrifts, and broker dealers (see AAA tranches, table 2-1).

The net result of all this was that the global banking balance sheet grew twofold between 2004 and 2007, but its risk appeared small. The LCFIs had, in effect, taken a highly undercapitalized one-way bet on the housing market, joined in equal measure by the U.S. government's own shadow banks—Fannie Mae and Freddie Mac—and by AIG, the world's largest insurer. While these institutions seemed individually safe, collectively they were vulnerable. And as the housing market crashed in 2007, the tail risk materialized, and the LCFIs crashed too, like a house of cards. The first big banks to fail were in the shadow-banking world. They were put on oxygen in the form of federal assistance, but the strains in the interbank markets and the inherently poor quality of the underlying housing bets, even in commercial bank portfolios, meant that when the oxygen ran out in the fall of 2008, some banks had to fail. A panic ensued internationally, making it clear that the entire global banking system was imperiled. The system needed a taxpayer-funded lifeline—and markets expected that this lifeline would be provided.

In the aftermath of this disaster, governments and regulators began to cast about for ways to prevent—or render less likely—its recurrence. The crisis created focus and led first to a bill in the House of Representatives, then one in the Senate, which were combined and distilled into the Dodd-Frank Act. The critical task for the act was to address the increasing propensity of the financial sector to put the entire system at risk and, eventually, to expect to be bailed out at the taxpayer's expense. Here are the highlights of the act:

—*Identifying and regulating systemic risk:* Sets up a council that can deem non-bank financial firms as systemically important, regulate them, and as a last resort, break them up; also establishes an office under the Department of the Treasury to collect, analyze, and disseminate relevant information for anticipating future crises.

—*Proposing an end to too big to fail:* Requires funeral plans and orderly liquidation procedures for unwinding systemically important institutions, ruling out taxpayer funding of wind-downs, and instead requiring that the management of failing institutions be dismissed, that wind-down costs be borne by shareholders and creditors, and if required, that ex post levies be imposed on other (surviving) large financial firms.

Table 2-1. *Distribution, U.S. Real-Estate Exposures, by Holder or Risk Bearer, 2004*

Holder or risk bearer	Loans	HELOC[a]	Agency MBS[b]	Nonagency			Total	Percent
				AAA tranches	CDO sub.[c]	Non-CDO sub.[c]		
Banks and thrifts	2,020	869	852	383	90	...	4,212	39
GSEs[d] and FHLB[e]	444	...	741	308	...	...	1,493	14
Brokers and dealers	...	...	49	100	130	24	303	3
Financial guarantors	...	62	...	...	100	...	162	2
Insurance companies	...	...	856	125	65	24	1,070	10
Overseas	...	...	689	413	45	24	1,172	11
Other	461	185	1,175	307	46	49	2,268	21
Total	2,925	1,116	4,362	1,636	476	121	10,680	...
Percent	27	10	41	15	4	1	...	...

Source: Lehman Brothers (2008).

a. Home equity line of credit.

b. Mortgage-backed security.

c. Collateralized debt obligation, subordinated.

d. Government-sponsored enterprise.

e. Federal home loan bank.

—*Expanding the responsibility and authority of the Federal Reserve:* Grants the Federal Reserve authority over all systemic institutions and the responsibility for preserving financial stability.

—*Restricting discretionary regulatory interventions:* Prevents or limits emergency federal assistance to individual nonbank institutions.

—*Reinstating a limited form of Glass-Steagall (the Volcker rule):* Limits bank holding companies to de minimis investments in proprietary trading activities, such as hedge funds and private equity, and prohibits them from bailing out these investments.

—*Regulation and transparency of derivatives:* Provides for central clearing of standardized derivatives, for the regulation of complex ones that can remain over the counter (that is, outside of central clearing platforms), for transparency of all derivatives, and for the separation of nonvanilla positions into well-capitalized subsidiaries, all with exceptions for derivatives used for commercial hedging.

In addition, the act introduces a range of reforms for mortgage lending practices, hedge fund disclosure, conflict resolution at rating agencies, skin-in-the-game requirement for securitization, risk taking by money market funds, and shareholder say on pay and governance. And perhaps its most popular reform, albeit tangential to the financial crisis, the act creates a Bureau of Consumer Financial Protection that will write rules governing consumer financial services and products offered by banks and nonbanks.

The Dodd-Frank Act: An Overall Assessment

The first reaction to the act is that it certainly has its heart in the right place. It is highly encouraging that the purpose of the new financial sector regulation is explicitly aimed at developing tools to deal with systemically important institutions. And it strives to give prudential regulators the authority and the tools to deal with this risk. Requiring funeral plans to unwind large, complex financial institutions should help demystify their organizational structures—and the attendant resolution challenges when they experience distress or fail. If the requirement is enforced well, it could serve as a "tax" on complexity, which seems to be another market failure, in that private gains from it far exceed the social ones.

In the same vein, even though the final language in the act is a highly diluted version of the original proposal, the Volcker rule limiting proprietary trading investments of LCFIs provides a more direct restriction on complexity and should help simplify their resolution. The Volcker rule also addresses a moral hazard, which is that direct guarantees to commercial banks are largely designed to safeguard payment and settlement systems and to ensure robust lending to households and corporations but that, through the bank holding company structure, they effectively lower the costs for more cyclical and riskier functions, such as making proprietary investments and running hedge funds or private equity funds, where there are thriving markets and a commercial banking presence is not critical.

Equally welcome is the highly comprehensive overhaul of derivatives markets aimed at removing the veil of opacity that has led markets to seize up when a large derivatives dealer experiences problems (Bear Stearns, for example). The push for greater transparency of prices, volumes, and exposures—to regulators and in aggregated form to the public—should enable markets to deal better with counterparty risk, in terms of pricing it into bilateral contracts as well as understanding its likely impact. The act also pushes for greater transparency by making systemic nonbank firms subject to tighter scrutiny by the Federal Reserve and the Securities and Exchange Commission (SEC).

However, the act requires over 225 new financial rules across eleven federal agencies. The attempt at regulatory consolidation has been minimal. In the end, the financial sector will have to live with unresolved uncertainty until various regulators (the Federal Reserve, the SEC, and the Commodity Futures Trading Commission) spell out the details of implementation.

Perhaps more important, from the standpoint of providing an economically sound and robust regulatory structure, are the act's weaknesses on at least four important counts, as I explain below. The net effect of these four basic faults is as follows: implicit government guarantees to the financial sector will persist in some pockets and escalate in others, and capital allocation may migrate in time to these pockets and newer ones that will develop in the future shadow-banking world and, potentially, sow seeds of the next significant crisis. The implementation of the act and future regulation may guard against this danger, but that is not certain.

Government Guarantees Remain Mispriced, Leading to Moral Hazard

In 1999 economists John Walter and John Weinberg, of the Federal Reserve Bank of Richmond, performed a study of how large the financial safety net was for U.S. financial institutions. Using fairly conservative criteria, they reported 45 percent of all liabilities ($8.4 trillion) received some form of guarantee. A decade later, the study was updated by Nadezhda Malysheva and John Walter, with staggering results: now, 58 percent of all liabilities ($25 trillion) was protected by a safety net. Without appropriate pricing, government guarantees are highly distortionary: they lead to subsidized financing of financial firms, moral hazard, and the loss of market discipline, which in turn generate excessive risk taking. Examples include FDIC insurance provided for depository institutions, implicit backing of government-sponsored enterprises (GSEs), such as Fannie Mae and Freddie Mac, and the much discussed too-big-to-fail mantra of the LCFIs.[1] The

---

1. The involvement of Fannie Mae and Freddie Mac is described in detail in Acharya and others (2011b).

financial crisis of 2007–09 exposed the depth of the problem with the failure of numerous banks and the need to replenish FDIC funds, the now-explicit guarantee of GSE debt, and the extensive bailouts of the LCFIs.

The Dodd-Frank Act makes little headway on the issue of government guarantees. While admittedly such guarantees have been a problem for many years, the act nonetheless makes little attempt to readdress the pricing of deposit insurance. And while the GSEs are the most glaring examples of systemically important financial firms whose risk choices went awry given their access to guaranteed debt, the act makes no attempt to reform them.[2] The distortion here is especially perverse, given the convenience of having them around to pursue such political objectives as boosting subprime homeownership and using them as "bad" banks to avoid another titanic collapse of housing markets. Finally, there are several large insurance firms in the United States that can—and did in the past—build leverage through minimum guarantees in standard insurance contracts. Were these to fail, there is little provision in the act to deal adequately with their policyholders. There are currently only tiny state-guaranteed funds, which would never suffice for resolving failure on the part of large insurance firms. Under the act, there would be no ex ante systemic risk charges on these firms, but it is highly unlikely that their policyholders will be wiped out or that the large banks will be made to pay for these policies (as the act proposes)! Taxpayer bailout of these policies is the more likely outcome. These institutions remain too big to fail and could be the centers of the next excess and crisis.

Of course, proponents of the act would argue that at least the issue of too big to fail has been dealt with once and for all through the creation of an orderly liquidation authority (OLA). But when one peels back the onion of the OLA, it is much less clear. Choosing an FDIC-based receivership model to unwind such large and complex firms creates much greater uncertainty than would a restructured bankruptcy code for LCFIs or the forced debt-to-equity conversions inherent in living wills. Time will tell whether the OLA is considered credible enough to impose losses on creditors (FDIC-insured depositors aside), but market prices of LCFI debt will be able to provide an immediate answer through a comparison of yield spreads with not-too-big-to-fail firms.

Individual Firms Are Not Sufficiently Discouraged from Putting the System at Risk

Since the failure of systemically important firms imposes costs beyond their own losses—to other financial firms, households, the real estate sector, and potentially other countries—it is not sufficient to simply wipe out their stakeholders: management, shareholders, and creditors. These firms must pay in advance for contributing to the risk of the system. Not only does the act rule this out, but

2. For the role played by the GSEs in the housing boom and bust in the United States, see Acharya and others (2011b).

it makes the problem worse by requiring that other large financial firms pay for the costs, precisely at a time when they likely face the risk of contagion from failing firms. This is simply poor economic design for addressing the problem of externalities.

It is somewhat surprising that the act shies away from adopting an ex ante charge for the systemic-risk contributions of LCFIs. And in fact it most likely compromises its ability to deal with their failures. It is highly incredible that, in the midst of a significant crisis, there will exist the political will to levy a discretionary charge on the surviving financial firms to recoup losses inflicted by the failed firms. It would, in fact, be better to reward the surviving firms from the standpoint of ex ante incentives and relax their financing constraints ex post to boost the flagging economic output in that scenario. Under the proposed scheme, therefore, the likely outcomes are that the financial sector will most likely not pay for its systemic-risk contributions—as happened in the aftermath of this crisis—and that to avoid any likelihood that they have to pay for others' mistakes and excesses, financial firms will herd together by correlating their lending and investment choices. Both of these would increase, not decrease, systemic risk and financial fragility.

Equally problematic, the argument can be made that the act actually increases systemic risk in a financial crisis. While it is certainly true that the Financial Stability Oversight Council of regulators has more authority to address a systemic crisis as it emerges, there is the implicit assumption that the council will have the wherewithal to proceed. Given the historical experience of regulatory failures, this seems like a tall order. In contrast, the act reduces the ability of the Federal Reserve to provide liquidity to nondepository institutions and, as mentioned above, provides no ex ante funding for solvent financial institutions hit by a significant event. The council will be so restricted that its only choice in a liquidity crisis may be to put systemically important firms through the OLA process, which, given the uncertainty about this process, could initiate a full-blown systemic crisis. Much greater clarity on exact procedures underlying the OLA would be necessary to avoid such an outcome.

The Act Falls into the Familiar Trap of Regulating by Form, Not Function

The most salient example of this trap is the act's overall focus on bank holding companies, after clarifying that nonbanks may be classified as systemically important institutions too—and be regulated accordingly. As explained, the act allows for provision of federal assistance to bank holding companies under certain conditions but restricts such assistance to other systemically important firms—in particular, large swap dealers. This will create a push for the acquisition of small depositories just as nonbanks anticipate trouble, undermining the intent of restriction. There are also important concentrations of systemic risk that will develop, for instance, as a centralized clearing of derivatives starts being implemented. And when their systemic risk materializes, employing the Federal Reserve's lender-of-last-resort function may be necessary, even if temporarily so, to ensure orderly resolution.

Consider a central clearinghouse of swaps (likely credit default swaps, to start with, but eventually several other swaps, including interest rate swaps). As Mark Twain would put it, it makes sense to put all your eggs in one basket and then "watch that basket." The act allows for prudential standards to watch such a basket. But if the basket were on the verge of a precipitous fall, an emergency reaction would be needed to save the eggs—in this case, the counterparties of the clearinghouse. Any restriction on emergency liquidity assistance from the Federal Reserve when a clearinghouse is in trouble will prove disastrous, as an orderly liquidation may take several weeks if not months. The most natural response in such cases is to provide temporary federal assistance, the eventual pass-through of the realized liquidation losses to participants in the clearinghouse, and its private recapitalization through capital contributions from participants. Why force intermediate liquidity assistance to go through a vote of the council and have the markets deal with discretionary regulatory uncertainty?

Large Parts of the Shadow-Banking Sector Remain in Current Form

The story of the financial crisis of 2007–09 is that financial institutions exploited loopholes in capital requirements and regulatory oversight to perform risky activities that were otherwise meant to be well capitalized and closely monitored. Examples are numerous. First, financial firms chose unqualified regulatory agencies to oversee them (for example, AIG's choice of the Office of Thrift Supervision for its financial products group). Second, so-called AAA-rated securities were loaded up in a regulatory setting ripe for conflicts of interest among rating agencies, security issuers, and investors. Third, a parallel banking sector was developed that used wholesale funding and over-the-counter (OTC) derivatives to conduct identical banking activities, as commercial banks were not yet subject to the same rules and regulations.

To be fair, the Dodd-Frank Act does not ignore all of this in its financial reform. For example, it makes major steps forward to deal with the regulatory reliance and conflict-of-interest problem with rating agencies, OTC derivatives are brought back into the fold, and leverage-enhancing tricks like off-balance-sheet financing are recognized as major issues. But the basic principle that similar financial activities—or for that matter, economically equivalent securities—should be subject to the same regulatory rules is not core to the act.

For example, several markets, such as sale and repurchase agreements that now constitute several trillion dollars of intermediation flows, have been shown to be systemically important. In what sense do these markets perform different functions than demand deposits? And why aren't they regulated as such? Moreover, these markets can experience a freeze if a few financial firms are perceived to be risky but their exact identity is unknown. An orderly resolution of a freeze and the prevention of fire-sale asset liquidations in these markets remains unplanned. The same can be said for the way the act deals with runs on money market funds, whose redemption risk following the collapse of Lehman brought finance to a standstill. That a collection, or herd, of small contracts and markets can be systemically important is essentially not recognized by the Dodd-Frank Act, as its focus is almost exclusively on the too-big-to-fail financial institutions.

Assessment Summary

In conclusion, while the Dodd-Frank Act does represent the culmination of several months of sincere effort on the part of the legislators, their staffers, the prudential regulators, academics, policy think tanks, and of course, the financial industry (and lobbyists!), it is important to recognize that the most ambitious overhaul of financial sector regulation in our times does not fully address the private incentives of individual institutions to put the system at risk, leaves a great deal of uncertainty as to how future crises will be resolved, and has been anachronistic right from the first day of its adoption.[3]

Basel III Requirements

In response to the systemic effect of the failure of the relatively small German bank Herstatt, in 1974, the central-bank governors of the G-10 established the Basel Committee on Banking Supervision. While having no statutory authority, the Basel Committee has emerged over the past thirty-five years as the go-to group to formulate international standards for banking supervision, and especially capital adequacy requirements. This thirty-five-year Basel process started with the 1988 Basel Accord (Basel I), which imposed the now infamous minimum ratio of capital to risk-weighted assets of 8 percent. The committee produced a revised framework in June 1999, which culminated in the implementation of the new capital adequacy framework in June 2004 (Basel II). Basel II expanded Basel I's capital requirement rules and introduced internal risk assessment processes. As a result of the financial crisis, the Basel Committee is at it again with proposals for new capital adequacy and liquidity requirements, denoted Basel III. In terms of specifics, before outlining the broad strokes of the Basel III agreement, it is helpful to briefly review the earlier accords, as Basel III works iteratively off these.

The purpose of the Basel accords is to provide a common risk-based assessment of bank assets and required capital levels. Basel I separated assets into

---

3. Not all is lost, though, and these limitations can be fixed in due course. See a possible road map for addressing these limitations in Acharya and others (2010b).

categories and gave risk weights ranging from 0 percent to 100 percent to each category. The risk-weighted assets are calculated by multiplying the sum of the assets in each category by these risk weights. Banks then should hold a minimum ratio of 8 percent of capital to risk-weighted assets.

Because the risk analysis of Basel I was quite crude, Basel II refined this by adding further gradations of risk categories; allowing for internal, and more sophisticated, risk models; and incorporating value at risk-based capital charges for trading books. Even with the apparent improvements of Basel II, LCFIs, armed with their too-big-to-fail funding advantage, easily exploited the conflicts of interest of rating agencies, played off external versus internal risk models, and minimized value at risk, though not systemic risk. Arguably, because the Basel II approach measured individual bank risk but ignored systemic risk (the primary rationale for bank regulation), and in addition did not address the fragility that was developing on the bank liability side in the form of uninsured wholesale deposit funding, the financial sector had a race to the bottom in risk taking and economic leverage and ended up in poor shape during the crisis.

Basel III recognizes that there are two types of risks that cause a financial firm to fail. These are solvency, or capital, risk—that is, the market value of the firm's assets falls below its obligations; and liquidity risk—that is, the firm cannot convert assets into cash to pay off its obligations because asset markets have become illiquid. Funding liquidity risk means that the firm is unable to roll over its maturing debt obligations with immediacy at some point in the future.

These risks can spread quickly through fire sales, counterparty risk, or contagious runs, and systemic risk can engulf the financial sector in no time. To the extent that Basel I and II focused almost exclusively on solvency risk, and little on the liquidity risk, Basel III constitutes an improvement. However, Basel III is disappointing in that it never makes an effort to identify when an institution's solvency risk or liquidity risk is likely to lead to systemic risk. By not differentiating so, it directly subsidizes those solvency and liquidity risks that contribute to systemwide risks versus those that do not.

In particular, while Basel III tries to correct some of these areas, the basic approach to regulation is essentially a follow-up to Basel II. Specifically, Basel III is stricter on what constitutes capital; introduces a minimum leverage ratio and, to be determined, higher capital requirements (possibly countercyclical in nature); it also creates liquidity ratios that banks will eventually have to abide by.

With respect to systemic risk—the real issue at hand—the July 2010 Basel Committee report states that the committee will "undertake further development of the 'guided discretion' approach as one possible mechanism for integrating the capital surcharge into the Financial Stability Board's initiative for addressing systemically important financial institutions." One would think systemic risk *should* be the primary focus of the regulatory guidelines, but somewhat surprisingly, even after the recent crisis, it is not.

Table 2-2. *Basel III Capital Adequacy Standards Risk-Weighted Assets,*
by Year of Effect
Percent

Capital adequacy standard	2013	2019
Minimum equity capital ratio (pure stock)	3.5	4.5
Minimum tier-1 capital (equity + other instruments, including some hybrid bonds)	4.5	6.0
Minimum total capital + new capital conservation buffer	8.0	10.5

Capital Requirements

The Basel III standards regarding capital endorsed by the Group of Twenty leading economies are summarized in table 2-2.[4] In particular, several hybrid instruments are eliminated as eligible forms of capital, and tier-3 capital is eliminated altogether, inducing a significant shift in bank liability structure, away from hybrid capital, whose growth (especially in Europe) was substantial in the pre-2007 period. In response to the severe criticism received by those using the risk-weighted approach, the standards put a floor under the buildup of leverage in the banking sector by requiring that the ratio of capital to (unweighted) assets be at least 3 percent. In addition, the plan is to introduce additional safeguards against model risk and measurement error by supplementing the risk-weighted assets measure with a simpler measure that is based on gross exposures.

In other—more specific but not fully spelled out—changes, the risk coverage of the capital framework will be strengthened by two requirements. One is to strengthen capital requirements for counterparty credit exposures arising from banks' derivatives, repossession, and securities financing transactions; to raise the capital buffers backing these exposures; to provide additional incentives to move OTC derivative contracts to central counterparties (probably clearing houses); and to provide incentives to strengthen the risk management of counterparty credit exposures. The second is to introduce measures to promote the buildup of capital buffers in good times that can be drawn upon in periods of stress.

These measures would have several goals: to dampen excess cyclicality of the minimum capital requirements, to promote forward-looking provisions, and to conserve capital to build buffers at individual banks and in the banking sector. They would have the broad macroprudential goal of protecting the banking sector from periods of excess credit growth, using long-term data horizons to estimate probabilities of default; downturn loss, given default estimates; improved calibration of the risk functions, which convert loss estimates into regulatory capital requirements; stress tests that include widening credit spreads in recessionary

4. For a full description of Basel III rules, see Saunders (2011).

scenarios; stronger provisioning practices; and accounting standards with an expected-loss approach.

Liquidity Requirements

As discussed before, financial distress arises not just from capital risk but also from liquidity risk. The financial crisis of 2007–09 shows that liquidity risk deserves equal footing. The problem arises because regulated institutions as well as their unregulated siblings have fragile capital structures in that they hold assets with aggregate risk and long-term duration or low liquidity but highly short-term liabilities. Arguably, the current crisis became a pandemic when there was a run on investment banks and money market funds after Lehman Brothers failed.

One solution is to impose liquidity requirements on financial institutions that are similar in spirit to the way capital requirements are imposed: that is, with the intention of reducing runs. The basic idea would be to require that a proportion of short-term funding must be in liquid assets—that is, assets that can be sold immediately in quantity at current prices. This requirement might be sufficient to prevent runs, as it will in effect increase the cost of financial institutions taking on carry trades and holding long-term, asset-backed securities.

The original December 2009 proposal in Basel III outlined two new ratios that financial institutions would be subject to—a liquidity coverage ratio (LCR) and a net stable funding ratio (NSFR). The LCR is the ratio of a bank's high-quality liquid assets (such as cash and government securities) to its net cash out-flows (such as retail deposits and wholesale funding) over a thirty-day period during a severe systemwide shock. This ratio should exceed 100 percent. The NSFR is the ratio of the bank's available amount of stable funding (its capital, longer term liabilities, and stable short-term deposits) over its required amount of stable funding (value of assets held multiplied by a factor representing the asset's liquidity). This ratio should exceed 100 percent.

The introduction of the LCR and the NSFR as prudential standards has merit. Consider the example of the super senior AAA-rated tranches of collateralized debt obligations relative to a more standard AAA-rated marketable security (say, a corporate bond). Specifically, assume that the probability and magnitude of losses (the expected mean and variance) associated with default are similar between the two classes of securities. What are the implications of an LCR and an NSFR on these holdings?

Liquidity risk refers to the ability of the holder to convert the security or asset into cash. Even before the crisis started, the super senior tranches were considered to be less liquid than standard marketable securities and more of a hold-to-maturity type of security. The fact that these securities offered a spread should not be surprising, given that there are numerous documentations of a price to illiquidity. For instance, consider the well-documented spread between off-the-run and on-the-run U.S. Treasuries. The LCR would most likely count the AAA-rated collateralized debt obligation (CDO) less favorably in terms of satisfying liquidity risk.

Funding risk refers to the mismatch in the maturities of assets and liabilities. There is a tendency for financial institutions to hold long-term assets using cheap short-term funding, a kind of carry trade. But this exposes the institution to greater risk of a run if short-term funding evaporates during a crisis. These two points suggest that it would be useful to know the liquid assets that the financial institution holds against short-term funding. One could imagine that the higher the ratio, the less an institution is subject to a liquidity shock, and therefore the less risky it is. The NSFR would help answer this question—and again would be less favorable for the AAA-rated CDO versus the AAA-rated marketable security.

Basel Capital Requirements: An Assessment

From a conceptual standpoint, the Basel capital requirements are a flawed macro-prudential tool. Here's why. First and foremost, a macroprudential tool should be concerned with—and attempt to address—the systemic-risk contributions of financial firms. Basel requirements, for the most part, are focused instead on the individual risk of financial firms.

Second, the very act of reducing the individual risk of financial firms can, in principle, aggravate systemic risk. For instance, if institutions cannot diversify perfectly but are encouraged to do so at all costs, then they can all be left holding the same aggregate risk as they diversify away all idiosyncratic risk. If the costs to bank failures are nonlinearly increasing in the number of failures, then diversification could in fact be welfare reducing in this form. A good analogy to this general point is banks with AAA-rated tranches to hold a diversified bet on the housing market, since such a diversified bet was rewarded by Basel requirements in terms of capital regulations relative to holding the underlying mortgages on banking books.

Third, even if one ignored the possibility of individual financial firms becoming more correlated as they reduce their own risks, Basel requirements ignore the *endogenous* or *dynamic* evolution of risks of the underlying assets. Consider again the case of AAA-backed residential mortgage-backed securities. By providing a relative advantage to this asset class, the Basel requirements explicitly encouraged greater lending in the aggregate to residential mortgages. As banks lent down the quality curve, they made worse mortgages (for example, in terms of loan-to-value ratios). Hence, even though the residential mortgage as an asset class had historically been stable, a static risk weight that favored this asset class made it endogenously riskier.

Finally, just as Basel requirements ignore that they increase correlated investments and endogenously produce deteriorating asset quality on a risk-favored asset class, they also ignore that, when the risk of this asset class materializes (since the financial firms are overleveraged in this asset class and in a correlated manner), they face endogenous liquidity risk. For instance, as each financial firm attempts to deleverage by selling its AAA mortgage-backed securities, so is every other financial firm attempting the same thing, implying that there is not enough capital in the system to deal with the deleveraging. In this way, systemic risk is created not only ex ante but also ex post. Thus Basel requirements induce pro-cyclicality over and above the fact that risks are inherently procyclical.

In economic parlance, the Basel risk-weights approach is an attempt to target relative prices for lending and investments by banks, rather than an approach that restricts quantities or asset risks directly. Regulators—in the absence of the price discovery provided by day-to-day markets—can have little hope of achieving relative price efficiency that is sufficiently dynamic and reflective of underlying risks and their changing natures. In contrast, concentration limits on asset-class exposure for the economy as a whole, or simple leverage restrictions (assets to equity of each financial firm not greater than 15:1, for instance), or an asset risk restriction (the loan to value ratio of mortgages not to exceed 80 percent, for instance), are more likely to be robust and countercyclical macroprudential tools. They do not directly address systemic risk, but at least they offer the hope of limiting risks of individual financial firms and asset classes.

To understand what went wrong from a *regulatory* capital point of view in the pre-2007 period, note that the LCFIs took their leveraged bets using regulatory arbitrage tricks as a direct result of Basel I and II.[5] First, they funded portfolios of risky loans via off-balance-sheet vehicles (conduits and structured investment vehicles). These loans, however, were guaranteed by sponsoring LCFIs through liquidity enhancements that had a lower capital requirement by Basel; so the loans were effectively recourse but had a lower capital charge, even though the credit risk never left the sponsoring LCFIs. Second, they made outright purchases of AAA tranches of nonprime securities, which were treated as having low credit risk and zero liquidity and funding risk. Third, they enjoyed full capital relief on AAA tranches if they bought "underpriced" protection on securitized products from monolines and AIG (both of which were not subject to similar prudential standards). Fourth, in August 2004 investment banks successfully lobbied the SEC to amend the net capital rule of the Securities Exchange Act of 1934, which effectively allowed for leverage to increase in return for greater supervision. This lobbying was in direct response to the internal risk-management rules of Basel II.

The net effect of such arbitraging by financial firms of Basel's capital requirements was that global banking balance sheets doubled from 2004 to 2007 with only a minor increase in Basel-implied risk.[6] This fact alone should have been a red flag to regulators. When one combines this fact with the growth in short-term shadow-banking liabilities from $10 trillion to $20 trillion between 2000 and 2007 (compared to $5.5 trillion to $11 trillion in traditional bank liabilities),

---

5. See the discussion in Acharya, Schnabl, and Suarez (forthcoming).
6. International Monetary Fund (2008), box 1.3, p. 31.

it is clear in hindsight that the focus of Basel capital requirements over the prior thirty years has been misplaced.

In fact, financial firms that had the best regulatory capital ratios (effectively, due to substantial regulatory arbitrage) fared the worst in terms of market-capitalization declines during the crisis.[7] In other words, their high regulatory capital ratios (such as low unweighted assets to risk-weighted assets ratios), were not a sign of their financial stability but were, ironically, a sign of their propensity to hold onto systemically risky assets with maximum economic leverage (such as by holding AAA-rated residential mortgage-backed securities that had little Basel capital charge).

Somewhat surprisingly, rather than the Basel Committee providing a mea culpa, its response has been to offer a new set of rules and guidelines that, in many ways, mirror the previous two attempts. While the Basel III process focuses on using more stringent capital requirements to get around some of these issues, it ignores the crucial market and regulatory failures of the financial system:

—While recognizing the systemic risk of financial firms, the Basel approach very much remains focused on the risk of the individual institution and not on the system as a whole. In other words, the level of a firm's capital requirements in Basel I, II, and III does not depend on its interaction with other financial firms.

—Whatever capital or liquidity requirements are placed on one set of financial institutions—say banks and bank holding companies—it is highly likely that the financial activities affected by these requirements will just move elsewhere in the shadow-banking system. That is, without the understanding that the whole financial system must be looked at and treated in unison, Basel III will run into the same shadow-banking issues that arose with Basel I and II.

—There seems to be no recognition of the role government guarantees play in the allocation of capital. Ceteris paribus, the more guarantees a firm receives, the lower its costs of debt funding. This artificially increases the relative cost of nonguaranteed funding like equity, preferred stock, and possibly subordinated debt (under a credible resolution authority).

Also problematic is that the Basel process sticks with tired old definitions of capital and leverage not entirely suitable for modern-day financial firms and for reducing excessive systemic risk. At the time they were designed, the primary purpose of the Basel capital requirements was to guard the retail deposit base of commercial banks from unexpected losses on their loan portfolios. While Basel II made improvements over Basel I by addressing OTC derivative positions, and Basel III tightened the treatment of off-balance-sheet financing, the focus is still not on the measurement of quantities that actually reflect systemic risk, such as the change in the value of the financial firm's assets given a macroeconomy-wide shock and the impact such a shock has on its liability and funding structure.

7. International Monetary Fund (2008), figure 21.17, p. 19.

That liquidity risk is now at the forefront of Basel III, and presumably future financial regulation in the United States as a result of the Dodd-Frank Act, is clearly a step forward. The LCR and NSFR liquidity adequacy standards are reasonable approaches toward the regulation of liquidity risk. For example, the focus of the LCR on a systemwide stress scenario is the appropriate way to think about the systemic consequences of holding fewer liquid assets or funding those assets with short-term liabilities.

That said, the approach is eerily similar to that of Basel I and II for setting capital requirements. All the adjustment factors and weights used in calculating the LCR and the NSFR have their counterpart in the risk weights of capital ratios. Without a doubt, implementation of the liquidity ratios will push banks toward regulatory arbitrage of the liquidity weights and in particular to the *best-treated* illiquid securities and systemically risky funding. Of course, the unintended consequence will be a concentration into these activities. Regulators should be acutely aware of this problem and be prepared ex ante to adapt in an expedited way.

The other problem is that the liquidity rules do not seem to take into account the impact a liquidity problem at one bank has on the financial sector as a whole, especially in a crisis. In other words, banks that contribute more to systemwide liquidity events (in a crisis) should be charged for this negative externality.

Further, regulators need to be aware that once the LCR and the NSFR are imposed on a subset of financial institutions, then these activities will migrate to a part of the financial sector not subject to these requirements. Regulators need to look at the financial system in the aggregate.

Finally, a significantly problematic issue with Basel III's specific implementation of liquidity risk management is whether the risk weights on government bonds are suitably calibrated for the emerging sovereign credit risk in eurozone countries, which implies that many securities that would traditionally have been both liquid and safe are now liquid (due to central bank collateral qualification) but significantly credit risky.

Contrast of Basel III with the Dodd-Frank Act

Consider the contrast between Basel III and the Dodd-Frank Act. As part of the broad mandate given to regulators, the Dodd-Frank Act calls for stricter prudential standards for systemically important institutions. Moreover, these standards should be increasing in stringency based on factors such as leverage, off-balance-sheet exposures, amount of short-term funding, interconnectedness, and so on. These additional standards may include

—risk-based capital requirements
—leverage limits
—liquidity requirements
—credit exposure reporting requirements and a resolution plan

—concentration limits

—a contingent capital requirement

—enhanced public disclosures

—short-term debt limits

—overall risk-management requirements.

Of these nine recommendations for stricter regulation, note that five include additional capital, contingent capital, or liquidity requirements.[8] The basic idea is that, to the extent these stricter standards impose costs on financial firms, these firms will have an incentive to avoid them and therefore be less systemically risky. While the underlying premise is promising from purely a systemic-risk viewpoint, our concern is that these standards may not be sufficient to get financial firms to internalize the costs of the systemic risk produced. *The glaring omission is any direct reference to the comovement of an individual firm's assets with the aggregate financial sector in a crisis.*

Also, like Basel III, Dodd-Frank provides for an explicit minimum leverage ratio (capital over total assets) along with minimum capital ratios—(capital over risk-weighted assets). Specifically, the Dodd-Frank Act states that

> The appropriate Federal banking agencies shall establish minimum leverage (and risk-based) capital requirements on a consolidated basis for insured depository institutions, depository institution holding companies, and nonbank financial companies supervised by the Board of Governors. The minimum leverage (and risk-based) capital requirements established under this paragraph shall not be less than the generally applicable leverage (and risk-based) capital requirements, which shall serve as a floor for any capital requirements that the agency may require, nor quantitatively lower than the generally applicable leverage (and risk-based) capital requirements that were in effect for insured depository institutions as of the date of enactment of this Act.

In other words, the risk-based capital and leverage capital ratios applicable to FDIC-insured depository institutions will be applied to bank holding companies and systemically important institutions. Since these ratios represent a minimum standard, other regulatory guidelines, such as Basel III, could still be viable as long as their rules were stricter. Table 2-3 provides the current ratios for depository institutions. Of some note, these requirements are to be enacted within eighteen months, though small institutions are generally exempt. Also important is the case in which, to the extent a financial institution is deemed systemically important, the Federal Reserve may exempt that institution if the capital and leverage requirements are not appropriate.

While the definitions of capital in the Dodd-Frank Act and Basel III do not perfectly coincide (so the comparison is not perfect), the proposed leverage ratio

8. See Acharya, Kulkarni, and Richardson (2010).

Table 2-3. *Capital Adequacy Standards, Dodd-Frank Act*
Percent

	Well capitalized	Adequately capitalized
Tier 1 (risk-based capital ratio)	6	4
Total (risk-based capital ratio)	10	8
Leverage ratio	5	4

in Basel III is actually 3 percent lower. The Dodd-Frank Act goes further still by requiring that bank holding companies with at least $50 billion in assets or systemically important institutions "maintain a debt-to-equity ratio of no more than 15 to 1 (or a leverage ratio of at least 6.5%), upon a determination by the Council that such company poses a grave threat to the financial stability of the United States and that the imposition of such requirement is necessary to mitigate the risk that such company poses to the financial stability of the United States."[9]

Along with the possible recommendation for more stringent capital requirements for systemically important financial institutions, the act explicitly calls for additional capital requirements for depository institutions, bank holding companies, and systemically important nonbank financial companies that address systemic risk arising from the following:

(i) significant volumes of activity in derivatives, securitized products purchased and sold, financial guarantees purchased and sold, securities borrowing and lending, and repurchase agreements and reverse repurchase agreements; (ii) concentrations in assets for which the values presented in financial reports are based on models rather than historical cost or prices deriving from deep and liquid two-way markets; and (iii) concentrations in market share for any activity that would substantially disrupt financial markets if the institution is forced to unexpectedly cease the activity.[10]

Further, and much unlike Basel III, Dodd-Frank recognizes that the systemic risk of assets and balance sheets can vary over time, due both to a change in the underlying risk of assets and to collective shifts in the risk choices of financial firms. A possible approach to dynamically adjust to such variations is to periodically project losses of the financial sector into infrequent but plausible future scenarios, to assess whether the financial sector has the capital to be able to withstand these losses, and in case of capital shortfalls, to decide on an early recapitalization plan. In order to be able to project into infrequent future scenarios, such scenarios need to be modeled and considered in the first place. An attractive

9. HR 4173, Title I, Subtitle C, Sec. 165, "Enhanced supervision and prudential standards for nonbank financial companies supervised by the Board of Governors and certain bank holding companies."
10. HR 4173, Title I, Subtitle C, Sec. 171.

way of dealing with such projection is to conduct stress tests along the lines of the Supervisory Capital Assessment Program (SCAP) exercise conducted by the Federal Reserve in 2009 for bank recapitalization, in 2010–11 for determining which banks could resume dividend payouts, and in 2012 (currently under way) for assessing bank solvency as it relates to the U.S. stock market, housing market, and unemployment rate. To report the objectives and findings of the first of these stress tests, I quote from the SCAP report:

> From the macro-prudential perspective, the SCAP was a top-down analysis of the largest bank holding companies (BHCs), representing a majority of the U.S. banking system, with an explicit goal to facilitate aggregate lending. The SCAP applied a common, probabilistic scenario analysis for all participating BHCs and looked beyond the traditional accounting-based measures to determine the needed capital buffer. The macro-prudential goal was to credibly reduce the probability of the tail outcome, but the analysis began at the micro-prudential level with detailed and idiosyncratic data on the risks and exposures of each participating BHC. This firm-specific, granular data allowed tailored analysis that led to differentiation and BHC-specific policy actions, e.g., a positive identified SCAP buffer for 10 BHCs and no need for a buffer for the remaining nine.[11]

The Dodd-Frank Act calls for systemic institutions to be subject to periodic stress tests: "The Board of Governors, in coordination with the appropriate primary financial regulatory agencies and the Federal Insurance Office, shall conduct annual analyses in which nonbank financial companies supervised by the Board of Governors and bank holding companies described in subsection (a) are subject to evaluation of whether such companies have the capital, on a total consolidated basis, necessary to absorb losses as a result of adverse economic conditions."[12]

Moreover, systemically important financial institutions are required to perform semiannual tests. Such assessments should be done more frequently in a crisis and may complement the firm's own test. The exercise of SCAP 2009 resulted in valuable knowledge and experience, and this could be built upon by the regulators in the United States. The recent decision to determine whether bank holding companies should resume dividend payouts, and by how much, was done based on a stress test (though the transparency of this stress test in 2011 was lower than that of SCAP in 2009). Bank of America was one bank holding company that was not allowed to resume its dividends, whereas most others were.

---

11. See the Federal Reserve Bank of New York report on the SCAP exercise (Hirtle, Schuermann, and Stiroh 2009).

12. HR 4173, Title I, Subtitle C, "Additional Board of Governors Authority for Certain Nonbank Financial Companies and Bank Holding Companies," Sec. 165, "Enhanced supervision and prudential standards for nonbank financial companies supervised by the Board of Governors and certain bank holding companies."

One specific, and generally sensible, rule that appears in both the Dodd-Frank Act and Basel III is that "In establishing capital regulations . . . the Board shall seek to make such requirements countercyclical, so that the amount of capital required to be maintained by a company increases in times of economic expansion and decreases in times of economic contraction, consistent with the safety and soundness of the company."[13] While Basel III is currently short on specifics, it is clear that countercyclical capital adequacy standards will be a key component of both Dodd-Frank and Basel III.

One way of implementing countercyclical regulation is to ensure that financial firms are well capitalized against their losses in stress tests, where stress scenario severity is not adjusted to be moderate even in good times or booms. Another way—and what is appearing to be the proposed Basel III approach—is to expand (or shrink) the size of the capital conservation buffer in each economy if there is a positive (or negative) deviation of the credit-to-GDP ratio with respect to certain prespecified thresholds, such as its trend. (In addition, other macroeconomic variables or groups of variables are also candidates "to assess the extent to which in any given jurisdiction there was a significant risk that credit had grown to excessive levels.") While research is being conducted to determine if these are sensible ideas, emerging evidence suggests that tying capital requirements to GDP growth rather than to credit-to-GDP deviations from trend produces more countercyclical capital buffers.

On liquidity requirements, while the Dodd-Frank Act explicitly calls for the regulator to take into account "the amount and types of the liabilities of the company, including the degree of reliance on short-term funding" in setting prudential standards for systemically important institutions, and for these standards to include "liquidity requirements" and "short-term debt limits," there are no other specifics. These are left to the Federal Reserve and other regulators. It is reasonable to infer, however, that U.S. regulators will look to the new liquidity requirements as part of Basel III.

Overall, the details of Dodd-Frank implementation are, perhaps rightly so, left to the regulators. While the act's recommendations will be implemented later by the Federal Reserve, it is clear that bank holding companies with more than $50 billion in assets, or systemically important nonbank financial companies (as designated by the Financial Stability Oversight Council), will be subject to these additional, yet unknown, capital and liquidity adequacy standards.

That said, it does seem to be the case that some significant improvements can be made possible by closing major capital loopholes and relying less on rating agencies. With respect to the loopholes, a good rule of thumb is that if off-balance-sheet financing is effectively a recourse for the banks, then the capital

13. HR 4173, Title VI, "Improvements to Regulation of Bank and Savings Association Holding Companies and Depository Institutions," Sec. 616, "Regulations Regarding Capital Levels."

at risk should be treated as such. Moreover, counterparty credit risk exposures to financial firms, including OTC derivatives and securities financing transactions, should also be taken into account. While Basel II did expand the notion of risk for financial institutions, in hindsight the accord chose simplicity over accuracy in the determination of how capital should be treated. As for the reliance on ratings, it seems reasonable to consider not only the credit risk of defaultable assets (as defined by rating agencies) but also liquidity (funding and market) and specification risks.

The Dodd-Frank Act does make considerable progress on these fronts:

—Addressing the conflict of interest inherent in the rating agency business model and the government's regulatory reliance on ratings.[14]

—Including off-balance-sheet activities in computing capital requirements.[15]

—With respect to derivatives, requiring margins that are centrally cleared or over the counter, reporting to data repositories with real-time price-volume transparency, and providing authority for prudential regulators to consider setting position limits and penalizing engagement in derivatives whose purpose is "evasive."[16]

On balance, the Dodd-Frank Act leaves open greater possibilities for the regulators to address systemic risk through capital requirements—for instance, by identifying systemically important financial institutions (SIFIs) and by undertaking periodic stress tests to ensure that these institutions are well capitalized in aggregate stress scenarios.

On November 4, 2011, the Bank for International Settlements and the Financial Stability Board released a list of global SIFIs (G-SIFIs), consisting of twenty-nine institutions: eight are headquartered in the United States (Bank of America, JPMorgan Chase, Citigroup, Wells Fargo, Goldman Sachs, Morgan Stanley, Bank of New York Mellon, State Street); four in the UK (HSBC Holdings, Barclays, Lloyd's Banking Group, and Royal Bank of Scotland); four in France (BNP Paribas, Crédit Agricole, Société Générale, and Banque Populaire); three in Japan (Mitsubishi UFJ Financial Group, Mizuho Financial Group, Sumitomo Mitsui Financial Group); two in Germany (Deutsche Bank AG, Commerzbank AG); two in Switzerland (UBS AG, Credit Suisse AG); and one each in Peoples's

14. HR 4173, title 9, "Investor Protection and Improvements to the Regulation of Securities," subtitle C, "Improvements to the Regulation of Credit Rating Agencies."

15. HR 4173, title 1, subtitle C, "Additional Board of Governors Authority for Certain Nonbank Financial Companies and Bank Holding Companies," sec. 165, "Enhanced Supervision and Prudential Standards for Nonbank Financial Companies Supervised by the Board of Governors and Certain Bank Holding Companies."

16. Missing from the Dodd-Frank Act, however, is any recognition (except in the case of OTC derivatives) that, once these standards are imposed on one set of financial institutions, financial activity most likely will move elsewhere in the financial system to firms not subject to these standards. Of course, this reallocation would not be a problem if the systemic risk is reduced by separating it from core functions of financial intermediaries. The recent financial crisis, however, tells a different tale, as much of the systemic risk emerged from the shadow-banking system that is both less regulated and less subject to capital and liquidity requirements, albeit with weaker government guarantees.

Republic of China (Bank of China Limited), Italy (Unicredit Group SA), Spain (Banco Santander SA), Belgium (Dexia SA), Sweden (Nordea AB), and the Netherlands (ING Groep NV).

While the Basel Committee has designated a list of G-SIFIs, the overall Basel III approach is to rely primarily on risk-weighted assets, with a capital conservation buffer. The Basel Committee on Banking Supervision does mention stress tests but at the bank level. The committee chooses not to subject the banking sector as a whole to common stress, which would be necessary for tying capital requirements to systemic risk. It is still reviewing—with no immediate clarity—the need for additional capital, liquidity, or supervisory measures to reduce the externalities created by systemically important institutions (G-SIFIs).

Current Implementation Status of Dodd-Frank and Basel III Reforms

The long-term implementation of these reforms started in the fall of 2010. The Dodd-Frank Act sets a variety of deadlines for rule making on the prudential regulators, mostly at one-year time points from when the law was enacted (July 2010). For instance, the designation of financial institutions as systemically important ones, which derivatives will be cleared centrally and on what platforms, the FDIC's orderly liquidation authority for systemically important institutions, and the separation of proprietary trading from bank holding companies were released in terms of initial proposals in the second half of 2011.[17] However, many of these rules are up against a public opinion and appeals period, and implementation would follow in the few years after the rules were finalized. In a nutshell, considerable uncertainty still remains.[18]

The Basel III rules are largely laid out (with further clarity to be provided on the capital conservation buffer, especially its countercyclical implementation), on the basis of whether contingent capital—a form of debt capital that converts to equity based on predesigned triggers—would be part of its requirements. Given the lengthy implementation phase (from now until 2013 for the first installment and then until 2019), it is quite likely that rules may undergo some changes, even on core capital and liquidity requirements.

While the Dodd-Frank Act, with all its limitations, represents a comprehensive overhaul of financial sector reforms in the United States, such clarity is missing elsewhere in the Western economies. The United Kingdom has set up

---

17. See, for instance, the one-year update on the Dodd-Frank Act in Acharya and others (2011a).

18. Some useful links concerning implementation of the Dodd-Frank Act are http://seclawcenter. pli.edu/category/dodd-frank-act/; www.reedsmith.com/_db/_documents/Dodd-Frank_Rulemaking_ Calendar_-_Proposed_Rules.pdf; www.americansecuritization.com/uploadedFiles/ASFDodd-Frank_ Rulemaking_Schedule.pdf; www.sec.gov/spotlight/dodd-frank/dfactivity-upcoming.shtml; http:// dodd-frank.com/sec-falls-short-on-rulemaking-agenda/.

the Independent Banking Commission, under the guidance of John Vickers of Oxford University, to come up with proposals for reforming the UK's financial sector. In the UK, structural reform along the lines of Glass-Steagall's separation of trading activities from commercial banks (an idea supported by the Bank of England's Governor Mervyn King) is still under debate. The UK is also among the few countries where the idea of relatively high bank capital ratios—in excess of 15 percent against unweighted assets—is still being debated. There is much less clarity on derivatives reforms in the UK, though before its inclusion into the Bank of England, the Financial Services Authority did present a view; somewhat surprisingly it did not push for centralized clearing and counterparties for derivatives markets. Whether this reluctance is due to an international race to attract greater flow in markets such as credit derivatives, where London thrived, is open to debate. Finally, the UK—even before the crisis—had stricter liquidity requirements (holdings of sterling at banks based on one-week projected cash flow needs) than other parts of the world. These requirements have been strengthened, but Basel III is likely to supersede these over time.

Finally, there is even less clarity as far as reforms in Europe are concerned. On one hand, Europe is likely to adhere to the Basel III reforms. On the other hand, there are a number of institutional changes taking place in the eurozone. For instance, a European Systemic Risk Board has been set up with an academic advisory council to guide its efforts to identify systemically risky institutions and, more broadly, to design macroprudential regulation. Similarly, a college of supervisors has been put in place to provide a pan-eurozone body that can share information about banks across regions and geographies. The current focus, however, is on resolving sovereign credit-risk issues in the eurozone, for which too a pan-European stabilization fund has also been set up. These sovereign risk issues in the eurozone are intertwined with bank solvency issues, and until they are resolved, European financial sector reforms are likely to be up in the air. After all, a significant crisis triggered by the restructuring of debt of a eurozone country is not only possible, but highly probable in these times.

Lessons for Emerging Markets from the Crisis, Dodd-Frank, and Basel III

The lessons to be learned from the present financial crisis and the efforts to lessen its effects can be divided into four groups: government guarantees, regulation of risk, macroprudential regulation, and fiscal policy and debt management.

Government Guarantees

Explicit and implicit government guarantees such as deposit insurance and too-big-to-fail policies can generate significant moral hazard in the form of risk-taking incentives. Even absent other market failures, this moral hazard can lead to excessive systemic risk and financial fragility. Consider the analysis of the lessons learned from the current crisis for the United States. Deposit insurance enacted in the 1930s in the wake of the Great Depression had long-term success only because significant protections were put in place in terms of insurance charges, regulation (mostly in the form of capital requirements and wind-down provisions), and restrictions on bank activity. As these protections began to erode, the moral hazard problem resurfaced.

To some degree, this lesson was already known in emerging markets. The number of countries offering explicit deposit insurance increased from twelve to seventy-one in the thirty-year period starting in the 1970s. Research looking at a large cross section of countries in the post-1980 period concludes that deposit insurance increases the likelihood of a banking crisis. Moreover, the likelihood and severity of the crisis are greater for countries with weaker institutional and regulatory environments and greater coverage for depositors. The incentive problems associated with the moral hazard from deposit insurance can be partially offset by effective prudential regulation and loss-control features of deposit insurance. However, in many Asian economies, including India, the charging method for deposit insurance is poor, if at all present.

In fact, to the extent that significant parts of financial sectors are state owned, guarantees from the government exceed just deposit insurance. State ownership also brings with it the bailout "genie." As the Irish example during 2008–11 illustrates, unlimited depositor guarantees and regulatory forbearance increase the fiscal costs of financial crises. Moreover, these actions increase the expectation that this will be the government's solution for future crises, thus killing market discipline and increasing the chances of risk shifting among financial institutions.

Of course, many analysts might point to the apparent success of the guarantees employed in the United States in the current financial crisis—and even more to the stellar success stories of India and China and the government backing they put into place. Let us analyze these latter cases as examples in emerging markets.

Consider India first. A significant part of the Indian banking system is still state owned. While they are generally considered less efficient and sophisticated than private sector banks, public sector banks in India in fact grew in importance during the financial crisis (which for India could be considered as the year 2008). The reason is simple and somewhat perverse: There was a "flight to safety" away from private sector banks, which have limited deposit insurance, to public sector banks, which are 100 percent government guaranteed (effectively so, as with the government-sponsored enterprises in the United States). This is because the relevant law (the Bank Nationalization Act) explicitly places 100 percent liability for public sector banks on the government.

Hence, when the financial crisis hit India—especially in the autumn of 2008, by which time the Indian stock market had plummeted by more than 50 percent and corporate withdrawals from money market funds threatened a chain of liquidations from the financial sector—there was a flight of deposits to state-owned banks.[19] In the period January 1, 2008, through February 24, 2009, public sector banks' market capitalizations fell by 20 percent less than that of private sector banks. Interestingly, this occurred even though, based on a precrisis measure of systemic risk (the marginal expected shortfall measure), public sector banks were substantially more likely than private sector banks to lose market capitalization during a marketwide downturn.[20] In addition, among private sector banks, those with higher systemic risk suffered more during the economywide crisis of 2008 (as the systemic-risk measure would predict), whereas among public sector banks, those with higher systemic risk in fact performed better! This divergence in behavior of public and private sector banks strongly suggests a role of government guarantees in boosting weak public sector banks at the expense of similar-risk private sector banks.

The trend of benefits to the state-owned banking sector at the expense of the privately owned banking sector continues. Reports suggest that loan growth among private sector banks in India was low in 2009, whereas such growth among public sector banks was as high as 10 percent (vehicle-backed finance). In essence, government guarantees have created an unlevel playing field that is destabilizing for two reasons. First, it has weakened those institutions that are in fact subject to market discipline. Second, it has raised prospects that the "handicapped" private sector banks (handicapped due to lack of comparable government guarantees) may have to lend—or take other risks—more aggressively in order to maintain market share and generate comparable returns to shareholders. Bank regulation in India tends to be on the conservative side, often reining in risk taking with overly stringent restrictions. However, the debilitating effects of government guarantees can travel quickly to the corporate sector and other financial firms reliant on banks, which are not directly under bank regulators' scrutiny or legal mandate.

In China's case, as a part of its fiscal stimulus, the Chinese government essentially employed its almost entirely state-owned banking sector to lend at large to the economy. From July 2008 to July 2009, lending by the Chinese banking sector grew by 34 percent. While this has clearly helped the Chinese economy recover quickly from the effect of the financial crisis in the United States—and its consequent effects on global trade—much of the growth in banking sector loans mirrors the growth in corporate deposits. In other words, loans are often sitting idle on corporate balance sheets, a phenomenon that is generally associ-

19. In a notable incident, Infosys, the bellwether of Indian technology and a NASDAQ-listed company, moved its cash in hand from ICICI Bank, one of the largest private sector banks, to State Bank of India, the largest public sector bank.

20. Acharya and others (2010a); Acharya and Kulkarni (2010). In particular, the marginal expected shortfall was calculated as follows. The worst 5 percent of days for the S&P's CNX Nifty Index (or Bombay Stock Exchange's Sensex) were taken during 2007. On these days, the average return of a financial firm was measured. This average return is the marginal expected shortfall for that financial firm. The results are available from the authors upon request.

ated with severe agency problems in the form of excessive investments. While some of the excess may be desirable as part of the stimulus, especially if it is in public goods such as infrastructure projects, estimates suggest that the excess liquidity is also finding its way into stock market and real estate speculation. It is not inconceivable that such lending through state-owned banks would be reckless and sow the seeds of asset-pricing booms and, perhaps, the next financial crisis. The moral hazard is clear: China has bailed out its entire banking system more than once before.

The examples of India and China highlight the classic risks that arise from government guarantees. First, they create an uneven playing field in banking sectors, where some banks enjoy greater subsidies than others. This invariably causes the less-subsidized players to take excessive leverage and risks, to compensate for a weak subsidy, and the more subsidized players to simply make worse lending decisions, given the guarantees. Second, government-guaranteed institutions are often employed to disburse credit at large to the economy, but this invariably ends up creating distortions, as the costs of the guarantees are rarely commensurate with risks taken.

Both of these problems festered because of government guarantees and contributed to the financial crisis of 2007–09. India and China should not rest on their laurels of rapid recovery from this global economic crisis. Instead, they need to safeguard financial and economic stability by engaging in a rapid privatization of their banking sectors—or at least stop inefficient subsidization of risk taking through state-owned banks. The genie of government guarantees brought out to deal with the crisis of 2008 needs to now be put back into the bottle, as these guarantees do not just weaken the banks that are guaranteed but also create systemic risk by weakening competing banks, subsidizing corporations, and fueling excessive asset speculation. And this is all true even leaving aside the natural risks stemming from politically motivated priority lending targets subjected to state-owned banks, their inevitable underperformance, and their eventual bailouts.

Systemic Risk of Emerging Markets and Their Coordinated Regulation

There are various ways that a financial institution produces systemic risk when the institution fails: counterparty risk, fire sales, and "runs." One of the principal conclusions from the analysis is that systemic risk is a negative externality on the system and therefore cannot be corrected through market forces. In other words, there is a role for regulation in order to force the financial institution to internalize the external costs of systemic risk. The exact same analogy for financial institutions within a domestic market can be made with respect to international markets, and especially so for emerging markets.

Even if a domestic regulator penalized a multinational financial firm for producing systemic risk locally, does this penalty carry through to all the international markets a firm operates in? In other words, should the penalty be more severe, as failure can lead to systemic consequences elsewhere? The issue becomes even more complicated because financial institutions have an incentive to conduct regulatory arbitrage across national jurisdictions; that is, if institutions are more strictly regulated in one jurisdiction, they may move (their base for) financial intermediation services to jurisdictions that are more lightly regulated. But given their interconnected nature, such institutions nevertheless expose all jurisdictions to their risk taking. Individually, jurisdictions may prefer to be regulation "lite" in order to attract more institutions and thereby jobs.

The poster child of the preceding crisis for being internationally interconnected is Iceland. Iceland, a tiny country with its own currency, allowed its banking sector to grow almost tenfold in terms of foreign assets compared to that of its own GDP. Its huge leverage aside, its survival was completely dependent on conditions abroad. The systemic risk of the three largest Icelandic banks (Kaupthing, Landsbanki, and Glitnir) also went beyond its own borders. Because the banks had fully exploited expansion within Iceland, they opened up branches abroad, in particular, in the UK and the Netherlands, by offering higher interest rates than comparable banks in those countries. When the Icelandic banks began to run aground and to face massive liquidity problems, in a now somewhat infamous event, UK authorities invoked an antiterrorism act to freeze UK assets. Essentially, Iceland as a country went into shutdown.

For at least several centuries the most common source of systemic risk is a run—a sudden withdrawal of capital. It is well known that, for many emerging markets, capital inflows are their lifeblood. There are numerous examples of capital flowing into new, emerging markets only to be withdrawn all of a sudden upon a crisis occurring. These runs can leave the corporate and banking sector of the developing country devastated, especially if there are currency, liquidity, or maturity mismatches between assets and foreign liabilities. An example from the recent crisis is that net private capital flows to emerging Europe fell from approximately $250 billion in 2008 to an estimated $30 billion in 2009. Not surprisingly, emerging Europe has been one of the hardest hit in terms of the impact of the crisis on GDP and internal institutions.

The current crisis was severe in both its financial effect (such as the spike in the risk aversion of investors) and economic impact (such as the large drop in global trade since World War II). Compared to past banking crises, therefore, it is quite surprising that emerging markets got through by and large unscathed. This can be partly attributed to better (or excess!) internal planning—a substantial stock of international reserves—and some to liquidity funding by international government organizations like the International Monetary Fund and the World Bank. Both of these elements suggest an approach to international coordination that mirrors how one might regulate systemic risk domestically.

Emerging markets need to coordinate with their larger brethren on prudent measures like leverage limits and currency reserves. As a reward, these markets could access international lender-of-last-resort facilities during a liquidity event and, in a systemic crisis in which there is a run on all financial institutions, employ loan guarantees and recapitalizations that are fairly priced and impose low costs on taxpayers. Of course, it would be necessary to shut down and resolve insolvent institutions to maintain the right incentives in good times.

If national regulators can agree upon a core set of sensible regulatory principles, then the constraints imposed by such alignment would reduce regulatory arbitrage through jurisdictional choice substantially. The central banks could present their proposals with specific recommendations to their respective national authorities and seek consensus internationally through the Financial Stability Board or the Bank for International Settlements. The lessons learned from this crisis should be especially useful to aid in these discussions.

Macroprudential Regulation: Leverage Restrictions
versus Sector Risk-Weight Adjustments

Given the various conceptual and implementation issues I have raised with the current Basel approach of charging capital requirements based on the *static* risk weights of assets, it is worthwhile considering the alternative macroprudential approaches. The most popular of these approaches is a direct leverage restriction. One variant of this is imposed and enforced at the level of each institution. No risk weights are attached, so that (perhaps with the exception of the highest rated government debt) all other assets are treated equally in terms of their potential risks. Then the leverage restriction is simply that the unweighted assets of the institution not exceed its equity value by more than a threshold, say 12:1 or 15:1. Alternately, leverage restriction can be imposed at the level of each asset class, for instance, mortgages cannot have loan-to-value ratios that are greater than 80 percent (as recently employed by the Reserve Bank of India against low-income housing mortgages with loans to value of over 90 percent).

While apparently simple, these restrictions in fact require a fair bit of regulatory oversight and sophistication. If enforcement is weak, the financial sector can evolve a shadow-banking system, as was the primary problem in the United States in the buildup to the crisis. Regulation must now ensure that all assets, both on and off the balance sheet, are suitably accounted for in leverage calculations (for instance, by charging the recently founded Council of Regulators in India to take a macroeconomic view of various assets and markets and by ensuring that commonly agreed-upon leverage restrictions are met). Similarly, if regulators have to use coarse leverage measurements on complicated securities and derivatives, regulatory arbitrage would push the financial sector toward innovation of such products. Again, this would call for sufficiently broad leverage requirements at the asset level. While it is conceivable that it would be useful to ban outright certain derivatives and innovation, there is no evidence that by and large this has worked. Regulators are often playing catch-up to the financial sector. Hence, more prudent enforcement would ensure that the regulatory perimeter is irrefutably enforced, so that *all* assets and risks in the financial sector are dealt with adequately, while limiting leverage of the system.

Another macroprudential approach used by some central banks in emerging markets (such as the Reserve Bank of India during 2006–07 in dealing with the housing boom) is the sector-weight adjustment approach. This approach requires the horizontal aggregation of financial institutions' balance sheets and risk exposures to identify over time—say each year—which asset classes are being "crowded in" as far as systemic-risk concentrations are concerned. For instance, if mortgages or mortgage-backed securities are increasingly picking up the lion's share of all risks on bank balance sheets, then the regulators could proactively react to limiting any further buildup. This could be achieved for instance by increasing the risk weights on future exposures to this asset class. In principle, stress tests could also be employed to glean such information about emerging pockets of risk concentrations.

One advantage of a dynamic sector risk-weight adjustment approach is that, if it is consistently implemented by regulators and anticipated by the financial sector, then it can act as a valuable countercyclical incentive. Financial firms anticipating the future risk in risk weights may stop adding exposure to an asset class once it is sufficiently crowded in. One disadvantage is that it may create a race to "get in first." Further, it relies heavily on regulatory discretion being prescient in identifying risk pockets and having sufficient will in good times to lean against the wind of fast-growing asset classes.

Of course, there is no reason why the various approaches outlined above could not be used in conjunction. Good regulation should look for robustness and resilience, both regarding its own potential errors and the arbitrage of regulation by the financial sector. Rule-based approaches, such as in the Basel capital requirements, free regulators from relying too much on discretion and therefore from being influenced by the industry; discretionary-based approaches counterbalance by making regulation sufficiently dynamic and adaptive as well as by creating constructive ambiguity within the industry about increasing correlated risks and leverage. My recommendation, however, is that discretionary approaches, such as sector-based risk adjustments, also be rule based to the extent possible, in terms of the principles of the framework guiding the adjustments.

Government Fiscal Policy and Debt Management

As the eurozone sovereign crisis has shown, when a full-fledged financial crisis hits an economy, the government balance sheet also gets embroiled, and the worse the starting condition of the government balance sheet (in terms of its debt-to-GDP ratio, for instance), the worse its ability to cope with the crisis.[21]

---

21. Acharya, Drechsler, and Schnabl (2010).

This effect on eurozone countries—and the somewhat muted but still significant effect on the United States—suggests that governments should manage their fiscal policies and debt levels in a manner that is countercyclical to the rest of the economy.

In the context of India, increasing fiscal deficits suggest a potentially worrisome path, where the high-growth and boom phase of the economy is coincident with a somewhat profligate government. India's financial sector is not yet too deep, in that fixed-income markets are currently poorly developed, so that there is great reliance on the banking sector. While the Reserve Bank of India has historically done a prudent job of containing the banking sector's potential excesses, and the well-developed equity market counterbalances to some extent the lack of thriving fixed-income markets, it is clear nevertheless that there is a great deal of "fat" in the government's fiscal condition. There are excessive subsidies to farming and fuel, there are explicit and implicit government guarantees to state-owned banks, and a number of state-owned enterprises and sectors are poorly run and managed. A tidying up of the government's balance sheet on pretty much all of its dimensions may be India's best preparation for any risks that it is exposed to, internally or externally.

References

Acharya, Viral, Itamar Drechsler, and Philipp Schnabl. 2010. "A Pyrrhic Victory? Bank Bailouts and Sovereign Credit Risk." Working Paper. NYU Stern School of Business.

Acharya, Viral, and Nirupama Kulkarni. 2010. "State Ownership and Systemic Risk: Evidence from the Indian Financial Sector during 2007–09." Working Paper. NYU Stern School of Business.

Acharya, Viral, Nirupama Kulkarni, and Matthew Richardson. 2010. "Capital, Contingent Capital, and Liquidity Requirements." In *Regulating Wall Street: The Dodd-Frank Act and the New Architecture of Global Finance,* edited by Viral Acharya and others. New York: John Wiley and Sons.

Acharya, Viral, Philipp Schnabl, and Gustavo Suarez. Forthcoming. "Securitization without Risk Transfer." *Journal of Financial Economics.*

Acharya, Viral, and others. 2010a. "Measuring Systemic Risk." Working Paper. NYU Stern School of Business.

———. 2010b. *Regulating Wall Street: The Dodd-Frank Act and the New Architecture of Global Finance.* New York: John Wiley and Sons.

———. 2011a. *Dodd-Frank: One Year On.* NYU Stern School of Business and Center for Economic and Policy Research, e-book (www.voxeu.org).

———. 2011b. *Guaranteed to Fail: Fannie Mae, Freddie Mac, and the Debacle of Mortgage Finance.* Princeton University Press.

International Monetary Fund. 2008. *Global Financial Stability Report, April.*

Lehman Brothers. 2008. New York: *Fixed Income Report, June.*

Saunders, Anthony. 2011. "Basel III: The Reform Proposals Summary." NYU Stern School of Business (http://pages.stern.nyu.edu/~sternfin/vacharya/public_html/Dodd-Frank-Basel-and-India-by-Viral-Acharya-2.pdf).

3

Global Financial Regulations and the Asian Financial System: Lessons from the Financial Crisis

YOSHINORI SHIMIZU

Responding to the financial crisis that occurred in 2008, a new regime of global financial regulations, Basel III, is being constructed. Its essence is to strengthen banks' capital regulations both quantitatively and qualitatively with additional surcharges to systemically important financial institutions (SIFIs). Capital regulation has been the main pillar of global bank regulations during the last quarter of a century, but it did not work to prevent the financial crisis. Regulatory strengthening is politically inevitable after such a critical financial crisis, especially due to taxpayers' intense criticism of the bailouts of large financial institutions and high remuneration for their management. But a cool-headed evaluation is now needed to check the theoretical validity and economic impact of such politically motivated and rushed reform.

The procyclicality of Basel III is responsible for the continued global economic downturn in 2012, which was triggered by the euro crisis, and Basel III, being a globally enforced regulatory reform, could have negative impacts on the growth of Asian countries, where the soundness of financial institutions has been maintained under a different business model than that of the United States and the United Kingdom, where the financial crisis originated. Although Basel I, initiated in 1988, aimed for a "level playing field," it actually created great inequalities in profits between financial institutions in these two countries, on the one hand (where securitization was developed with large capital markets), and those in Asian countries, on the other hand (where securitization was not developed).

In retrospect, the global financial crisis stemmed mainly from the regulatory defects intrinsic to U.S. and UK financial systems. A failure in the U.S.

monetary policy induced the U.S. housing price bubble and the expansion of
the shadow-banking system. The capital regulations of the Bank for International Settlements (BIS) was the main impetus for the shadow-banking system in the United States. The globally uniform financial regulatory regime
based on BIS capital regulations, introduced in 1988, is largely obsolete in a
world with such wide differences among countries' financial environments—
under the influence of rapid and uninterrupted technical progress in financial
markets.

Based on this perspective, this chapter points to the three lessons of the global
financial crisis which should be remembered when restructuring global financial regulations. In this context, the defects of the current capital-based bank
regulations are discussed, along with the challenge to Asia for funding its own
growth—foreseeing Asia as a world growth center in the coming decades. Finally,
based on the ongoing regulatory reform package, which was agreed upon during
the G-20 meeting in Seoul in 2010, three regulatory reform proposals for future
improvements are offered.[1]

Lesson 1: An Obsolete Financial Regulatory System

The most important lesson from the global financial crisis is the fact that the
existing global financial regulatory system, based on capital regulation, is already
fundamentally obsolete. The core of the global financial regulatory system over
the last quarter of a century has been BIS's capital adequacy regulation. Nevertheless, that the global financial crisis originated in the United States, whose
financial system was supposed to be the most advanced and well regulated, reveals
that the global regulatory system was not successful in preventing crises. In retrospect, the volume of bank capital, which was enforced by the BIS regulation,
did not perform its expected function as a buffer of losses. Governments of many
countries were forced to bail out large financial institutions, using tax money.
Figures 3-1, 3-2, and 3-3 show BIS capital ratios for large banks in the United
States, the EU, and Japan, respectively. All of them are stable at a level higher
than 10 percent throughout the period of financial crises, including banks that
were bailed out by public money injections. It is self-evident that the BIS capital
ratio did not represent the soundness of banks.

Proponents of the BIS regulation may attribute the cause of the U.S. financial
crisis to the fact that Basel II was not adapted to U.S. commercial banks. The
Basel II regulation, however, had been adopted by the five largest U.S. invest-

---

1. Basel Committee on Banking Supervision (2010).

Figure 3-1. *Bank for International Settlements and Market-Valued Capital Ratios, Large U.S. Banks, 2005–12*

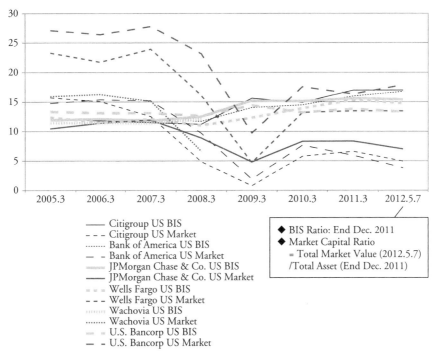

Source: Author's calculations.

ment banks before becoming commercial banks.[2] The fact that those five banks all failed during the financial crisis does not support the assertion that the financial crisis would not have happened if Basel II had also been adopted by U.S. commercial banks. Moreover, all three of the largest U.S. banks, Citigroup, Bank of America, and Goldman Sachs, that were bailed out by the public money injection had a very high BIS capital ratio, around 12 percent, up until the financial crisis and throughout the crisis as well. This level of capital ratio is much higher than the required Basel I and Basel II ratio of 8 percent and even higher than the required Basel III ratio of 10.5 percent. This fact seems to imply

2. Since 2004, based on Basel II, the U.S. Securities and Exchange Commission allowed the five largest investment banks the use of their own models in risk assessment and adopted a consolidated supervised entities program, waiving the adoption of the net capital rule, which restricts their assets to twelve times their capital. In this respect, the SEC adopted Basel II before adoption by U.S. commercial banks. Responding to the crisis of all these investment banks, the SEC suspended its adoption on September 26, 2008, just after the Lehman shock.

Figure 3-2. *Bank for International Settlements and Market-Valued Capital Ratios, Large EU Banks, 2005–12*

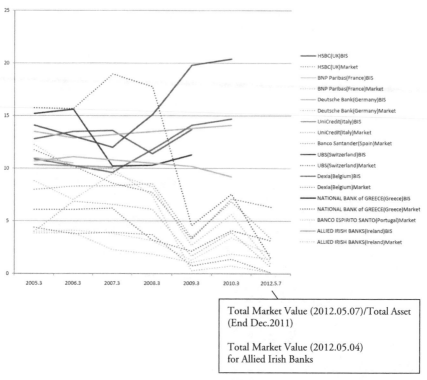

Total Market Value (2012.05.07)/Total Asset (End Dec.2011)

Total Market Value (2012.05.04) for Allied Irish Banks

Source: Author's calculations.

not only that financial crises cannot be curbed by tightening the required capital ratio and sophistication of capital calculation rules but also that the global financial regulatory system itself—with the BIS capital regulation as its core—has already been fundamentally outdated.

The core of the existing global financial regulatory framework has been and still is the bank capital adequacy regulation, which was introduced by the Basel Committee on Banking Supervision in 1988. Since then, the focus of financial innovations in the banking industry has been to create new business models to obtain higher profits with less capital. As a result, all kinds of new financial technologies were developed as a means of regulatory arbitrage, such as financial unbundling, off-balancing assets, securitization (such as collateralized debt obligation and asset-backed securities), credit default swaps to reduce risk weights, establishing unconsolidated structured investment vehicles, and investment fund growth. Since the BIS capital regulation is applicable only to banks in a single and consoli-

Figure 3-3. *Bank for International Settlements and Market-Valued Capital Ratios, Large Japanese Banks, 2003–12*

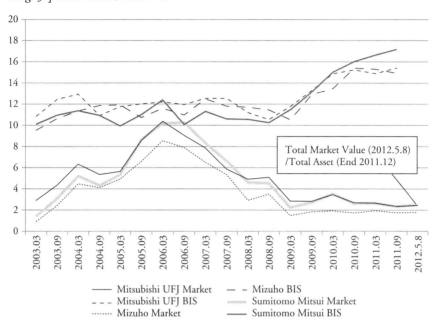

Total Market Value (2012.5.8) /Total Asset (End 2011.12)

——— Mitsubishi UFJ Market   — – Mizuho BIS
– – – Mitsubishi UFJ BIS   Sumitomo Mitsui Market
········ Mizuho Market   ——— Sumitomo Mitsui BIS

Source: Author's calculations.

dated financial and capital market, it is natural that banks' activities shifted toward financial markets that were less regulated. Bank risks thus spread to the whole financial market, and true risks in the market as a whole have been obscured.

Securitization was the trend in financial markets and became an important source of profits for financial institutions in countries with large capital markets, like in the United States and the United Kingdom. On the other hand, securitization has not been common in countries with relatively small capital markets, such as Asian countries. Due to differences among countries in their financial and capital markets, the same global capital regulation that aimed to establish a level playing field in fact created competitive inequalities among financial institutions in different countries. Capital adequacy regulation was rendered obsolete through regulatory arbitrage facilitated by the rapid financial innovations of the 1990s.

The existing regime of financial regulation thus has to be completely restructured. As mentioned, the capital adequacy regulation has proved to be ineffective, nor would a tightening of the same obsolete regulation do more than simply create regulatory procyclicality (as seen by the ongoing euro crisis). But there are problems with the BIS capital adequacy regulation. Although it was invented as a domestic regulation by UK and U.S. regulatory authorities as a means to prevent excessive risk taking by domestic banks, and although the Bank of England used the ratio of capital to risk-weighted assets as a guiding indicator of bank supervision since 1975, problems arose in the 1970s.[3] After several international bank failures, such as the Herstatt bank and debt crisis in Latin America in 1970s and 1980s, the focus of international bank regulations shifted from crisis management to crisis prevention.

The Basel Committee examined the use of this ratio as a base of international comparison. Governors of both the U.S. Federal Reserve Bank and the Bank of England agreed in 1986 to promote international bank regulation based on the capital ratio, which initiated a trend toward the Basel Accord in 1988. One factor that facilitated the accord was an increasing presence of Japanese banks in international banking in the late 1980s, which served to suppress objections to tighter regulations by U.S. and UK banks.

The required ratios in the United Kingdom were determined independently for each bank, depending on its risk taking and its risk management system and based on careful and detailed bank supervision, including interviews of the top management by the regulatory authority. The higher the risk taking, and the poorer the risk management system, the higher the required capital-asset ratio. In one case—of a small bank that took a high risk under a poor risk management system—the regulatory authority required a capital-asset ratio of 35 percent.

In the case of BIS capital regulation, an internationally uniform minimum ratio is enforced for all banks regardless of their level of risk taking. In this case, banks could take any level of risk once the minimum ratio is achieved. Given a level of capital, the Basel capital regulation could even facilitate a bank to take more risk to get higher profit.

The UK regulation took a level of risk taking as a benchmark and determined a necessary capital ratio for each bank separately. Although the capital adequacy regulation of the Basel Committee and that of the United Kingdom seems to be the same, the impact of each regulation is completely opposite. In this sense, the BIS capital regulation had a fundamentally flawed incentive mechanism from the beginning, and these problems need to be examined theoretically. First, how does the regulation enhance a bank's soundness? Second, is the regulation adequate as an internationally uniform regulation, which could be adopted by all countries regardless of their financial systems and business practices?

Lack of Theoretical and Empirical Rationale

The capital adequacy regulation intends to enhance a bank's soundness—that is, its corporate value—by regulating its debt structure through enforcing a capital ratio above a certain level. According to the Modigliani-Miller theorem, in prin-

3. Himino (2003).

ciple a debt structure of a corporation is irrelevant to its corporate value. Thus a theoretical rationale for BIS capital regulation in enhancing banks' corporate value has to be found in factors not considered by the Modigliani-Miller theorem, such as incomplete information, uncertainty, the transaction cost, and the effects on incentives of management.

Four types of theoretical analyses are offered. The first analysis focuses on a principal-agent problem between banks and the regulatory authority that provides deposit insurance.[4] This model, under the Modigliani-Miller theorem, supposes a case in which deposit insurance is provided proportionally to the amount of deposits. In this case, the value of a bank is equal to the total value of investment projects and the pure value of deposit insurance. When the deposit insurance premium is lower than the correct cost of insurance that reflects default risks, banks tend to have portfolios that involve excessive risks and impose excessive costs on the regulatory authority—costs that could be prevented by capital adequacy regulation.

In this case, accurate information on default probabilities and costs of deposit insurance is needed in order to find the best level of regulated capital ratio. This kind of information is, however, unavailable in practice. This is exactly the reason for deposit insurance. This argument implies that the appropriate capital ratio for each bank is different and thus cannot be a rationale for a uniform capital ratio.

The second approach treats the case of a bank as a risk averter and with investment projects that cannot be perfectly diversified.[5] This approach considers a bank's portfolio selection when a bank's risk-averting utility function depends on expected utility and variance, with no risk diversification among investment projects. In this case, it is possible to restrict its expected return and reduce default probability by imposing risk weights that correctly reflect a bank's investment projects and a minimum capital ratio. But in this case as well, information on the variance and covariance matrix of each investment project is required in order to calculate appropriate risk weights. When risk weights are not appropriate, default probability could increase. Nevertheless, this kind of information on the variance and covariance matrix of each investment project is unavailable in practice, and thus this approach is unrealistic as well.

The third model focuses on incomplete information and the moral hazard of bank managers.[6] This model presupposes three players: bank managers, shareholders who cannot observe the effort level of bank managers, and the regulatory authority as a representative of depositors. In a case of bad performance, bank managers tend to take excessive risks. In order to prevent this (using the capital ratio as a signal to judge management performance), a bank's management right

4. Buser, Chen, and Kane (1981).
5. Rochet (1992).
6. Dewtripont and Tirole (1994a, 1994b).

is transferred from bank managers to the regulatory authority, if its capital ratio has become less than a certain minimum level—thus preventing high-risk investments by bank managers. In this case, however, the probability distribution of returns is needed to determine the necessary capital ratio, which is impossible as well.

Fourth, and more generally, an encouraging effect on a bank manager's effort could be expected based on market valuation. This idea is based on a presumption that the regulatory authority, an outsider, cannot effectively regulate complex bank-risk management. It intends to give bank managers an incentive to enhance the bank's market valuation by letting the market evaluate its performance. The valuation criteria are its stock price. The higher its stock price, the easier it is to raise funds through new issues, and the easier it is to raise the capital ratio. Following this rationale, when stock prices are low, it is hard to raise the capital ratio. Thus using the capital ratio could be a meaningful criterion of market valuation. If this is so, stock prices per se are good market valuations, and so there is no need to depend on a bank's capital ratio.

Management indexes, such as the capital ratio, the rate of return, the bad loan ratio, and many others, are all on a trade-off relationship. The essence of bank management exists in how to choose the best mix of these indexes. The capital regulation that imposes a uniform restriction only on the capital ratio could deprive management of its freedom to find the best mix of indexes, thus possibly compromising its efficiency.

As discussed above, no persuasive theoretical rationale is available to justify capital regulation to enhance a bank's soundness and a bank's corporate value. From the empirical viewpoint, too, there is almost no evidence that shows the effectiveness of the Basel capital adequacy regulation in enhancing bank soundness.[7] The most direct and striking empirical evidence is the global financial crisis that began in the United States in 2008 and euro crisis ongoing since 2010.

It is surprising that a regulation that has neither theoretical nor empirical underpinnings has been extensively and globally used as the core of international banking regulations for a quarter of a century.

Problem of Internationally Uniform Regulation

The second problem stems from the internationally uniform enforcement of the same level of minimum capital ratio to banks of different countries with different portfolio structures and risk profiles. This point was in fact the most controversial problem to reach international agreement when the domestic capital regulation was made global. The level of 8 percent was determined as a compromise, so that banks in the major industrial countries (Japan, the United States, and certain European nations) were not all seriously affected.

7. See Santos (2000).

In the United States long-term funds are predominantly supplied through capital markets; banks supply mainly short-term funds. Banks' share in the financial system is thus far smaller than in Japan. Large and deep capital markets made it far easier for U.S. banks to securitize loan assets and to raise their capital ratios, compared to banks in Asian countries, where capital markets are not highly developed. In fact, the Basel capital adequacy regulation forcefully facilitated "financial unbundling" in the United States, leading to a higher rate of return for banks and to keeping the high capital ratios by specializing in originating loans and selling them to investors.

On the other hand, in Asian countries including Japan, banks have a dominant share in the funds supply, including long-term funds. In countries with smaller capital markets, the scope of financial unbundling is limited. A uniform capital standard for all economies, despite their characteristics, has an intrinsic problem. Differences in the availability of financial unbundling commodities, for example, creates huge differences in profits between banks in countries with large financial markets and those in countries that do not have such markets. A globally uniform regulation intended to level the playing field ironically created just the opposite.

It is argued that one of the motives behind the global uniform regulation was to suppress the growing presence of Japanese banks in the later 1980s.[8] Whatever the reasons for its introduction, the BIS capital adequacy regulation had serious negative impacts on the Japanese economy by prompting reductions in bank loans, which led to a prolonged deflation, beginning in the 1990s.[9]

Japanese banks are in a unique position, in which their funds are limited by the movement of stock prices. This is due to their large stock holdings, which are a source of hidden assets: 45 percent of them are counted as part of capital in the BIS capital regulation.[10] A Japanese bank's capacity for risk taking is therefore limited by stock prices and thus the business cycle.

Separately from the above point, the BIS capital regulation does not differentiate between individual shocks that can be controlled by each bank and macroeconomic shocks that cannot.[11] Bank managers should be responsible for each individual shock that is specific to their bank. But in times of bad performance due to macroeconomic shocks, which bank managers have no means to control, the BIS capital regulation could be too severe

---

8. See Himino (2003), chap. 3, for details.

9. Shimizu (2007b).

10. Banks holding stock is a historical characteristic of countries defeated in World War II, such as Japan and Germany. Since capital markets disappeared after the war, the only source of funds was banks that accepted deposits from the public. Reconstruction money had to be supplied to the industry by banks; these took the form of stock investments as well as loans.

11. Dewtripont and Tirole (1994b).

Procyclicality

The procyclicality of the BIS capital regulation is well recognized and a matter of international concern. Japan was directly and seriously affected by this characteristic in the late 1980s into the 1990s.[12] The same procyclicality is evident in the euro crisis, which is ongoing in 2012. The Basel capital regulation, agreed to in 1988, was adopted by Japan in 1993. Since Japanese banks started to prepare for its adoption even before 1993, it is hard to believe that an earlier adoption could have suppressed the bubbles of the late 1980s. On the contrary, at that time—when stock prices were rising—it could have encouraged a further expansion of the bubbles.[13]

This problem stems from the fact that the Basel capital adequacy regulation presupposes a constant and unchanged risk level, regardless of the stage of the business cycle. In order to avoid this problem, some measure of adjustment is needed to differentiate good times from bad times (this is partly, but insufficiently, accounted for in Basel III, discussed later).

Another important issue is that capital regulation reduces corporate demand for long-term funds. Banks are the last resort for their customer firms and are expected to supply funds, especially in bad times with lower stock prices. The Japanese medium- and small-sized firms that, in the 1990s, experienced credit crunches due to the capital regulation well recognize the possibility of another credit crunch, if lower stock prices cause banks to cut back on loans. Customer firms take all possible future events into account to make their long-term investment and financing strategy. Once they have even a slight concern for the future availability of funds, they are forced to make conservative investment plans, and this reduces demand for loans. This concern is an important factor curbing Japan's economic growth.

The Japanese regulatory authority took measures to ease the capital requirement so as to cope with drastic drops in stock prices—and thus capital—after the bursting of the bubble. These measures, which include subordinated debts and deferred tax assets, were necessary to offset the negative impacts of the procyclicality of capital regulation. It allowed, however, room for discretion and decay in the rule-based regulation.

In the calculation of the capital ratio, the regulatory authority has some discretion in the valuation of assets, which affects provision for loan losses and deferred tax assets. So it is believed that the uniform regulatory standard has a certain range of adjustment in its practical application in each country. In this sense, the capital regulation is not exactly a globally "uniform" regulation, since it is adjusted to the situation of each country and each economic situation.

---

12. See Shimizu (2007b).
13. Kashyap and Stein (2004) shows that this kind of phenomenon is globally common.

Figure 3-4. *Major Components of Tier 2: Ratios from Hidden Assets and from Debts, 1990–2002*

Average, major banks

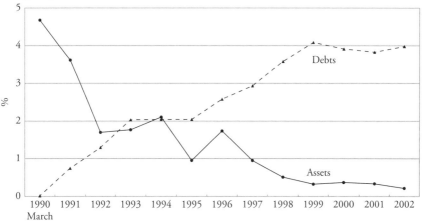

Source: Author's calculations.

Practical Application of the Basel Capital Regulation

The practical application of the capital regulation in Japan has largely diverged from the theoretical concept. During the financial crisis of the 1990s, the definition of *capital* was enlarged to meet the capital requirement of 8 percent.

The definition of capital in the original capital regulation contains two elements: tier 1, internationally common factors, and tier 2, complementary factors, which can be included discretionarily by each regulatory authority up to the amount of tier 1. Originally, an inclusion of 45 percent of hidden assets in stock holdings was agreed upon as a compromise, to account for the Japanese situation, in which the 8 percent level was not attainable without it. As stock prices kept falling after the bursting of the bubble, in the 1990s—when the required level could not be met—subordinate debts were approved to be counted in tier-2 capital to offset the fall. These ratios were completely reversed between 1990 and 2002 (figure 3-4). The inclusion of subordinate debts was key for major banks maintaining the 8 percent required ratio.

In 1998, 45 percent of the revaluation profit of held real estate was included in tier 2. Further, in March 1999 deferred tax assets, the amount equal to a 40 percent effective tax rate times future expected taxable income over five years, was counted in tier 2. Finally, in 1998–99, public money was injected into all large banks to maintain the required capital. This situation—of maintaining the required capital by enlarging the definition of capital and, finally, through public money injection—is practically the same as it would be in a situation without capital regulation. That is, without capital regulation, banks could still survive through government support but only for their financing needs, not for capital.

Nevertheless, this revision of capital definition should not be undervalued. This is a result of the effort and wisdom of the Japanese regulatory authority to protect the Japanese financial system. Without this revision, the Japanese financial crisis could have been much worse. The lesson is that each country should have enough discretion to cope with local crises by diverging from international uniform regulations, if needed. This actually happened in the United States when the U.S. authority suspended the mark-to-market accounting at the time of the U.S. financial crisis. In this sense, the original idea of achieving a level playing field in international banking based on capital regulations was not exactly met. In other words, it was an imaginary objective that was not realistic in practice.

In 1987 major countries in Europe objected to the internationalization of the joint proposal by the United States and the UK, and Japan asserted that the Basel Committee should allow for different standards and should recommend that banks increase capital, since an international capital standard was hard to achieve. In the actual implementation of the capital regulation in the 1990s, the Japanese assertion has been practically realized.

Thus the capital adequacy regulation is not exactly an internationally unified rule but in actual implementation is locally adjusted. It is natural, then, for Basel III to move toward even more flexibility. This is a lesson we should learn from the two-decade history of the international capital regulation.

Lesson 2: Liquidity Assurance and the Financial Crisis

The second lesson from the global financial crisis is the key importance of liquidity in avoiding crises. In the process of the regulatory reform toward Basel III, regulation of the liquidity coverage ratio has been discussed, but the details are still to be determined. A globally uniform regulation is, however, not suitable for liquidity assurance, because of wide differences among business models in different countries, such as deposit-based fundraising versus market-based fundraising.

Importance of Fundraising Capacity

U.S. and UK banks depend heavily on markets to raise their funds, while Asian banks depend mainly on deposits, which are more stable than market funds. Even with large liquidity holdings, the held liquidity may not be enough during a time of financial emergency. Then, what kind of concrete regulatory reform can be thought of regarding liquidity assurance?

The last resort of liquidity assurance exists in its capacity to raise funds from markets. In this sense, a bank's capacity to raise funds from markets should be regarded as its capacity to avoid failure, which can be interpreted as a measure

Figure 3-5. *Ratios, 1986–97, Hokkaido Takushoku Bank, Failed November 1997*

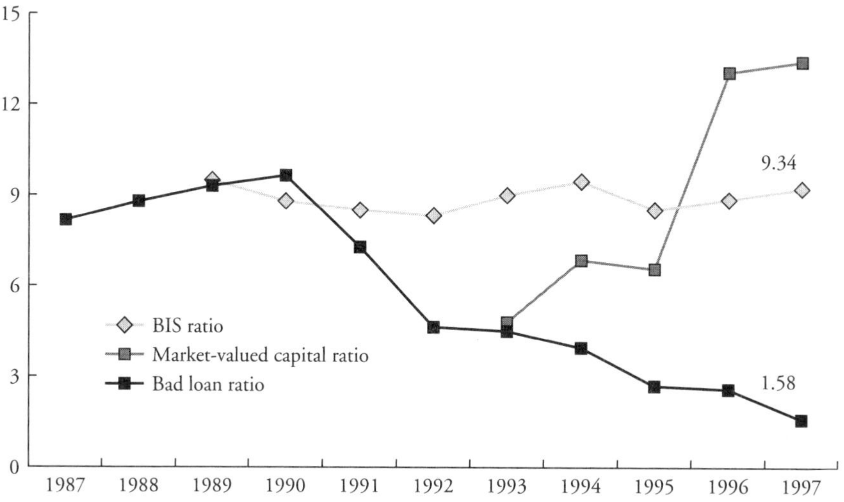

Source: Author's calculations.

of its soundness. Since the capacity of a bank to raise funds from markets can be judged based on its market valuation, the market-valued capital ratio (MVCR) (total market value of capital/total assets) is a good measure of its soundness—or in other words, its probability of survival (or probability of default, if converted) at a time of crisis.

The MVCR is a very simple measure and can be observed easily and immediately. On the other hand, the capital adequacy ratio is calculated according to the BIS's detailed specification and is impossible for outsiders to observe.

MVCR versus BIS Ratio: The Data

Let's take a look at the data to see the predictive power and the usefulness of the MVCR over the BIS capital ratio. Figures 3-5 through 3-10 show the MVCRs, the BIS capital ratios, and the bad loan ratios of five failed city banks in Japan.

The BIS ratio of the Hokkaido Takushoku Bank stayed over 8 percent up until the time of failure, in November 1997 (figure 3-5). On the contrary, its MVCR continued to fall after March 1991 and dropped to 1.58 percent in March 1997, eight months before its failure. At the same time, its BIS ratio was 9.34 percent, the highest level among all city banks at that time. The bad loan ratio reached over 13 percent. It failed just after its MVCR fell below 2 percent. The Nippon Long-Term Credit Bank's BIS ratio was 10.32 percent in March 1998, but it failed seven months later. Its MVCR was already below 8 percent in 1993 and continued to fall, to 2.20 by March 1998 (figure 3-6). Its bad loan ratio at that time was over 6 percent.

Figure 3-6. *Ratios, 1986–98, Nippon Long-Term Credit Bank, Failed October 1998*

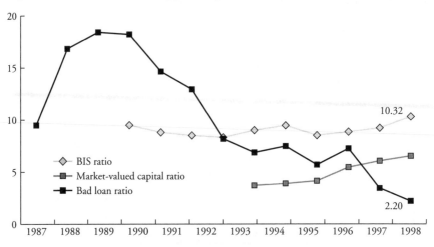

Source: Author's calculations.

The BIS ratio of Nippon Credit Bank suddenly dropped to 2.99 percent in March 1997, after staying over 8 percent up until that time (figure 3-7). Responding to public money injection, it sharply recovered, to 8.25 percent in March 1998 and 8.19 percent in September 1998. However, it failed in December, only three months later. Its MVCR kept falling after 1991, to 7.86 percent by March 1992. In March 1998 it was 3.66 percent. The bank failed in December 1998. Its bad loan ratio reached 16 percent in March 1998.

Figure 3-7. *Ratios, 1986–98, Nippon Credit Bank, Failed December 1998*

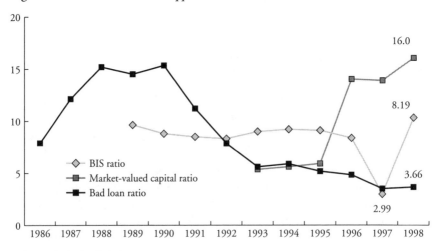

Source: Author's calculations.

Figure 3-8. *Ratios, 1986–98, Ashikaga Bank, Failed September 2003*

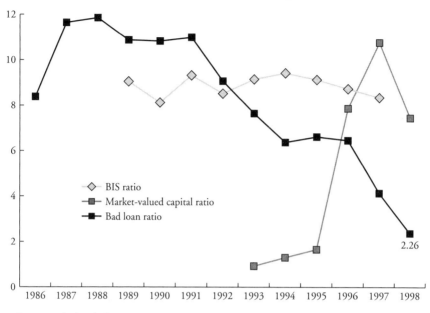

Source: Author's calculations.

Figure 3-9. *Ratios, 1986–2006, Risona Bank, Failed April 2003*

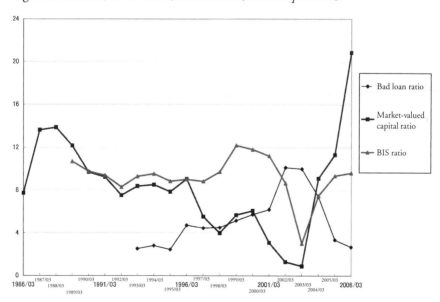

Source: Author's calculations.

Figure 3-10. *Ratios, 1986–2006, Average, All City Banks*[a]

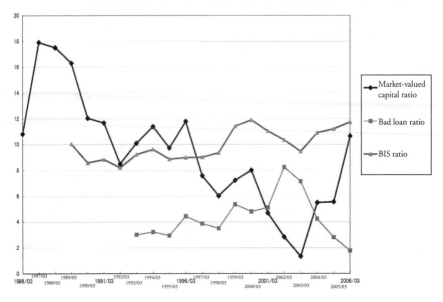

Source: Author's calculations.
a. Banks were merged in 2001–02.

Ashikaga Bank's BIS ratio was consistently above 8 percent up until the time
of the bank run in the autumn of 1997 (figure 3-8). It got a public money injection in 1999 but finally failed due to a denial of deferred tax assets by the auditing
agency; it was nationalized in 2003. Its BIS ratio was announced as 4.54 percent
at the time of failure, but it later turned out to be negative, according to a subsequent examination. Its MVCR fell below 8 percent by March 1993 and continued to fall thereafter. It was 2.26 percent in March 1997.

Risona Bank failed in 2003 when its BIS ratio suddenly dropped to
2.93 percent, from 8.60 percent in the previous year (figure 3-9). Its MVRC
fell below 8 percent by March 1997. (Risona Bank is a merged bank made
up of Daiwa Bank and Asahi Bank. Daiwa's MVCR and Asahi's MVCR fell
below 8 percent after 1995 and 1997, respectively.) Risona's MVRC dropped
to 0.90 percent in 2003. Once public money was injected and the bank was
nationalized in 2003, its MVCR sharply jumped to 9.09 percent in 2004 and
reached 20.8 percent, the highest ratio among all city banks, in 2006. This rise
in MVCR reflects the government policy of public money injection without
capital reduction. This event was believed to have had a positive impact on
other city banks as evidence of the government's policy of possibly bailing out
large banks.

Figure 3-10 shows the weighted average by asset size of the same ratios for
all city banks. In the 1980s there were twenty-one large banks, both city banks

and long-term credit banks. They merged into four large city banks by 2003. They are Mizuho FG, Mitsubishi-UFJ FG, and Sumitomo-Mitsui FG (which are considered megabanks), and Risona bank. During the years 1986 to 2006, their BIS ratio consistently stayed over 8 percent and in fact shows a rising trend. Even at the worst time of the financial market—in 2003, when many mergers took place—it was 9.46 percent. Hikes in 1998 and 1999 reflect the public money injection to all city banks in these years. The MVCR was above 8 percent during the first half of the 1990s, but it fell sharply after 1997 and, except for a temporary hike in 1998 and 1999 reflecting public money injection to all city banks, continued to fall, reaching 2 percent in March 2003. In the year 2003 a large-scale restructuring of city banks took place, forming four very large banks. As shown in figure 3-3, in 2006, when the public money was repaid, the MVCRs of all three megabanks recovered to above 10 percent. Between 1997 and 2005, a period of Japanese financial crisis, the MVCRs were less than 8 percent (except for March 1999, when it was exactly at 8 percent, a reflection of public money injection). The MVCR has a high negative correlation with the bad loan ratio, while the BIS ratio does not.

The BIS ratios for Japan's three megabanks have been consistently above 10 percent since the merger in 2003, and the trend is rising (figure 3-3). Their MVCRs recovered by March 2006 but started to fall afterward. In fact, once their MVCRs fell to 2 percent or less, all of these banks failed in some way. These failures took the form of mergers and acquisitions, public money injections, nationalization, or large-scale restructuring.[14]

In all three of these banks, their MVCRs sharply contrasted with their BIS ratios. Their MVCRs predicted their failure far before their actual failure. In this sense, market valuation has a power to see through to a bank's true soundness. The BIS ratios, on the contrary, were still high and stable up until failure happened or even in the middle of and throughout a financial crisis. In contrast, banks with high MVCRs (more than 8 percent) did not have serious funding problems even during the crisis in the United States.

Table 3-1 shows a regression analysis comparing the relationship of the BIS ratio and the MVCR, respectively, with a bad loan ratio and the rate of return on assets. The MVCR has a positive significant correlation with return on assets and a strongly significant negative correlation with a bad loan ratio. On the contrary, the BIS ratio does not have any correlation with either index. This is another reason to doubt that the BIS ratio is an indicator of bank soundness.

Thus the best strategy for a bank—and probably the only way to avoid bank failure—is to raise its MVCR as high as possible during normal times so that it can keep the market's confidence in order to raise funds even at a time of crisis.

---

14. For more details on MVCR and its implications, see Shimizu (2007a, 2007b).

Table 3-1. *Effect of the Market-Valued Capital Ratio and the Bank for International Settlements Ratio on Return on Assets and the Bad Loan Ratio*[a]

Measure	Return on assets	Bad loan ratio	t value	R_2
MVCR	7.340		3.77**	0.435
		−1.266	−3.24*	0.488
BIS ratio	0.699		0.799	0.004
		0.015	0.08	0.0005

**Significant at the 0.1 percent level.
*Significant at the 1 percent level.
a. Regression is based on data of all individual Japanese large banks that make up the aggregated weighted average data on figure 3-10.

The MVCR is a useful and powerful indicator of not only a bank's soundness but also that of corporations in any business field. For the MVCR to correctly reflect a bank's soundness, it is necessary for the market to be transparent enough that market participants can make correct valuations. For that reason, market infrastructure and regulation improvements are necessary. In the case of the global financial crisis, a lack of transparency due to too much and too complex information on securitized commodities, such as subprime loans, was cited as a cause of the crisis.

In the end, a regulatory reform leading toward liquidity assurance eventually facilitates correct market valuation through rules, regulations, and improvements in the informational infrastructure of the market.

Stability of the MVCR as a Measure of Soundness

Skepticism could arise regarding the stability of the MVCR as a measure of bank soundness, since market valuation is not stable and could change from time to time. But bank soundness itself would not necessarily be stable over time. It should change day by day, reflecting the market situation sensitively. If a large loan by a bank suddenly became a bad loan due to, for example, war or accident, then the soundness of the bank would be threatened and would become fragile immediately. In such a case, a bank's MVCR would drop quickly, showing that its soundness had deteriorated. Then, if a government guaranteed to support the bank financially, the bank's soundness would recover immediately, and the MVCR would rise again. This is what happened to Risona Bank in April 2003 (figure 3-9) as well as U.S. banks bailed out by the government in 2009 (figure 3-1).

Every day and every minute, the market will (and should) affect the soundness of a bank. This kind of sensitivity is key if a measure of bank soundness is to be useful. It is important that the market, in this way, act as a supervisor of a bank's behavior. The BIS ratio, on the other hand, is stable regardless of a bank's real soundness. This is exactly why the BIS ratio is not useful as a measure of soundness. Skepticism regarding the stability of the MVCR is inconsistent with its essential role as a measure of soundness.

Capital as a Buffer against Bank Failure

Bank capital is thought, erroneously, to be a buffer against bank losses and therefore against its failure. In truth, bank capital is simply an accounting concept; a bank with a high capital ratio does not necessarily have enough liquidity to prevent failure. Corporate failure occurs when liquidity is lost, such as when defaults on loans outpace its capital. The direct trigger is a lack of suppliers of liquidity due to information regarding bank losses. In reality, as seen above, all failed banks in Japan had more than an 8 percent BIS capital ratio. This ratio was more than 12 percent for U.S. troubled large banks, a ratio higher than that required by Basel III. In reality, when large losses are disclosed to the public, bank capital is already lost and cannot work as a buffer to prevent failure.

Even in such cases, if a government or a central bank, when announcing a bank bailout, also announces a government guarantee, the bank could get liquidity from the market and survive. This is what happened in both Japan and the United States during their financial crises. This is an important lesson for future improvements of the regulatory system.

Lesson 3: Global Regulations in Question

The global financial crisis has revealed many defects in risk diversification in the U.S. and UK financial systems. The shadow-banking system is an integral part of their unified financial systems, but it has been mostly untouched by regulation.

The biggest problems for the United States are the concept of "too big to fail" and also monopolies in specific financial markets, since risk diversification, the essential function of any financial market, cannot be achieved in a monopolistic environment. The market for credit default swaps, for example, was practically monopolized by one insurance company, AIG, and the U.S. government was forced to bail out the company, since its failure could have led to even larger bank failures. The too-big-to-fail problem is a serious threat to a sound financial system, but it is not unique to the financial industry. It is common also in insurance, investment funds, and the automobile and airline industries.

Because of their advanced financial technologies and high profits through efficient risk diversification, the U.S. and UK financial systems have been role models for Asian financial institutions. But since the global financial crisis, this is no longer the case: risk diversification through capital markets is seen as not necessarily superior to the Asian financial system, in which banking is the dominant form of finance.

In a modern financial market, like that of the United States and the United Kingdom, financial, capital, and insurance markets as well as shadow banking are complexly connected, forming a unified and consolidated single market. The problem of monopoly and oligopoly (too big to fail) is a threat to global financial markets. Once a big corporation is in trouble, the government will be forced to bail it out to avoid massive negative social impacts. The management of such companies, in choosing their business strategies, may well take this outcome into account. The U.S. airline and automobile industries are examples.

The U.S. financial regulatory system, long believed to be a model for Asian countries to follow, is now understood to be a source of the crisis, due to the lack of smooth information exchange and coordination among regulatory authorities in each field. Similarly, in the United Kingdom a return to a detailed, rule-based regulatory system became necessary after the failure of the once-esteemed principle-based regulatory system that relied on the self-regulation of financial institutions. The regulatory systems of both of these countries need to be fundamentally restructured and thus are no longer role models for Asian countries.

Asian financial markets were relatively lightly affected by the global financial crisis. Their business models are based on stable funds from deposits and are characterized by self-disciplined business practices. The strengthened U.S. and UK banking regulations are indicators that these countries are patterning their business practices upon Asian models. This is not to say that global adoption of the Asian model is recommended. As discussed, each country should construct a regulatory system best suited to the characteristics of its own financial market.

In U.S. and UK financial markets, as noted, the cause of the financial crisis was attributable to excessive risk taking by financial institutions. In Asian markets, on the contrary, risk taking could have been insufficient, which could lead to lower than potential growth. However, this is not to suggest the adoption of regulations like those of the United States and the United Kingdom. Global regulatory authorities, such as the Financial Stability Board and the Basel Committee on Banking Supervision, make global rules and regulations, but once a financial crisis has occurred, they have no power to resolve it. Each government is forced to deal with the crisis, without any help from the global regulatory authority. Then, each government has the liberty to regulate its own financial institutions with the necessary and minimum international coordination. A global financial regulation should allow larger degrees of freedom in adopting and implementing to each country. This is the third lesson from the global financial crisis.

Basel III: An Evaluation

Any evaluation of Basel III must begin with the causes of the 2008 collapse of the global economy, and that requires an examination of U.S. monetary policy leading up to the crisis. A look at the costs and benefits of regulations provides background, as does an examination of the Asian economies.

Figure 3-11. *Home Price Indexes, 1988–2010*

Source: Standard & Poor's Case-Shiller Home Price Indices; Fiserv.

Failure of Monetary Policy

Well before the outbreak of the global financial crisis in 2008, there was a risk of a housing price bubble (figure 3-11). John Taylor pointed out that U.S. monetary policy failure was creating a housing price bubble, which led eventually to the global financial crisis (figure 3-12). According to Taylor, the Federal Reserve Bank delayed tightening its policy for two years because it had lowered interest rates in 2000 in response to the bursting of the information technology bubble. This two-year delay in tightening monetary policy caused the housing price bubble and the global financial crisis. The episode exactly matches the Japanese experience of the late 1980s and 1990s.

In the autumn of 1987, facing an unusual hike in land prices, the Bank of Japan was about to shift its policy to a monetary tightening. Just before its implementation, on October 19, the Black Monday crash of the U.S. stock market occurred. As a result, the U.S. government strongly opposed Japan's plan of monetary tightening, leading Japan to abandon it. In the middle of 1988, the Bank of Japan again planned a monetary tightening, following the example of Germany, which raised interest rates in the middle of 1988 regardless of U.S. opposition. But the introduction of a consumption tax (in April 1989) now emerged as the biggest political issue in Japan. Due to political pressure from the government—afraid of a possible recession before its introduction—the Bank of Japan again

Figure 3-12. *Federal Funds, Actual and According to the Taylor Rule, 2000–06*

Percent

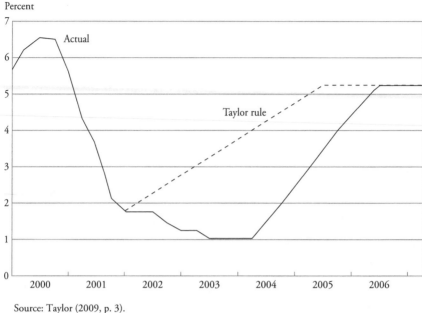

Source: Taylor (2009, p. 3).

delayed its tightening policy (until the end of May 1989). This nineteen-month delay was responsible for the worst of the Japanese real estate bubble.[15]

Given this history, one fundamental cause of the global financial crisis is obviously the failure of U.S. monetary policy. The direction of global regulatory reform should be informed by this fact. The importance of macroeconomic prudence has been mentioned frequently since the crisis; it is a perspective that will eventually lead to the appropriate management of monetary policy.

Common both to the late-1980s crisis in Japan and to the crisis in the late 2000s in the United States is an overvaluation of the consumer price index and an undervaluation of real estate prices as reference measures of monetary policy. Unlike those two countries, Germany sharply raised its interest rate in the middle of 1988, thereby preventing a bubble in its economy, although bubbles occurred in many developed countries at that time.[16] Asset prices, especially prices of real estate (which is most people's largest asset), are the key indicator of monetary policy management. For the future management of monetary policy, it is a challenge for monetary authorities to reflect the movement of asset prices in their monetary policy. It is essentially a challenge specifically for the United States and the United Kingdom.

15. For the details, see Shimizu (1997, chap. 13).
16. Shimizu (1997, chap. 13).

Nevertheless, politicians are forced to do something visible in response to such a big global crisis. Voters are very critical of bailouts of large financial institutions as well as of high remuneration of their management. So, at a time of crisis, an excessive reaction may well be better than an insufficient one. A regulatory reform proposal that is seemingly very severe may be better from a political perspective than a less severe one. The proposed tightening of capital regulations, for example, could restrict banks' capacity for risk taking and delay recovery from the global financial crisis. A long grandfathering period would therefore be both appropriate and wise. In the process of the adoption of Basel III, these outlooks should be accounted for. This still leaves the too-big-to-fail and shadow-banking problems untouched.

Each government should carefully and cautiously evaluate the details of Basel III, so that it does not have any negative impacts on their economies. There may well be another regulatory arbitrage, especially in the financial institutions in the United States and the United Kingdom, even under Basel III regulations. Asian countries need to be careful in implementing the new global regulations so that their economies do not experience any negative impacts. This point has become clearly visible through the ongoing euro crisis. Euro banks are being forced to reduce their assets, resulting in procyclical negative pressures on the EU and the global economy.

Costs and Benefits of Regulations

As mentioned earlier, the capital adequacy regulation is already obsolete. Basel II introduced three improvements: pillar 1 brought a sophistication of capital regulations; pillar 2, a voluntary upgrading of risk management by large financial institutions; and pillar 3, enhancement of market discipline. Even for pillar 1, however, the market invented such new commodities as credit default swaps in order to circumvent the regulation allowing banks to take larger risks based on the BIS specification of risk calculations. Because of this newly invented financial commodity as a means of regulatory arbitrage, the U.S. government was forced to bail out AIG, an insurance company. The global financial crisis posed serious doubts about the efficacy of pillar 2.

Can Basel III enhance the robustness of the financial system by increasing the required capital ratio from 8 percent to 10.5 percent? Can it fundamentally change the resilience of the whole financial system, even though the failed large U.S. banks had all attained more than a 12 percent capital ratio at the time of the crisis? In reality, there may not be an alternative for the global regulatory authorities to choose, other than a tightening of the existing regulations. In this context, Basel III is only an intermediate and tentative regulatory reform, which needs to be constantly updated and revised.

In an environment in which many means of regulatory arbitrage have been developed, a simple tightening of the same capital regulations could lead to further risk taking by banks that are facing reduced profit opportunities and further expansion of shadow banking. Careful audits would be needed, especially of large U.S. banks.

As a general reaction to a financial crisis, some kind of regulatory tightening is inevitable. But we should not forget that regulatory tightening has costs, along with benefits. A benefit of regulatory tightening by Basel III is prevention of a financial crisis. Even if a financial crisis may happen rarely, probably once in a hundred years, it still needs to be feared because of the massive damage it can do to the global economy. The cost of regulatory tightening—that is, restricting banks' capacity to give loans—would be a long-term slowdown of the growth rate of the world economy. Since this growth slowdown would last over a pro-longed period, the accumulated cost could surpass the possible damage of this rare one-time crisis. In the implementation of Basel III, a careful evaluation of the cost and benefit structure is needed.

Asian Growth Potentials

In 2010 Asia had a population of 3.3 billion people, or half the world's population. Over the present decade the region is expected to experience the highest economic growth in the world. Asia's middle-income ($5,000–$35,000) population was estimated to increase from 936 million in 2010 by 2.1 times—to 2 billion—by 2020 (figure 3-13). The high-income (over $35,000) population is expected to increase from 152 million in 2010 to 481 million by 2020. Accordingly, Asia is seen as the land of opportunity for the world financial industry, with 38 percent of incremental global banking revenues predicted by 2014, the largest revenue increase surpassing that of the United States and Europe. By 2030 Asia is expected to have the highest share among the global top thousand banks.

When we look the world's history over 2,000 years, Asia had a half share of the world economy most of the time up until the Industrial Revolution in the late eighteenth century. Since then, Asia's share dropped drastically until only recently. After the Internet revolution in 2007, however, Asia's share started to recover quickly, and it is estimated that it will be back to half a share of the world's economy within a few decades (figure 3-14). For this growth potential to be realized, a stable supply of growth funds is indispensable, coupled with an appropriate regulatory environment, so that financial institutions can perform their function efficiently under adequate risk management.

Recommendations for Global Financial Regulatory Reform

Based on the above mentioned analysis, and provided the current status of the reform, I have three recommendations for Basel III financial reform.[17]

17. Research Group on the Financial System (2011). The author served as chairman to draft the proposal.

Figure 3-13. *Share of Global Financial Business, Top Thousand Banks, by Country or Region, 1990–2030*[a]

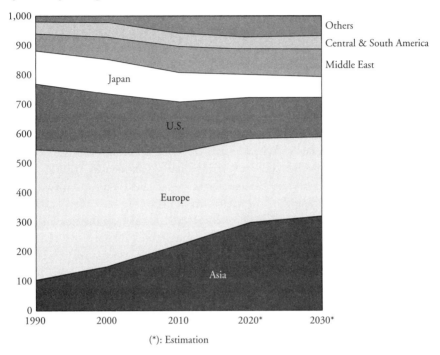

(*): Estimation

Source: The Banker, July 2010 (www.thebanker.com).
a. Numbers for 2020 and 2030 are estimates.

Figure 3-14. *Share of Global GDP through History, by Country or Region, Year 1 to 2007*

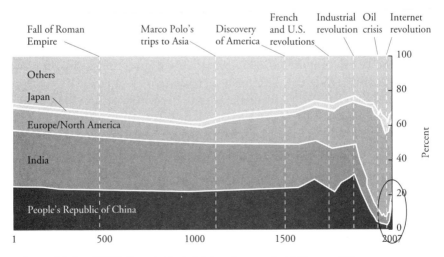

Source: Madison (2003); Deutsche Bank global market research; McKinsey and Co.

Recommendation 1

The new regulations should strive to achieve both prudence and stable economic growth by reflecting the unique characteristics of individual countries. Regulations should ensure that the financial sector can remain resilient. This is best done by acknowledging the variety of economic circumstances. The imposition of any regulations on SIFIs should be left to the discretion of the authorities in each country, who are best situated to understand the business conditions of individual financial institutions and the economic conditions of their jurisdiction.

Any financial regulatory reform package that would stabilize the financial sectors of the United States and the United Kingdom would not necessarily work in the best interest of other countries. Additional regulations on SIFIs and new regulations extending beyond capital adequacy rules will have the unintended consequence of impeding the flow of growth funds to industries and destabilizing the financial systems of other countries. This is particularly the case for Japan and such other countries whose primary banking model is commercial banking based on deposits. In these countries, sound economic growth has the highest priority, since it ensures the resilience of the financial sector and a reliable supply of funds. It is critical that global regulations take the different characteristics of individual countries into account.

Indeed, many of the side effects of the capital adequacy rules are already apparent. In Japan, these rules have reduced banks' risk taking capacity and constrained growth; in the United States, they set the backdrop for the expansion of the market for securitized instruments, which triggered the global financial crisis. The new rules do allow each country more discretion in enforcing the new package in specific aspects, such as countercyclical capital buffers. The focus of the package is, however, on capital adequacy rules. Without such flexibility in its enforcement, the potential for regulatory arbitrage and other adverse side effects could be real threats in the future.

Specifically, regulatory administration must be left to the discretion of authorities in the various countries. With respect to stronger regulations on SIFIs, it is important to recognize that each financial institution has unique features, and across-the-board regulations should be avoided. Policymakers must carefully and correctly assess the impact any such regulation will have on their own economies and be concerned about the potential for stronger regulations to produce contractions in financial institutions that could distort financial innovation.

Recommendation 2

The regulations should emphasize macroeconomic prudential supervision suited to the circumstances of the financial markets of individual jurisdictions. Rebuilding systems and organizations should be prioritized so that financial sector supervision is once again effective in the United States and Europe.

A proper balance between macroeconomic and microeconomic perspectives is critical to ensure multifaceted supervision of the entire range of increasingly sophisticated and complex financial systems. Supervision should contribute to the resilience of financial institution portfolios to domestic and international macroeconomic environments. Authorities in different jurisdictions should further strengthen their cooperation and coordination to improve both the depth and the speed of their response.

The recent financial crisis stemmed from a variety of issues not directly related to capital adequacy—for example, inappropriate behavior, such as excessive risk taking in creating securitized instruments and inappropriate reviews of loan structuring. The real problems were inadequacies in financial institutions' basic risk management practices and behavior contrary to management discipline. Addressing such problems must include a candid review of regulatory and supervisory regimes that overlooked or were unable to identify inappropriate practices. Rebuilding these regimes to function effectively should be prioritized. In the United States, where the financial crisis erupted, the Dodd-Frank Wall Street Reform and Consumer Protection Act attempts to strengthen the supervisory regime, at least in its regulatory structural form. The act establishes, for example, a Financial Stability Oversight Council, which comprises the secretary of the treasury, the Federal Reserve Board chair, and the Federal Deposit Insurance Corporation chair. The act does little or nothing, however, to change the complex matrix of sector, federal, and state regulations, and it remains to be seen whether the new regime will function effectively.

The biggest factors in the U.S. financial crisis were unique to the country's financial system, such as arbitrary consolidation standards and lending to unqualified borrowers. Another factor in the financial crisis was the failure of the supervisory authorities to understand that institutions were incorporating enormous risks into securitized and other complex instruments. Using varied channels, financial commodities were disseminated throughout the world, leading to large risks accumulated within global financial markets, including the initiating financial institutions.

Microeconomic prudence, focusing on the soundness of individual financial institutions, is inadequate for capturing the larger trends mentioned above. Instead, macroeconomic prudence must monitor risks across economic and sectoral boundaries. Effective programs are needed to improve the transparency of the entire financial sector—not only banks but also insurance companies and nonbank financial companies; these programs would monitor asset price trends, GDP, and other macroeconomic metrics. That is, they would perform appropriate risk analyses before these risks triggered a financial crisis. Clearly, implementing appropriate macroeconomically prudent policies without microeconomic information is impossible. Multifaceted supervision on the financial system should play a crucial role, with a balance of both macroeconomic and microeconomic perspectives.

In today's borderless financial markets, regulators must adapt with better coordination among domestic monetary and fiscal authorities as well. Improvements in both the extent and the speed of coordination and cooperation among countries are needed in order to prevent regulatory arbitrage on a global scale. From a macroeconomic prudential perspective, appropriate management of monetary policy is key. One primary cause of the housing bubble in the United States was that country's wrong monetary policy, as discussed above. It should be acknowledged that monetary policy must balance price stability and financial system stability; this might be difficult. In light of this, traditional monetary policy must be appropriately combined with the new policy tool of macroeconomic prudence.

In Japan the Financial Services Agency supervises financial institutions in all categories. The Bank of Japan manages monetary policy from a macroeconomic perspective and measures overall risk in the financial system through its day-to-day monetary regulation and its administration of the payment and settlement system. The two authorities work in close coordination, but the Ministry of Finance must participate in macroeconomic prudence. Each body's role and responsibility must be clear, and they must work together in both day-to-day policy administration and in times of crisis. The creation of a forum for detailed coordination among the three may also be desirable in order to highlight Japan's stance toward strengthening macroeconomic prudence both domestically and internationally.

The global financial crisis was partly due to large variances in interest rates, prices, and foreign exchange rates in Japan, the United States, and Europe. These disparities caused significant distortions in the international flow of funds. Specifically, large-scale funds flowed to the United States from Japan as well as to Europe from Japan and the United States. As money flowed into economies, asset prices and, most clearly, real estate prices surged. These distortions in the international flow of funds could not be corrected by the stronger capital and liquidity requirements of financial institutions.

A more effective solution, as pointed out, would have been better supervision based on macroeconomic prudence. Once regulators and central banks provide useful information on deviations between current economic circumstances and the undistorted long-term state based on the metrics of macroeconomic and international financial environments, an environment can be created in which financial institutions do not overreact to distortions in international finance. Individual financial institutions must also take steps to ensure that their portfolios are resilient to changes in domestic and international macroeconomic environments. These concrete and pragmatic efforts on the part of regulatory authorities to enhance financial market health would help prevent another global financial crisis.

Recommendation 3

Regulations should be reviewed and reassessed to better address the procyclicality problem. Strengthening the health of the financial sector will require not only voluntary efforts on the part of the financial institutions themselves but also the implementation of policies that encourage stable economic growth by individual governments. The imposition of multiple rules and regulations produces cumulative effects that could lead to unintended adverse economic consequences. If regulations are found to have unintended economic consequences, stable economic growth must be prioritized. Candid reviews and reassessments of regulations in order to better address the procyclicality problem are critical.

As noted at the beginning of this chapter, I commend the new financial regulatory reform package for providing long-term transitional grandfathering measures that give financial institutions time to prepare and mitigate adverse impacts on the real economy. Nonetheless, the new regulations essentially represent a substantial increase in capital adequacy. In order for necessary benefits to continue to accrue, both voluntary efforts on the part of financial institutions and stable economic growth are indispensable. For this purpose, each government should appropriately enforce the new regulatory package in a way suitable to the economic circumstances of each country. The new package also introduces new regulatory concepts and tools: liquidity regulation and countercyclical capital buffers. My view is that any package of regulations should focus on flexible enforcement of capital adequacy rules, because the rules themselves are clearly inadequate to prevent a crisis.

Individual regulations might have some positive effects. Nevertheless, the combined effect of these multiple regulations could lead to cumulative effects with unintended adverse consequences on the complex real economy. Regulators and supervisors must carefully monitor the impacts of the new rules once they are implemented. Authorities must be courageous enough to revise their regulations, if any signs of unintended economic consequences appear, such as a euro crisis. Since stable economic growth is the first priority, avoiding regulatory procyclicality should be a key concern for all regulatory authorities.

Conclusion

Financial system reforms are often made at times of financial crises. After the recent massive global financial crisis, regulatory and system reforms are inevitable. Another global financial crisis should be prevented by restructuring the U.S. and UK supervisory systems. It needs to be emphasized, however, that the Asian financial system was unrelated to the causes of the crisis. In spite of that—and mainly for political reasons—the intrinsically local regulatory reforms have been taken up by the G-20, with the aim of setting forth international common rules of financial regulation. These rules could affect even well-functioning financial systems. For this reason, this is not an reasonable financial regulatory reform.

The ongoing euro crisis is a clear example of the short-sightedness of a common regulatory reform process. This crisis threatens negative impacts on the global economy, including Asia. One of its costs will be in the form of slower world growth, since a credit crunch related to EU banks has become evident. Basel III's long grandfathering period (until 2019) was a wise decision, one that should be reevaluated in due time by the international regulatory authorities.

The global financial crisis has revealed that the Basel capital adequacy regulation, which was introduced a quarter of century ago, did not prevent the financial crisis. The defects of globally uniform regulations became more evident with conflicts among economies, including emerging economies. So it is unrealistic to establish any new regulatory regime to replace the existing one: a global financial regulatory system should be constructed through step-by-step improvements, working toward a more diversified system, with larger responsibilities and discretion assumed by each government.

References

Basel Committee on Banking Supervision. 2010. "Basel III: A Global Regulatory Framework for More Resilient Banks and Banking System." Bank for International Settlements. December (revised June 2011).

Buser, S., A. Chen, and E. Kane. 1981. "Federal Deposit Insurance, Regulatory Policy, and Optimal Banking Capital." *Journal of Finance* 36: 51–60.

Dewtripont, Mathias, and Jean Tirole. 1994a. *The Prudential Regulation of Banks.* MIT Press.

———. 1994b. "A Theory of Debt and Equity: Diversity of Securities and Manager-Shareholder Congruence." *Quarterly Journal of Economics,* pp. 1027–54.

Himino, Ryozo. 2003. *Kinnyuu Zaisei Jizyo Kennkyukai* [Inspection: BIS regulation and Japan].

Kashyap, A. K., and J. C. Stein. 2004. "Cyclical Implications of the Basel-II Capital Standard." In *Economic Perspectives, First Quarter,* pp. 18–31. Federal Reserve Bank of Chicago.

Madison, Angus. 2003. *The World Economy: Historical Statistics.* OECD Development Center.

Research Group on the Financial System. 2011. "Prudential Policy for Stable Economic Growth." Japan Banker's Association.

Rochet, J. C. 1992. "Capital Requirement and the Behavior of Commercial Banks." *European Economic Review* 36: 1137–78.

Santos, J. A. C. 2000. "Bank Capital Regulation in Contemporary Banking Theory: A Review of the Literature." BIS Working Paper 90. September. Monetary and Economic Department.

Shimizu, Yoshinori. 1997. *Keizaigakuno shinnpo to kinnyuu seisaku* [Progress of macroeconomics and monetary policy macro]. Yuhikaku.

———. 2007a. "BIS Regulation and Market Evaluation." *Shoken Analyst Journal* (April): 19–31.

———. 2007b. "Impacts of the BIS Regulation on the Japanese Economy." *Journal of Asian Economics* 18, no. 1: 42–62.

Taylor, John. 2009. *Getting off Track: How Government Actions and Interventions Caused, Prolonged, and Worsened the Financial Crisis.* Washington: Hoover Institution.

U.S. Department of the Treasury. 2009. "Financial Regulatory Reform—A New Foundation: Rebuilding Financial Supervision and Regulation." White paper. June, 17.

PART II

Promoting Financial Development and Inclusion

4

The Asian Financial System: Development and Challenges

CYN-YOUNG PARK

Surviving the event of the Lehman collapse in September 2008 and the post-crisis recession, the global economy struggles to regain strength. In response to the crisis, the G-20 leaders made firm commitments to "build a stronger, more globally consistent, supervisory and regulatory framework for the future financial sector, which will support sustainable global growth."[1] Yet the G-20 reforms, having thus far focused rather exclusively on strengthening the global regulatory system and restoring financial stability, paid limited attention to urgent development needs in many developing economies' financial systems, given the role of finance in supporting balanced and sustained growth.

Despite the often devastating effects of the crisis, finance remains central to economic growth and poverty reduction.[2] Theoretically, a well-functioning financial system has an important role to play in promoting economic growth and reducing poverty. The functions of the financial sector have been sorted into five broad categories: producing information about potential investment opportunities; mobilizing savings to the most productive investment; monitoring firms and exerting corporate governance; promoting risk diversification and sharing across individuals, firms, and countries; and facilitating the exchange of goods and services.[3] Development of the financial sector reduces the cost of

The author would like to thank Rogelio V. Mercado Jr. for excellent research assistance.

1. Group of Twenty (2009a).
2. Zhuang and others (2009) review the theoretical and empirical literature on the role of financial sector development in promoting economic growth and hence reducing poverty.
3. Levine (2005).

information collection, contract enforcement, and transactions, thereby increasing allocative efficiency and promoting economic growth.

Although not without contention, a large empirical literature has established a positive relationship between financial sector development and economic growth.[4] These studies demonstrate that financial sector development influences real economic activity by altering saving and investment decisions, capital accumulation, technological innovation, and hence income growth. Essentially, the financial sector pools and mobilizes savings into the most productive investment. Development of the financial sector can also ease constraints on credit to improve the efficiency of resource allocation, hence promoting productivity growth. Here the quality as well as the quantity of investment is an important factor for determining the productive capacity of an economy. An important function of financial services is therefore to produce information about potential investment.

The role of finance in achieving strong, sustainable, and balanced global growth seems more crucial than ever, as persistent weakness in advanced economies threatens the postcrisis global economic and financial stability. Risks remain large, with increased budget deficits, sovereign debt burdens, and incomplete household and banking sector restructuring in the United States and Europe. With the expectation of prolonged weakness in advanced economies, it is essential that emerging and developing economies in Asia strengthen their own domestic demand for the sources of growth. G-20 members with sustained, significant external surpluses also pledged to strengthen domestic sources of growth, including (depending on circumstances) increasing investment or consumption, reducing financial market distortions, boosting productivity in service sectors, improving social safety nets, and lifting constraints on demand growth.

In Asia the crisis effects differ across borders, depending on the degree of economic and financial openness as well as on the degree of dependency on external demand and credit. Although most Asian financial systems have exhibited remarkable resilience during the crisis, the inevitable changes in the postcrisis global economic and financial landscape require a revisit to the reform of national financial sectors.

Across Asia, financial sector development remains an important development agenda. In fact, in the wake of the global financial crisis and the consensus to support more balanced and sustainable global growth, further domestic and regional financial development in Asia is now imperative. Experience and research demonstrate that an appropriate level of development in finance is crucial to achieving the twin objectives of economic growth and financial stability.

---

4. See Levine (2005) for a literature survey.

This chapter examines the key development agenda of Asian financial systems in the face of a rapidly changing global financial landscape, shedding light on the challenges facing the region's policymakers. The following sections explain the salient features of the region's financial sector developments, discuss the challenges of financial sector development for balanced and inclusive growth in Asia, examine approaches to financial sector development for diversity and stability, and conclude with some policy implications.

Financial Sector Growth in Developing Asia

Developing Asia emerged as a new growth pole of the world economy when the traditional markets faltered during the global financial crisis. But such growth isn't new to developing Asia. Its economic rise has been spectacular for decades, having been bolstered by policies to promote export-oriented industrialization even while mobilizing a high level of savings.

As the world's fastest growing region, developing Asia outperformed not only industrialized economies but also other parts of the developing world. During 1980–2010, developing Asia's real GDP grew 7.3 percent annually on average, compared to the world average of 2.9 percent. The region's real GDP (measured in purchasing power parity) climbed from about $2.2 trillion in 1980 to $18.5 trillion in 2010. That is an increase of more than eight times, compared with about three times for the world economy during the same period. By 2010 the region accounted for 32.3 percent of world GDP; including Japan, the share reached 42.1 percent.

Developing Asia's economic and financial systems showed remarkable resilience to the global financial crisis, largely owing to their limited exposure to the toxic assets that sparked the crisis. In some part, however, the resilience also reflects the successful reforms and restructuring undertaken in the aftermath of the region's own crisis of 1997–98. The Asian crisis prompted a comprehensive reform of the macroeconomic policy framework and financial sector regulation. Reform of macroeconomic and financial management improved fiscal and external positions. The regulatory system was revamped, ensuring that financial institutions remained sound, with capital adequacy ratios well above international norms. In the aftermath of the Asian crisis, massive external deleveraging was undertaken by the private sector, including bank and nonbank financial institutions. As a result, the region's external vulnerability was reduced substantially. With current account surpluses from years of export-driven growth, the region had also accumulated international reserves, accounting for 45 percent of the world's total foreign exchange reserves as of 2010.

Financial sector reforms following the Asian financial crisis centered on bank rehabilitation and recapitalization, while also upgrading the prudential norms. Strong economic growth and profits strengthened banks' balance

Figure 4-1. *Banking Soundness Indicators, Developing Asia, 1997, 2005, 2010*[a]

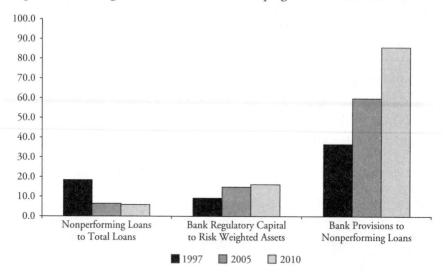

Source: Author's calculations using data from International Monetary Fund (2011b) and national sources.

a. Developing Asia includes Armenia; Bangladesh; People's Republic of China; Georgia; Hong Kong, China; India; Indonesia; Kazakhstan; Republic of Korea; Malaysia; Pakistan; Philippines; Singapore; and Thailand.

sheets, reduced nonperforming loans, and improved their resiliency against external shocks, as proven in the wake of the global financial crisis (figure 4-1). The crisis also prompted the development of financial systems beyond bank financing into, for example, government and corporate bonds, which aimed to improve financial resilience. The region's financial sectors and markets have broadened and deepened in the past decade (figure 4-2). The size of financial assets has increased significantly, with greater participation of nonbank financial institutions and capital markets, especially stock and government bond markets.

While the progress is commendable, the region's financial sectors and markets continue to face major developmental challenges, varying greatly in scope across and within borders. First, weak financial sectors and markets present a significant constraint on economic growth and development in many low- and middle-income developing economies. The development of the region's financial sectors and markets lags behind the real economy and is inadequate in funding and financial services for the private sector. The region's financial sectors are much smaller than those of advanced economies (figure 4-3). Although wide variation exists across economies, there is room for expansion even in the region's middle-income economies (figure 4-4). The situation is much worse in low-income and conflict-affected economies, where the size of financial assets is much smaller even

Figure 4-2. *Size of Financial Assets, Developing Asia, 2000–10*[a]

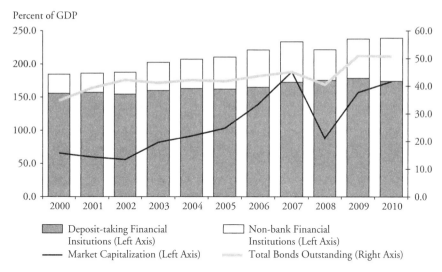

Percent of GDP

Source: Author's calculations using data from AsianBondsOnline, Bank for International Settlements, CEIC, World Federation of Exchanges, and International Monetary Fund (2012a).

a. Market capitalization data include listed stocks. Total bonds outstanding refer to domestic debt securities in local currency. Values estimated using available data. Developing Asia includes Bangladesh; People's Republic of China; Hong Kong, China; India; Indonesia; Kazakhstan; Republic of Korea; Lao PDR; Malaysia; Nepal; Pakistan; Philippines; Singapore; Sri Lanka; Taipei,China; and Thailand.

Figure 4-3. *Comparison of Financial Asset Sizes, 2010*[a]

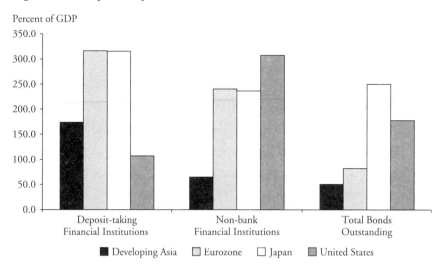

Percent of GDP

Source: Author's calculations using data from AsianBondsOnline, Bank for International Settlements, CEIC, World Federation of Exchanges, and International Monetary Fund (2012a).

a. Market capitalization data include listed stocks. Total bonds outstanding refer to domestic debt securities in local currency. Values estimated using available data. Developing Asia includes Bangladesh; People's Republic of China; Hong Kong, China; India; Indonesia; Kazakhstan; Republic of Korea; Lao PDR; Malaysia; Nepal; Pakistan; Philippines; Singapore; Sri Lanka; Taipei,China; and Thailand. Eurozone includes members of the euro system.

Figure 4-4. *Financial Sector Assets, Developing Asia, 2010*[a]

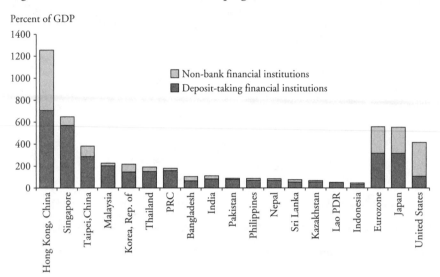

Percent of GDP

Source: Author's calculations using data from AsianBondsOnline, Bank for International Settlements, CEIC, World Federation of Exchanges, and International Monetary Fund (2012a).

a. Values estimated using available data. Developing Asia includes Bangladesh; People's Republic of China (PRC); Hong Kong, China; India; Indonesia; Kazakhstan; Republic of Korea; Lao PDR; Malaysia; Nepal; Pakistan; Philippines; Singapore; Sri Lanka; Taipei,China; and Thailand. The eurozone includes members of the euro system.

with a higher concentration in the banking sector. In addition, their banking systems have very limited physical presence (measured by number of branches and automated teller machines), thus failing to provide adequate access for the public (figure 4-5).[5]

Second, the region's financial systems remain structurally unbalanced, with high concentration in the banking system, which can undermine their structural resilience and systemic stability. The 1997–98 crisis highlighted the risk of heavy reliance on bank lending, which limited financial diversity and hence threatened financial stability. The absence of well-developed domestic capital markets constrains the availability of alternative sources for stable long-term corporate financing and thereby increases the risks to the overburdened banking system from maturity and currency mismatches. The lack of diversification in firms' capital and funding structure and investors' portfolios can also aggravate the financial position of corporate balance sheets, should an adverse economic condition dampen investment demand, triggering a sudden withdrawal of capital and a rush for credit.

5. CGAP and World Bank (2010).

Figure 4-5. *Access to Banking System, Eight Developing Asian Economies, 2010*

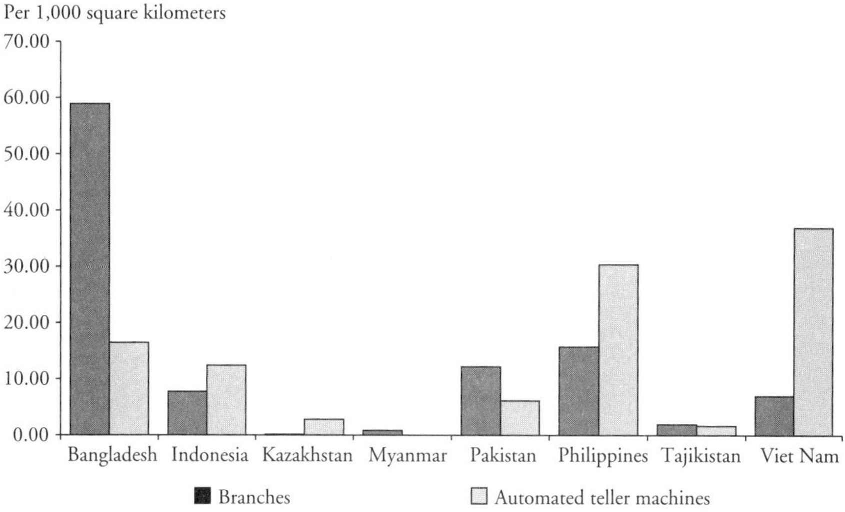

Per 1,000 square kilometers

Source: Author's calculations using data from International Monetary Fund (2012c).

Third, an underdeveloped financial infrastructure combined with lack of proper legal and regulatory framework hinders efficient functioning of the financial sectors and markets. Basic financial infrastructure is lacking in many developing economies in the region. Rapidly growing middle-income economies—for example, India, Indonesia, the Philippines, and Thailand—have in the past decade strengthened such financial infrastructure as electronic payment systems, credit information bureaus, and collateral registries. These changes helped significantly to enhance not only the efficiency of banking operations but also public confidence in the banking and financial systems. However, many low-income developing economies continue to suffer from inadequate basic financial infrastructure, including the necessary legal and institutional frameworks and governance systems.

Finally, the region's financial sectors and markets remain largely fragmented, hindering the deepening and broadening of regional financial markets and services and thus effectively constraining the mobilization of the region's savings for its vast investment needs. Asia as a whole is a net saver and exports a large amount of capital to advanced economies (table 4-1).[6] This already presents an irony—that capital flows from low-income to high-income economies. What is more ironical, however, is that a number of regional economies in need of external funding for their investment import these necessary funds from outside the

6. Petri (2007) reports that the advanced economies (especially the United States) imported, in 2005, about $0.7 trillion in capital, out of which $0.4 trillion came from Asia.

Table 4-1. *Developing Asia Savings and Investment, 2010*[a]
US$ billion except as indicated

Economy	GDP	Savings	GDCF	Net savings	Savings (% of GDP)	GDCF (% of GDP)	Net savings (% of GDP)
Japan	5,459	1,167	1,104	63	21.4	20.2	1.1
Emerging Asia	7,654	3,608	3,432	176	47.1	44.8	2.3
China	5,927	3,064	2,832	232	51.7	47.8	3.9
India	1,727	544	601	(57)	31.5	34.8	(3.3)
NIEs	1,878	639	497	142	34.0	26.5	7.6
Hong Kong, China	224	66	53	13	29.5	23.7	5.8
Korea, Rep. of	1,014	324	296	28	32.0	29.2	2.8
Singapore	209	108	50	58	51.7	23.9	27.8
Taipei,China	430	140	98	42	32.6	22.8	9.8
ASEAN 5	1,569	508	445	63	32.4	28.4	4.0
Indonesia	707	241	230	11	34.1	32.5	1.6
Malaysia	238	93	51	42	39.1	21.4	17.6
Philippines	200	37	41	(4)	18.5	20.5	(2.0)
Thailand	319	106	83	23	33.2	26.0	7.4
Viet Nam	106	30	41	(11)	28.3	38.7	(10.4)
Total	16,559	5,922	5,478	444	35.8	33.1	2.7

Source: Author's calculations using data from World Bank (2011); Directorate General of Budget, Accounting, and Statistics for Taipei,China (http://eng.dgbas.gov.tw/mp.asp?mp=2).

a. GDCF = gross domestic capital formation; NIE = newly industrialized country. For Taipei,China, the GDCF value is equal to total gross fixed-capital formation plus total increase in stocks. Values in parentheses are negative.

region. This reflects the inability of the region's financial systems to effectively channel the surplus funds within the region, leaving the region vulnerable to swings in external credit and financial conditions.

Achieving Global Balance

The global financial crisis highlighted the risk of substantial global savings and the investment imbalances at its root. Working out these imbalances is paramount to sustaining the postcrisis recovery momentum and safeguarding financial stability. Moreover, since Asia has been a major player behind the global imbalances, rebalancing the region's economy should be a key element in global rebalancing. The crisis has made it clear that multiple sources of growth are needed for a more balanced and resilient global economic expansion. Asia has pulled the global economy out of recession, and its strong growth is expected to contribute to that. Given the expectations of prolonged weaknesses in external demand, accelerating the shift in the sources of demand toward domestic and regional demand would be also largely in the region's self-interest.

Financial sector development is essential to increasing private investment and consumption, hence contributing to the rebalancing process. Across Asia, there is a clear need to focus efforts on financial sector development to support inclusive and balanced growth. The region's predominantly bank-based financial systems have made considerable progress in broadening the reach, and improving the efficiency and stability, of financial services since the 1997–98 Asian financial crisis.[7] In many developing economies, however, the limited access of the poorest population and also of small and medium-sized enterprises (SMEs) to formal credit remains an important constraint on achieving growth, development, and poverty reduction.

The promotion of financial access for these traditionally underserved sectors is therefore a high priority. Banks need to extend their reach to the broader public, including through the continued development of microfinance markets. The use of new technology needs to be positively considered and pursued in a way to broaden the public's access to banking without adding too much pressure on banks' operation costs. Even now, in some developing countries—including India and Bangladesh—mobile banking is actively promoted as a part of "inclusive banking" and used to extend the reach of banking services to the people not covered by banks due to either geographical or economic barriers.[8] In many

---

7. Ghosh (2006).

8. The Reserve Bank of India (RBI) has been promoting financial inclusion of the unbanked segment and passed several directives or recommendations to major banks in India to augment financial inclusion by making available basic, no-frills banking accounts. The RBI has introduced mobile banking in a phased manner since it first issued guidelines for mobile banking transactions in October 2008.

developing economies with low population density or disconnected geography, Internet or mobile banking can extend banks' reach without their incurring the cost of setting up branch networks. Mobile payment, prepaid debit cards, and other innovative payment methods might also allow more efficient fund mobilization, especially by lowering fees for remittances.

The priorities on the financial sector development agendas may differ among countries, depending on country-specific conditions and level of development. For example, in middle-income economies, where bank-based financial systems have made notable strides, efforts can be made to develop the nonbanking sector and capital markets to diversify the financial systems. For low-income developing economies, whose banking systems are underdeveloped and public access to banking and formal credit is significantly weak, however, the focus should be on strengthening the banking systems and broadening public access to basic financial services.

Increasing microcredit facilities requires particular attention in low-income developing economies in order to support more balanced and inclusive growth. Poor households typically have uncertain income sources, and their limited savings are often in perishable assets. They also face substantial difficulty in managing their financial risks due to limited access to any formal financial sector, including insurance, while relying heavily on social networks and their offspring. It is often very expensive for banks to reach out to the poor. And the problem is only compounded by the poor's lack of pledgeable assets or collateral and credit information. Under such circumstances, it would be important to create an environment in which private microfinance institutions can thrive by removing unnecessary legal and regulatory hurdles to market entry and undue administrative burdens on their operations.

SME financing in general is another important issue. In many emerging and developing economies, SMEs are the main pillars of production and job creation. Despite SMEs' economic importance, however, banks are reluctant to lend to them because of their generally high business risks, lack of reputation, inadequate credit information and history, and lack of collateral. The relatively high number of nonperforming loans made by SMEs and the higher costs associated with managing a large number of small accounts also discourage banks from lending to them.

The progress of SME finance varies widely across the region. The most visible progress has been made in the region's middle-income economies, where secured and nonsecured lending regimes have been established with their own collateral management systems and credit information bureaus. But in low-income developing economies, lack of legal and regulatory frameworks, inadequate information and market transparency, weak corporate governance, and underdeveloped financial infrastructure continue to hamper effective SME finance.

In order to enhance financial access by the poor and by micro, small, and medium-sized enterprises (MSMEs), strong policy intervention and support is necessary. First, legal and regulatory reforms as well as capacity building can support financial institutions to provide more efficient microfinance services. In many developing economies in the region, state-owned financial institutions offer commercial microfinance services. However, their limited ability to assess credit risk and to manage the risk—as well as their weak corporate governance—hamper their efficiency and leave them prone to financial losses and bankruptcy. Inadequate monitoring and supervision of these institutions add another layer of complication. Hence it is imperative to strengthen the legal and regulatory system through clear and transparent property rights, proper insolvency arrangements, and bankruptcy procedures, while enhancing credit assessment, risk management, and corporate governance.

Second, building critical financial infrastructure such as web-based collateral registers or credit information systems is essential to ensuring the efficient functions of microfinance markets. It is particularly important to build institutional and systemic support for effective risk management. Credit risk managers in emerging markets have a difficult task, as necessary information on credit ratings and traded security prices, for example, can be hard to come by. Microfinance institutions often have very limited data on the credit and default histories of their clients. There is also little infrastructure support, such as credit information bureaus. Even where there is some data availability, drastic changes in the economic environment in which banks and financial institutions have operated across Asia since the mid-1990s make it difficult to gauge default probabilities or exposures to defaults in the current situation.

Third, it is important to encourage innovative ways to provide a better array of financial services and products that cater to the needs of small entrepreneurs and investors. Securitization is an important financial innovation and is potentially very useful to pool assets or future incomes for necessary funding for SME investment. Securitization was used increasingly in the wake of the Asian financial crisis as a means to address loan losses by financial intermediaries or as a device to help bring about market-based financial sector restructuring. However, the global financial crisis of 2008–09 put a rather abrupt stop to the growth of securitization markets worldwide. Given its great potential in facilitating the mobilization of savings for investment by increasing the degree of freedom for both savers and investors to customize their financial positions to fit their risk profiles and preferences, the use of securitization for SME funding needs to be reviewed within a proper regulatory and monitoring framework. Similarly, securitization can help strengthen households' financial positions by, for example promoting housing finance and mortgage markets. Very little effort has been made to introduce mortgage schemes and to systemically assist housing finance development.[9] Securitizing the mortgage assets and selling them to a wider group of investors can allow housing finance and mortgage markets to grow.

Finally, developing diverse market segments such as venture capital, factoring, and lease markets would be a good way to improve SMEs' access to finance. The Republic of Korea successfully developed a well-functioning stock market for start-up SMEs to raise capital through publicly traded shares. Singapore established an impact investment exchange—a social stock exchange that provides a trading platform and an efficient capital-raising mechanism for social enterprises (which include microfinance entities). With a substantial portion of Asian SMEs in export industries, providing effective financial assistance in hedging against foreign-exchange volatility and trade financing is also valuable.

Achieving Diversity and Stability

For Asia, where banks are the main channel for financial intermediation, building a strong banking sector is a priority. There has been great improvement in terms of their diversity, efficiency, inclusivity, and stability over the period 2000–10 (table 4-2, figures 4-6a, 4-6b). Despite banks' dominant role in domestic financial systems, however, the scope of banking businesses and services is still limited. Authorities need to promote greater public access to banking, encourage banks and other financial institutions to develop diverse savings instruments and provide credits to traditionally underserved sectors such as households and SMEs, and allow a wide array of products and markets to develop for better risk management. Although the region's banking systems exhibited remarkable resilience during the latest crisis, recent developments in global financial markets and some notable changes in the region's banking business—such as increasing household lending and securities transactions—also require special attention.

Reforming the banking and financial sector should start with the development of a central bank. Weak central banks often compound the problems of weak financial sectors and markets as well as providing inadequate financial supervision in many low-income and crisis-affected developing economies. In particular, the inability of the central bank to properly monitor the economy, formulate and conduct appropriate monetary policy, and effectively supervise banks is a major obstacle to the development of the banking and financial sector. Particularly in low-income or crisis-affected countries, public confidence in the banking systems

9. Two exceptions are Malaysia and Thailand. In 1986 Malaysia established Cagamas, the National Mortgage Corporation, as a special vehicle to mobilize low-cost funds to support the national home ownership policy and to spearhead the development of the private debt securities market. In Thailand a specific-purpose financial institution, the Government Housing Bank, provided finance, with lower interest rates, for people seeking to purchase their own homes, especially those in low- and middle-income groups. In 1997 the Secondary Mortgage Corporation was established to promote and develop the secondary mortgage market.

is very low. Another important complication is the prevailing dollarization in a number of transitional economies (Cambodia, the Lao People's Democratic Republic, Kazakhstan, the Kyrgyz Republic, Tajikistan, and Viet Nam). The impact of dollarization on financial sector development is still being debated, but still it is clear that dollarization can be a serious threat to fiscal and monetary policy effectiveness. Studies also find that a high dollarization of banks' assets may increase banks' solvency and liquidity risks.[10]

Asian banking systems began to realize profits and a stronger operational efficiency following the reforms after the 1997–98 crisis (figures 4-7a through 4-7f). Earnings increased, with commercial banks venturing into new areas such as credit cards, mortgages, insurance, and other retail financing. Profit performance generally improved on strong growth in noninterest income, as banks strengthened their fee businesses. Banks also reduced operational expenses. The net interest margin has gradually come down since the mid-2000s (albeit at high levels), reflecting efficiency improvement, even as funding costs declined to historically low levels over the extended period of low interest rates and strong liquidity conditions. However, the expansion of the banking business into unfamiliar areas may entail new types of risk. As the banking system extends its reach beyond the traditional customer base and takes on new risks, it is essential to strengthen prudential regulation and supervision to ensure the stability of the system.

The region's banking systems need to further enhance their systemic resilience and financial strength. Strengthening the regulatory and supervisory framework is particularly important for developing economies with relatively weak financial market infrastructure, so as to support credit risk assessment and effective risk management. It is critical that the minimum capital requirements are met for regulated financial institutions. But more important, a rigorous supervisory review process needs to be implemented to ensure that banks maintain sound balance sheets and exercise due vigilance in their risk management practice. Regulators also need to strengthen their capacity—and be fully empowered—to evaluate banking soundness against the rapidly evolving financial environment and to assess the impact of new developments on the micro- and macroprudential soundness of financial institutions, risk management, investor protection, and systemic financial stability.

Rapid penetration of financial innovation in some of the region's underdeveloped financial systems is a significant regulatory concern, and even some of the more advanced regional economies need to remain vigilant against their banking system's exposures to new financial products and services. Asia's banks held up well compared to their Western counterparts in large part because of their relatively low degree of financial innovation and sophistication. But the

10. See Asel (2010), Duma (2011), and Menon (2007) for dollarization experiences in developing Asia.

Table 4-2. *Size and Composition of Financial System, Developing Asia,*
2000, 2005, 2010
Percent of GDP

	Financial sector assets [b]								
	Deposit-taking financial institutions			Nonbank financial institutions			Market capitalization [c]		
Economy [a]	2000	2005	2010	2000	2005	2010	2000	2005	2010
Bangladesh	52.2	52.0	65.5	3.9	9.5	39.9	2.5	5.0	14.9
Hong Kong, China	505.5	524.2	705.7	188.3	390.4	548.9	368.6	593.5	1,209.5
India	53.9	69.8	83.4	16.3	18.0	28.5	67.8	134.9	196.2
Indonesia	71.2	40.7	34.9	9.0	11.6	11.8	16.2	28.5	50.9
Kazakhstan	17.3	59.5	55.2	7.6	11.0	13.5	7.3	18.4	41.0
Korea, Rep. of	130.5	136.9	146.4	41.9	48.1	70.9	27.8	85.0	107.6
Lao PDR	38.3	23.7	51.5	0.6	0.2	1.2	...	...	...
Malaysia	154.2	178.3	202.3	17.1	21.0	24.4	120.6	130.8	171.9
Nepal	56.8	60.3	70.0	5.5	10.7	15.1	13.8	16.4	30.8
Pakistan	73.7	86.1	78.9	10.0	11.6	10.4	8.9	41.9	21.6
Philippines	92.9	78.5	70.7	22.4	19.0	17.1	31.2	38.6	78.8
PRC	157.5	159.0	158.4	5.1	15.5	21.3	48.9	24.6	76.9
Singapore	635.4	604.7	569.6	75.3	81.3	77.8	164.5	205.2	284.6
Sri Lanka	61.9	64.1	54.2	5.0	29.2	22.5	6.3	23.4	40.2
Taipei,China	256.0	310.4	286.4	29.4	67.1	94.8	75.9	130.5	190.3
Thailand	132.3	143.5	150.5	20.7	30.7	41.3	23.8	70.2	87.1
Average	**155.6**	**162.0**	**174.0**	**28.6**	**48.4**	**65.0**	**65.6**	**103.1**	**173.5**
Median	**83.3**	**82.3**	**81.2**	**13.1**	**18.5**	**23.5**	**27.8**	**41.9**	**78.8**
Addendum									
Eurozone	230.6	272.6	316.5	159.9	188.4	240.7	79.6	59.3	48.0
Japan	240.8	255.0	315.3	263.1	273.1	236.7	66.7	104.2	74.7
United States	79.2	92.6	107.2	278.8	305.4	307.6	152.1	136.5	119.0

Source: Author's estimates using data from national sources accessed through CEIC (2012); Bank for International Settlements (2012); World Federation of Exchanges (2012); World Economic Outlook (2011); International Monetary Fund (2012a, 2012b, 2012c).

a. PDR = People's Democratic Republic; PRC = People's Republic of China.

b. Values are estimates based on available data from various sources accessed through the CEIC database, IMF reports, and national sources. In years when data are unavailable, they refer to the closest value available.

c. Data derived using U.S. dollar values of stock market capitalization and nominal GDP.

d. Data refer to domestic debt securities by sector and residence of issuer as reported by the Bank for International Settlements.

... = data not available.

Total bonds outstanding[d]

Government			Corporate			Total		
2000	2005	2010	2000	2005	2010	2000	2005	2010
...	10.0	7.6	...	...	...	...	10.0	7.6
9.0	9.9	38.9	17.0	18.1	15.5	26.0	28.0	54.5
23.4	33.1	38.1	0.4	1.4	6.3	23.8	34.5	44.3
31.0	16.4	12.8	1.4	2.3	1.6	32.5	18.8	14.4
...	...	...	...	...	...	...	...	...
21.4	45.5	46.8	49.4	51.1	62.7	70.8	96.6	109.5
...	...	...	...	...	...	...	...	...
30.2	38.9	59.5	33.5	41.2	60.7	63.7	80.1	120.1
13.3	14.9	12.4	...	...	...	13.3	14.9	12.4
36.1	31.0	32.4	...	...	...	36.1	31.0	32.4
25.5	39.0	30.9	0.3	0.9	1.1	25.8	39.9	32.1
9.2	27.3	27.4	7.7	12.6	23.8	16.9	39.8	51.1
26.5	37.4	45.2	18.0	17.1	10.9	44.5	54.5	56.1
...	...	...	...	...	...	...	...	...
14.1	26.6	36.5	23.7	26.1	23.5	37.7	52.8	60.0
14.0	30.5	52.4	11.5	10.9	13.2	25.5	41.5	65.6
21.2	**27.7**	**33.9**	**16.3**	**18.2**	**21.9**	**34.7**	**41.7**	**50.8**
22.4	**30.5**	**36.5**	**14.3**	**14.8**	**14.4**	**29.3**	**39.8**	**51.1**
39.7	36.0	41.8	26.2	29.5	43.0	65.9	65.5	84.8
76.5	144.5	211.9	44.0	38.6	38.3	120.5	183.1	250.2
41.3	53.5	81.5	96.8	109.2	96.3	138.0	162.7	177.8

Figure 4-6a. *Real Estate Loans, Selected Asian Countries and the United States,
2000–10*

Percent of total loans

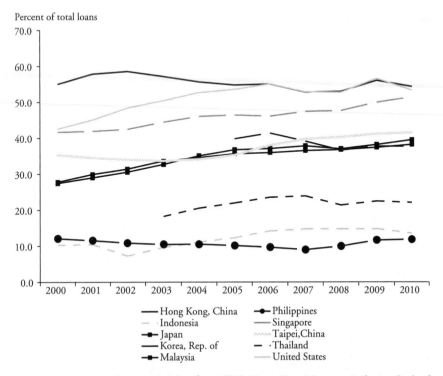

Hong Kong, China   Philippines
Indonesia   Singapore
Japan   Taipei,China
Korea, Rep. of   Thailand
Malaysia   United States

Source: Author's calculations using data from CEIC, Hong Kong Monetary Authority, Bank of
Indonesia, Bank of Japan, Bank Negara Malaysia, U.S. Federal Reserve Board, and Taipei,China's central
bank.

region continues to embrace the wave of financial globalization and sophistication brought by various factors, including the increasing participation of foreign
investors, the tightening global network with the revolution in information and
communications technology, and the introduction of new financial products
and services.

Innovations need to be tailored to fit market-specific conditions. In developing countries, regulatory capacity should also be an important element for
consideration when innovations are introduced. Financial globalization and
imported innovation can complicate local authorities' tasks of effectively regulating and supervising financial institutions. Despite its potential to create more
efficient and resilient financial markets, financial innovation entails significant
risks and uncertainties by changing the ways financial intermediation and markets function. Past episodes of financial crises showcase the risk of innovation
that challenged market participants' and regulators' understanding of risk while
generating overly optimistic views about its benefits. A lack of institutional

Figure 4-6b. *Securities Investment of Commercial Banks, Selected Asian Countries, the United States, and the European Union, 2000–10*

Percent of total bank assets

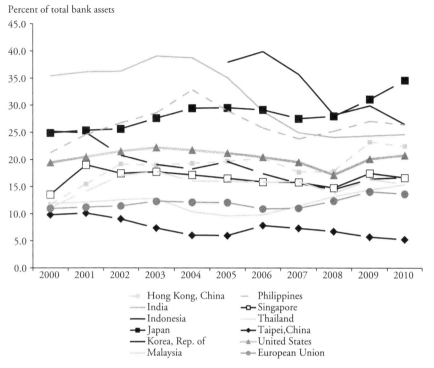

Hong Kong, China — Philippines
India — Singapore
Indonesia — Thailand
Japan — Taipei,China
Korea, Rep. of — United States
Malaysia — European Union

Source: Author's calculations using data from CEIC, Hong Kong Monetary Authority, Bank of Indonesia, Bank of Japan, Bank Negara Malaysia, U.S. Federal Reserve Board, and Taipei,China's central bank.

capacity among both financial institutions and regulators is another factor that can hamper effective risk monitoring and control.

The crisis also highlighted the importance of adequate information on cross-border financial activities and effective knowledge sharing. The region's regulatory authorities need to have adequate information on cross-border financial activities and promote effective knowledge sharing, perhaps through formal regional policy dialogues, which can also ensure adherence to international standards and minimum regulatory principles by adding peer pressure.

The lack of necessary infrastructure and institutional support continues to impair the development of the region's banking sector. Many low-income developing economies with less developed financial systems face longer term development issues. These include establishing a legal and institutional infrastructure for finance such as creditor rights, prudential regulations, and insolvency regimes; building an information and governance infrastructure such as credit information systems, accounting and disclosure rules, and internal and external auditing

Figure 4-7a. *Return on Assets, Developing Asia and the G3, 2000, 2005, 2010*[a]

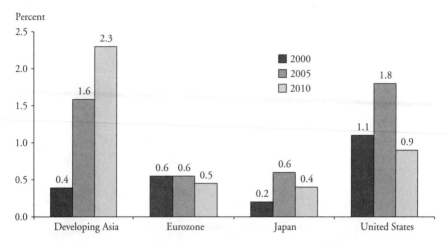

Source: Author's calculations using data from national sources, European Central Bank, and International Monetary Fund (2012b).

a. Developing Asia includes Armenia; Bangladesh; People's Republic of China; Georgia; Hong Kong, China; India; Indonesia; Kazakhstan; Republic of Korea; Malaysia; Pakistan; Philippines; Singapore; and Thailand. The eurozone includes members of the euro system. The G3 refers to the eurozone, Japan, and the United States. Data definitions follow, to the extent possible, the methodology of the Financial Soundness Indicators Compilation Guide.

Figure 4-7b. *Return on Equity, Developing Asia and the G3, 2000, 2005, 2010*[a]

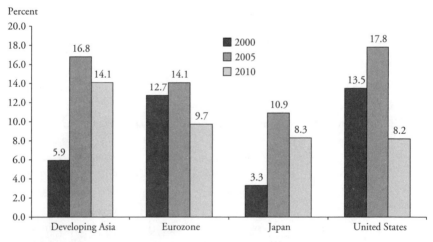

Source: Author's calculations using data from national sources; European Central Bank, and International Monetary Fund (2012b).

a. Developing Asia includes Armenia; Bangladesh; People's Republic of China; Georgia; Hong Kong, China; India; Indonesia; Kazakhstan; Republic of Korea; Malaysia; Pakistan; Philippines; Singapore; and Thailand. The eurozone includes members of the euro system. The G3 refers to the eurozone, Japan, and the United States. Data definitions follow, to the extent possible, the methodology of the Financial Soundness Indicators Compilation Guide.

Figure 4-7c. *Net Interest Margin: Net Interest Income as Share of Average Assets, Developing Asia and the G3, 2000, 2005, 2010*[a]

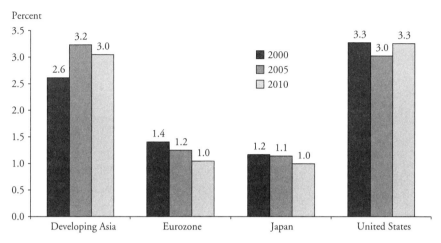

Source: Author's calculations using data from national sources accessed through CEIC and OECD database on bank profitability.

a. Developing Asia includes India; Indonesia; Republic of Korea; Malaysia; Nepal; Philippines; Taipei,China; and Thailand. The eurozone includes France, Germany, and Italy. The G3 refers to the eurozone, Japan, and the United States. Net interest margin refers to the difference between interest income and interest expense as percentage of total assets.

Figure 4-7d. *Share of Interest Income to Average Assets, Developing Asia and the G3, 2000, 2005, 2010*[a]

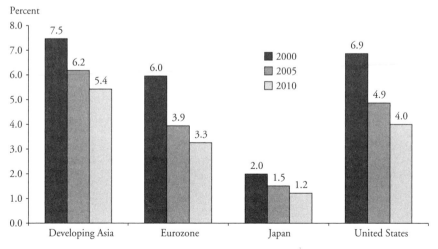

Source: Author's calculations using data from national sources accessed through CEIC and OECD database on bank profitability.

a. Developing Asia includes India; Indonesia; Republic of Korea; Malaysia; Nepal; Philippines; Taipei,China; and Thailand. The eurozone includes France, Germany, and Italy. The G3 refers to the eurozone, Japan, and the United States.

Figure 4-7e. *Share of Noninterest Income to Average Assets, Developing Asia and the G3, 2000, 2005, 2010*[a]

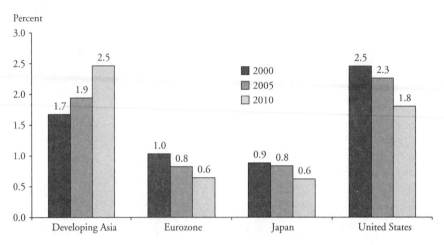

Source: Author's calculations using data from national sources accessed through CEIC and OECD database on bank profitability.

a. Developing Asia includes India; Indonesia; Republic of Korea; Malaysia; Nepal; Philippines; Taipei,China; and Thailand. The eurozone includes France, Germany, and Italy. The G3 refers to the eurozone, Japan, and the United States.

Figure 4-7f. *Share of Operating Expenses to Average Assets, Developing Asia and G3, 2000, 2005, 2010*[a]

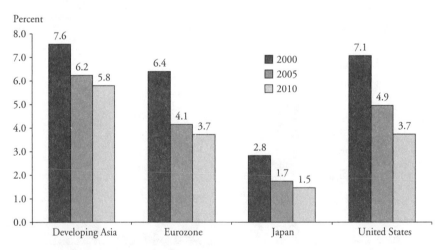

Source: Author's calculations using data from national sources accessed through CEIC and OECD database on bank profitability.

a. Developing Asia includes India; Indonesia; Republic of Korea; Malaysia; Nepal; Philippines; Taipei,China; and Thailand. The eurozone includes France, Germany, and Italy. The G3 refers to the eurozone, Japan, and the United States.

systems; and strengthening the role of central banks to provide systemic liquidity support through effective monetary operations and efficient payments and settlement systems. Such institution building is also an important prerequisite to financial liberalization without undermining financial stability.

As the economy matures and its demand for financial services becomes more diverse, authorities must also foster a broader range of financial sectors and markets—including nonbank financial institutions, debt and equity capital markets, securitization, and derivatives—to enhance systemic resilience and promote financial stability. A diversity of financial systems—while meeting the demand from the society for diverse financial services by accommodating the various risk preferences of savers and investors—helps reduce the risk of overreliance on banks and hence promotes financial stability.

In the region's many developing economies, growth in the nonbanking financial sector hasn't picked up, while capital market development is often biased toward equities. Nonbank financial institutions such as private investment funds, mutual and pension funds, hedge funds, insurance and leasing companies, and venture capital firms, albeit growing rapidly in the region's relatively more advanced economies, remain largely underdeveloped.[11] The region's equity markets have grown robustly (on the back of strong foreign capital inflows) and have emerged as an important source of corporate funding in a few large developing economies, such as the People's Republic of China (PRC) and India. However, the development of local currency bond markets has lagged, with government debt markets yet to be fully functioning across the region—with the notable exceptions of Hong Kong, China, the Republic of Korea, and Singapore.

Developing domestic capital markets and contractual savings is important to the financing of long-term investments. A transition from short- to medium- and long-term funding, however, requires certain policy initiatives with a long-term view, such as gradually extending the tenures of government and corporate bonds and accelerating the processing of pension reforms. The development of pension and insurance sectors has an added value of strengthening the nation's social security system. As shown in table 4-3, the pension systems in most Asian middle-income economies are relatively new and have limited coverage.[12] In recent years, some larger middle-income countries, including the PRC, Indonesia, Thailand, and Viet Nam, established national pension systems or strengthened their existing schemes by extending coverage and improving benefits. Private pension funds are, however, still at an embryonic stage of development even in middle-income countries in Asia. With the concern of aging populations in some large middle-income countries (notably the PRC and Thailand), pension reform needs to accelerate.

11. Lee and Park (2008).
12. Park (2009).

Table 4-3. *Pensions in the Asia Pacific Region, by Income*
Percent except as indicated

Economy[a]	Gross replacement rate (2008)	Labor force coverage rate[b]	Ratio of total pension assets to GDP[c]	Year pension system introduced[d]
High income				
Hong Kong, China (private DC)	38.5	78.0	21.0	1971
Japan (public DB)	36.3	95.2	25.4	1941
Korea, Republic of (public DB)	46.9	49.5	27.0	1973
Singapore (public DC)	12.7	62.9	61.9	1953
Taipei,China (public DB)			14.7	1950
Upper-middle income				
China (public DC)	82.5	20.7	2.1	1951
Malaysia (public DC)	30.4	50.0	83.0	1951
Thailand (public DB)	50.0	22.5	5.7	1990
Lower-middle income				
India (public DB and DC)	72.4		5.4	1952
Indonesia (public DC)	14.1	15.5	2.0	1977
Pakistan (public DB)	80.0		0.01	1976
Philippines (public DB)	90.5	27.1	1.0	1954
Sri Lanka (public DC)	48.5		21.1	1958
Viet Nam (public DB)	67.4	13.2		1961

Source: Author's calculations using data from Central Provident Fund Board (2011); Economist Intelligence Unit (2011a, 2011b, 2011c, 2011d, 2011e, 2011f, 2012); International Organization of Pension Supervisors (2009a, 2009b); Mandatory Provident Fund Authority (2011); Organization for Economic Cooperation and Development (2009, 2011a, 2011b); U.S. Social Security Administration and International Social Security Association (2011).

a. DB = defined benefit, DC = defined contribution.
b. Figures are for 2002 for Indonesia; 2004 for India, Pakistan, and Sri Lanka; 2005 for the PRC, Thailand, Viet Nam, Japan, and Republic of Korea; and 2008 for Hong Kong, China, Malaysia, Philippines, and Singapore.
c. Figures are for 2010 except for India (2007) and Pakistan (2008).
d. Year of introduction of the first law covering the regulatory framework for old age, disability, and survivors.

Figure 4-8. *Government and Corporate Bond Issuance, Developing Asia, 2008–11*[a]

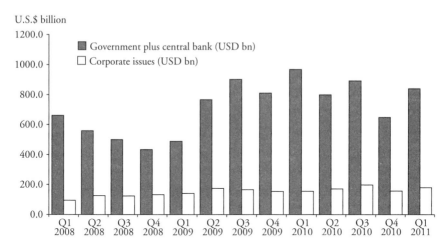

Source: Author's calculations using data from AsianBondsOnline, Asian Development Bank (2011a), and Bloomberg LP.

a. Government figures include central bank issuances. Data include local currency bond issuance of the People's Republic of China; Hong Kong, China; India; Indonesia; the Republic of Korea; Malaysia; the Philippines; Singapore; Thailand; and Viet Nam.

Broadening and deepening domestic financial markets remains an important long-term agenda for more efficient and resilient financial systems. Some of Asia's stock markets are now as large as—or even larger than—those of other regional emerging markets at similar income levels. However, growth is uneven across segments of capital markets. This is especially true of short-term money and fixed-income markets, which are often shallow and fragmented. Except in Japan and the Republic of Korea, local currency bond markets account for a smaller share of GDP than in the United States and Europe. Although it is undeniable that growth has been phenomenal for local currency bond markets, this has been driven primarily by government bond markets (figure 4-8). Development of the corporate bond markets has lagged considerably behind that of government bond markets, suggesting that much remains to be done.

Development of local currency bond markets can help improve resource allocation in several ways: by allowing greater scope for market-determined interest rates to accommodate the various risk profiles of the issuers; by providing essential market indicators for credit and market risks, thus improving the risk management of financial institutions; and by promoting risk sharing and debtor monitoring among a large number of creditors. Especially, liquid and well-functioning local currency bond markets provide a venue for the long-term financing of infrastructure investment. The region's bank-dominated and underdeveloped capital markets present a difficult hurdle to the funding of long-term development (particularly infrastructure) needs and thus to achieving sustained high growth. An important issue in bank financing of infrastructure is the asset-liability mismatches. While infrastructure is typically a long-term project, banks' main funding sources are short-term deposits. Therefore, funding infrastructure investment will naturally create significant asset-liability mismatches in bank balance sheets. This mismatch problem is particularly acute in emerging Asia, where banks remain a major source of corporate funding.

A liquid government bond market serves as an anchor to the development of domestic credit markets. By providing an essential benchmark yield curve, a government bond market facilitates the introduction of new financial products and services. More often than not in emerging markets, government securities also provide crucial market liquidity for secondary-market trading and lay a foundation for market infrastructure. The existence of primary issues on certain benchmark maturities, however, would not necessarily create benchmarks or a benchmark yield curve, while the quoted price remains only indicative.

Without active secondary trading, the price discovery process is largely stalled, unable to provide reliable prices. Especially in many emerging markets, liquidity is often concentrated in some of the benchmark issues, failing to create a continuous benchmark yield curve. In order to enhance market liquidity in the secondary market and induce firm prices for benchmark issues, authorities should establish a conducive environment for market making, such as providing hedging tools for primary dealers. To enhance liquidity in the secondary market, market infrastructure, including the trading, depository, clearing, and settlement systems, needs to be strengthened. Rationalizing tax impediments is also important, while streamlining regulation and accounting practices ensures equal tax treatment for different savings vehicles.

Development of the asset management industry will foster the retail investor segment of the market, enhancing demand and market liquidity. (For examples of the growth of assets under management between 2006 and 2009 in various Asian countries, see figure 4-9.) Mutual funds and various investment funds can help channel retail demand to the short- and medium-term segment of the market. Well-developed pension and insurance sectors will also have the desirable demand impact on the long-term segment of local currency bond markets, as the maturity of instruments gradually extends. Some middle-income countries—including India, Indonesia, Malaysia, the Philippines, and Thailand—have promoted investment funds for the growth of the pension and insurance sector, but the size of assets managed by the region's institutional investors remains much lower than that of Europe and the United States. A strong presence of domestic institutional investors with long-term horizons—such as funded national pension schemes, mutual funds, and domestic insurance companies—has an added benefit. Apart from mobi-

Figure 4-9. *Assets under Management, Selected Asian Countries, 2006 and 2009*

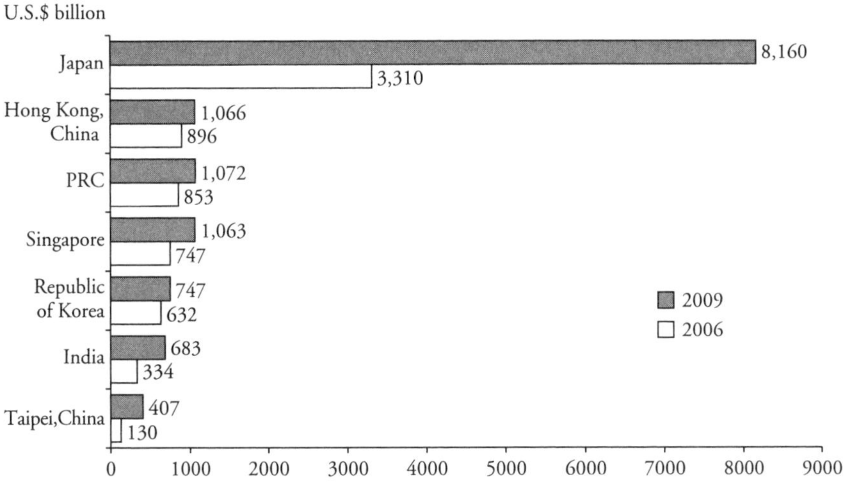

U.S.$ billion

Source: Author's calculations using data from CEIC, Central Provident Fund Board (2011), Economist Intelligence Unit (2011a, 2011b, 2011c, 2011d, 2011e, 2011f, 2012); Matrix Services Limited, and Organization for Economic Cooperation and Development (2012b).

lizing long-term savings for long-term investment, institutional investors also reinforce market discipline as they exercise the right of creditors in oversight of the firm performance.

The development of related investment instruments—including repurchase agreements (repos), forwards, interest rate swaps, and futures—should enhance risk management, thereby contributing to financial stability. The development of a private repo market is crucial for improving market liquidity and thus facilitating price discovery. A well-established repo market also provides a link between collateral and money markets, thus strengthening the market infrastructure. Establishment of a futures market may present a great opportunity for enhancing market liquidity and transparency at an early stage of bond market development. By concentrating liquidity on certain generic products such as government bond futures, reliable and centralized price information facilitates trading activities in the secondary market.

In the aftermath of the 1997–98 financial crisis, East Asian economies in particular took various steps to improve the domestic financial system and promote regional financial integration. They took the crisis as an opportunity to deepen financial cooperation and integration—both as a safeguard against the spillovers of global market instability and to provide a platform for regional financial market development. Some regional initiatives are noteworthy, such as the ASEAN+3 Economic Review and Policy Dialogue, the

Chiang Mai Initiative, the Asian Bond Market Initiative, and the Asian Bond Fund Initiative.[13]

However, there is much room for improvement in the region's financial integration. A number of studies find that the region's financial markets remain largely fragmented and provide evidence that the region's financial markets are integrated more with the global markets than with each other.[14] Fragmentation and the limited availability of regional financial products aggravate the depth and liquidity conditions of the region's financial markets, hampering efficient mobilization of regional savings for regional investments.

The region's authorities should work further in three major areas to support regional financial cooperation and integration: strengthening regional economic surveillance; deepening regional capital markets, particularly through local currency bond market development; and establishing a regional mechanism for crisis prevention and management as well as liquidity support in times of crisis.

First, Asia should continue strengthening regional policy cooperation and promote regional economic and financial integration to ensure financial stability. Difficult access to external funding sources could cause severe disruptions in the region's currency and asset markets. However, national mechanisms to stem the spread of financial panic proved to be largely inadequate, ineffective, and inefficient in the face of massive deleveraging in advanced economies, tight international liquidity, and worsening growth prospects. The large scale and volatility of capital flows at times also seems to be a source of instability, motivating the region's economies to accumulate reserves further and hence exacerbating the situation of global imbalances.

The multilateralization of the Chiang Mai Initiative (CMIM) is a good example of regional initiatives to create a regional framework for liquidity provision.[15] Strong regional macroeconomic and financial surveillance is an essential element for the effective operation of such regional financing arrangements. To this end, the establishment of an independent regional surveillance unit— the ASEAN+3 Macroeconomic Research Office (AMRO)—is expected to strengthen regional surveillance. Looking forward, these regional surveillance mechanisms can forge an explicit cooperative relationship with the global (multilateral) surveillance system to generate synergy.

Second, Asia needs to take further steps to develop and integrate its capital markets. On the back of strong economic growth, developing Asia's capital markets have shown a rapid expansion and have played an increasingly important role

---

13. See Asian Development Bank (2008) for details.

14. See Kim, Lee, and Shin (2008); Hinojales and Park (2011); and Park and Lee (2011).

15. A $120 billion foreign-currency reserve arrangement among the ten ASEAN members, the PRC, Japan, and the Republic of Korea came into effect in March 2010. In May 2012, ASEAN+3 agreed to double the size of the regional emergency reserve pool to $240 billion to further bolster the region's financial safety net in a bid to underpin financial stability.

in fostering economic development. Ensuring the sound operation of markets is all the more important if the region's capital markets are to expand further. After the global financial crisis, widespread regulatory reform is expected to continue. The reform in Asian capital markets has to take the form of smarter (not necessarily stronger) regulation and greater liberalization, simultaneously. Improving corporate governance and market transparency is a key priority to attract more investors. Across the region's still developing capital markets, effective disclosure, high-quality accounting standards, and sound regulations are needed to prevent financial irregularities and to protect investors. The region's authorities have already taken measures to address a wide spectrum of problems and potential weaknesses in accounting and governance practices, but more needs to be done in these areas.

Despite the risks associated with market liberalization, the region's authorities also need to enhance their efforts to liberalize their domestic markets and integrate them across the region. Fragmentation of the region's capital markets constrains cross-border investment opportunities for the region's investors, hence limiting the potential benefits of portfolio diversification. The regional investors' investment portfolios are still largely in stocks, particularly concentrated in their own local domestic stocks. This strong home bias is partly driven by regulations on investing abroad and the sale of foreign equities in local markets. Further integration of regional capital markets would also require the liberalization of capital accounts, the promotion of common standards for financial transactions, and the establishment of a financial infrastructure that can support cross-border transactions.

The development of local-currency bond markets is particularly important in light of the lessons from both the 1997–98 Asian financial crisis and the 2008–09 global financial crisis. Deep, liquid, and well-functioning local-currency bond markets can provide domestic investors with an alternative both to local bank loans and to offshore bonds. This will help the investors better manage their funding portfolio by matching the revenues and the debts in their currency and maturity structures, contributing to greater stability in the region's financial system. The region needs to continue working to expand and standardize its bond markets so that investors and issuers are able to tap into regional markets. A new road map for the Asian Bond Market Initiative, approved by ASEAN+3 in 2008, provides plans and strategies to assist the member countries to increase issuance and demand for local currency bonds and to improve the regulatory framework and market infrastructure.

Finally, the crises (both in 1997 and in 2008) revealed the region's vulnerability to financial instability arising from rapid financial globalization, large swings in short-term capital flows, exchange-rate volatility, and lack of crisis control mechanisms. With the increase in the frequency and severity of financial crises, the number and size of regional financing arrangements has expanded to form a solid defense against a financial crisis.

East Asia is at the forefront, accelerating its institution building for cooperation—within ASEAN and ASEAN+3, specific initiatives like CMIM have contribution shares, voting rights, and multiples worked out. Together with the AMRO, its new monitoring and surveillance arm, CMIM plants a seed of institutional foundation for a regional financial mechanism supporting regional and global financial safety nets. The further strengthening of these institutions with the aim of bolstering their roles beyond crisis resolution and toward crisis prevention is a must.

Reform of the global financial architecture is under way. It is also important to create synergy between emerging regional institutions and established global institutions such as the International Monetary Fund (IMF). Several proposals are under consideration to enhance cooperation and synergy between these regional financing arrangements and the IMF. For example, the CMIM could have qualification under the updated flexible credit line and the new precautionary credit line for member countries satisfy the IMF link and thus allow them to qualify for CMIM disbursements. Deeper institutional reform would be essential for effective coordination, for example, establishing clear and coherent mechanisms that regional financing arrangements can engage the IMF.

Policy Implications

The experience of the global financial crisis underscores the need for wide-ranging regulatory reform to address challenges associated with the rapidly changing financial environment with innovation and globalization, in which financial institutions do business and markets function. Following the crisis, and the G-20 responses to it, significant reforms have already been put in place, focusing on strengthening global regulatory guidelines (such as the Basel III standards), on filling regulatory gaps, and on broadening coverage.[16] Despite the critical nature of these reforms for the future financial landscape worldwide, however, their impact on the region's still developing financial sectors and markets has not been adequately analyzed and discussed.

With the ongoing talk of regulatory reforms globally, the impact of overseas regulation may be considerable. New regulations have been adopted in the United

16. In the wake of the unprecedented global financial crisis, the G-20 gathered in Washington in November 2008. Under the premise of the G-20's guiding principles, the Financial Stability Board and its constituents sculpted specific reform proposals to strengthen financial stability. The Basel III package of capital and liquidity reforms—the first concrete outcome of such reforms—was endorsed by the G-20 at its November 2010 Seoul Summit and was to be implemented beginning January 2013 and, in full, by January 1, 2019. Further reform is ongoing in the areas of strengthening macroprudential policy frameworks; studying regulation and supervision of commodities and futures markets; improving market integrity and efficiency; enhancing consumer protection; strengthening regulation and supervision of shadow banking; and assessing regulatory reform issues, which are especially relevant to emerging markets and developing economies.

States and Europe, with potentially significant impact on the activities of various Asian financial institutions and markets. U.S. regulatory agencies, including the Securities and Exchange Commission, have been issuing rules to implement provisions of the Dodd-Frank Wall Street Reform and Consumer Protection Act of 2010. Substantially increased regulatory requirements for information and transparency and associated costs of reporting will add to the burden of regulation. There are already concerns about its impact on international remittances and mobile banking, which tend to be less documented. For developing countries, the risk of adopting standardized—and poorly suited—regulations from overseas is also a genuine concern, since their financial sectors and markets are too important to their economic growth for them to be foolhardy. The wave of (re)regulation should not lead to overregulation or to regulations that do not take adequate account of their country-specific conditions.

Two important reform priorities, in the context of financial stability in Asia, should be, first, economic growth and development and, second, inclusive growth, to support social stability and equity. Therefore, when considering issues related to financial sector development and regulatory reform, these twin objectives must be central.

Reform efforts should not overlook the enormous development challenges faced by the region's low- and middle-income countries and the different conditions that they face in terms of financial sector and market development, regulatory capacity, availability and flow of information, and financial openness. For Asia's emerging and developed economies, special attention needs to be paid to the balance between growth and stability and to that between financial innovation and regulation. In this respect, appropriate sequencing of reforms is important to support financial development and economic growth. Below are some important elements in the context of country-specific development stages and socioeconomic needs when considering appropriate sequencing.

Supporting Economic Growth and Development

Asia's underdeveloped financial systems remain an important constraint on funding necessary development and ensuring sustained high growth. There is a clear need to focus efforts on financial sector development to support growth in the context of establishing the necessary foundations of finance and financial infrastructure, such as effective payment systems, clear and transparent property rights, information systems, corporate governance structures, and strong legal and regulatory frameworks, including insolvency and dispute resolution systems. Particular attention needs to be paid to developing economies' financial needs for infrastructure and small and medium-sized enterprises. In the context of banking, it is important to extend banking services to reach micro, small, and medium enterprises, including through continued development of microfinance markets. For middle-income economies, where demand for financial services can be diverse and complex, the development of nonbank financial sectors and markets should be a priority. Infrastructure, transparency, and corporate governance are central to such development (as well as to stability).

Promoting Financial Inclusion

Financial inclusion empowers people—particularly the poor, women, and marginalized sectors of society—to participate in business and economic activity. At the Pittsburgh Summit in 2009, the G-20 committed to improving access to financial services for the poor.[17] Fresh and further efforts need to be made to increase public access to banking; to promote financial literacy and consumer protection; to provide adequate credit to promote entrepreneurship; to diversify savings instruments; and to develop appropriate products and markets for better risk management. Authorities should encourage innovation and the adoption of new technology in the marketplace to enhance financial inclusion. Necessary legislative and regulatory reform can also help financial institutions and markets provide affordable credit, savings accounts, and basic insurance to the financially excluded sectors.

Balancing Regulation and Innovation

The key challenge for regulators in emerging and developing economies is how to encourage and manage financial market development without stifling innovation. Regulators should be wary of complex innovations that make the underlying risks of products or services more difficult to assess or trace—whether by bank management, regulators, or investors. However, an important distinction should be made between the basic elements for financial market development and risky financial innovation. For many developing economies, simple innovation—such as mobile banking, securitization, and basic (plain vanilla) derivatives—could be very useful to broaden access to finance and promote financial efficiency. At the low stage of development, such basic financial innovation may deliver substantial efficiency gains and allow better risk management. Improved profits and risk management capacity in turn contribute to stability in the banking and financial systems. Technology and innovation often take off before proper regulation is in place. Excessive early regulation could smother innovation, but delayed regulation may allow innovations to become systemically entrenched and too complex to monitor. Regulators should work with market players to make sure that the new products and services do not operate in a regulatory vacuum. Proper regulations are crucial in facilitating the standardization and expansion of innovations, including mobile and Internet technology, especially given its network effects. The rapid penetra-

---

17. See Group of Twenty (2009b). It was agreed that the G-20 supports "the safe and sound spread of new modes of financial service delivery capable of reaching the poor and, building on the example of microfinance, will scale up the successful models of SME financing."

tion of innovation is a challenge, nonetheless. Regulators in developing countries need to learn quickly how to deal with innovations with adequate understanding of their potential risks to ensure there will be no abuse of innovation—for example, using innovation for regulatory avoidance and arbitrage.

Strengthening Crisis Prevention and Management Mechanisms

The global financial crisis highlighted the need for an effective national, regional, and global framework to ensure financial stability. At the national level, it implies that sound macroeconomic policies should be implemented at all times, even while building a comprehensive framework for macroprudential oversight and preparing a contingency plan for financial institution failures, including consumer protection measures such as deposit insurance. At the regional level, establishing regional and subregional forums would support regional economic and financial cooperation, policy coordination, and crisis assistance, while complementing and augmenting the role of the G-20 and the Financial Stability Board. Asia also needs to actively participate in the reform of the international financial architecture and in the establishment of global financial safety nets to enhance crisis prevention and management.

References

Asel, I. 2010. "Financial Sector Development and Dollarization in the Economies of Central Asia." Final Report for Grant RRC IX-69. Washington: Global Development Network (www.cerge-ei.cz/pdf/gdn/RRCIX_69_paper_01.pdf).

AsianBondsOnline. 2012. *Bond Market Indicators* (http://asianbondsonline.adb.org/regional/data.php).

Asian Development Bank. 2008. *Emerging Asian Regionalism: A Partnership for Shared Prosperity* (http://aric.adb.org.emergingasianregionalism/).

———. 2011a. *Asian Capital Markets Monitor* (http:asianbondsonline.adb.org/publications/adb/2011/acmm_2011.pdf).

———. 2011b. "Financial Sector Operational Plan" (http:beta.adb.org/sites/default/files/financial-sector-operational-plan.pdf).

Bank for International Settlements. 2012. *BIS Statistics* (www.bis.org/statistics/index.htm).

Bloomberg LP. Accessed Subscription 2012.

CEIC. 2012. *CIEC Database* (www.ceicdata.com/).

Central Provident Fund Board. 2010. *Annual Report 2010* (http://mycpf.cpf.gov.sg/CPF/About-Us/Ann-Rpt/AnnualReport_PDF_2010.htm).

CGAP and World Bank. 2010. *Financial Access 2010: The State of Financial Inclusion through the Crisis*. Washington: Consultative Group to Assist the Poor and The World Bank (www.cgap.org/p/site/c/financialindicators/).

Directorate-General of Budget, Accounting, and Statistics for Tapei,China (http://eng.dgbas.gov.tw/mp.asp?mp=2).

Duma, N. 2011. "Dollarization in Cambodia: Causes and Policy Implications." IMF Working Paper 11/49. Washington: International Monetary Fund (www.imf.org/external/pubs/ft/wp/2011/wp1149.pdf).

Economist Intelligence Unit. 2011a. *China Country Finance Report* (http://country.eiu.com/
    FileHandler.ashx?issue_id=1258421110&mode=pdf).
————. 2011b. *Japan Country Finance Report* (http://country.eiu.com/FileHandler.ashx?
    issue_id=1838169768&mode=pdf).
————. 2011c. *Malaysia Country Finance Report* (http://country.eiu.com/FileHandler.ashx?
    issue_id=378648422&mode=pdf).
————. 2011d. *Singapore Country Finance Report* (http://country.eiu.com/FileHandler.ashx?
    issue_id=98417794&mode=pdf).
————. 2011e, *South Korea Country Finance Report* (http://country.eiu.com/FileHandler.ashx?
    issue_id=1457855930&mode=pdf).
————. 2011f. *Taiwan Country Finance Report* (http://country.eiu.com/FileHandler.ashx?
    issue_id=1258421110&mode=pdf).
————. 2012. *Hong Kong Country Finance Report* (http://country.eiu.com/FileHandler.ashx?
    issue_id=88785393&mode=pdf).
Ghosh, S. 2006. *East Asia Finance: The Road to Robust Markets.* Washington: World Bank
    (http://siteresources.worldbank.org/INTEAPREGTOPFINFINSECDEV/Resources/
    589748-1144293317827/full_report.pdf).
Group of Twenty. 2009a. "G20 Leaders' Statement: The Global Plan for Recovery and
    Reform." London. April 2 (www.g20.utoronto.ca/2009/2009communique0402.html).
————. 2009b. "G20 Leaders Statement." Pittsburgh Summit. September 24–25 (http://
    ec.europa.eu/commission_2010-2014/president/pdf/statement_20090826_en_2.pdf).
Hinojales, M., and C-Y Park. 2011. "Stock Market Integration: Emerging East Asia's Experi-
    ence." In *The Dynamics of Asian Financial Integration: Facts and Analytics,* edited by M. B.
    Devereux and others. London: Routledge.
International Monetary Fund. 2012a. *World Economic Outlook Database 2011* (www.imf.org/
    external/pubs/ft/weo/2011/01/weodata/index.aspx).
————. 2012b. *Financial Soundness Indicators* (http://fsi.imf.org/).
————. 2012c. *Financial Access Survey* (http://fas.imf.org/).
International Organization of Pension Supervisors. 2009a. *IOPS Country Profile—India*
    (www.iopsweb.org/dataoecd/63/43/39625861.pdf).
————. 2009b. *IOPS Country Profile—Pakistan* (www.iopsweb.org/dataoecd/3/6/44873831.
    pdf).
Kim, S., J-W Lee, and K. Shin. 2008. "Regional and Global Financial Integration in East
    Asia." In *China, Asia and the New World Economy,* edited by B. Eichengreen, Y. C. Park,
    and C. Wyplosz. Oxford University Press.
Lee, J-W, and C-Y Park. 2008. "Global Financial Turmoil: Impact and Challenges for Asia's
    Financial Systems." *Asian Economic Papers* 7, no. 1: 9–40.
Levine, R. 2005. "Finance and Growth: Theory and Evidence." In *Handbook of Economic
    Growth,* edited by P. Aghion and S. Durlauf. Amsterdam: Elsevier.
Mandatory Provident Fund Authority. 2011. *Annual Report 2010/2011* (www.mpfa.org.hk/
    english/quicklinks/quicklinks_pub/files/22_MPF_AR1011_E.pdf).
Matrix Services Ltd. 2012.
Menon, J. 2007. "Dealing with Dollarization: What Options for the Transitional Economies
    of Southeast Asia?" Discussion Paper 63. Tokyo: ADB Institute (http://aric.adb.org/pdf/
    workingpaper/WP19_Cambodias_Persistent_Dollarization.pdf).
Organization for Economic Cooperation and Development. 2009. *Pensions at a Glance:
    Special Edition Asia/Pacific* (www.oecd.org/dataoecd/33/53/41966940.pdf).
————. 2011a. *Pensions at a Glance 2011: Retirement-Income Systems in OECD and G20
    Countries* (www.oecd.org/els/social/pensions/PAG).

———. 2011b. *Pensions at a Glance Asia/Pacific* (www.oecd.org/dataoecd/37/41/49454618. pdf).

———. 2012a. *OECD Database on Bank Profitability* (http://stats.oecd.org/Index.aspx? DataSetCode=BPF1).

———. 2012b. *Institutional Investors' Assets* (http://stats.oecd.org/Index.aspx?DatasetCode= 7IA).

Park, C-Y, and J-W Lee. 2011. "Financial Integration in Emerging Asia: Challenges and Prospects." *Asian Economic Policy Review* 6, no. 2: 176–98.

Park, D. 2009. "Ageing Asia's Looming Pension Crisis." ADB Economics Working Paper 165. Manila: Asian Development Bank (www.adb.org/Documents/Working-Papers/2009/ Economics-WP165.pdf).

Petri, P. 2007. "Financing Asia's Future." Paper prepared for Asian Development Bank Institute 10th Anniversary Conference, Tokyo, December 4 (www.adbi.org/files/cpp.financing. asias.future.petri.pdf).

U.S. Social Security Administration and International Social Security Association. 2011. *Social Security Programs throughout the World: Asia and the Pacific 2010* (www.ssa.gov/policy/docs/ progdesc/ssptw/2010-2011/asia/ssptw10asia.pdf).

World Bank. 2011. *World Development Indicators 2010.* Washington.

World Economic Outlook. 2011. Database (www.imf.org/external/pubs/ft/weo/2011/02/ weodata/index.aspx).

World Federation of Exchanges. 2012. *World Federation of Exchanges Database* (www.world-exchanges.org/statistics).

Zhuang, J., and others. 2009. "Financial Sector Development, Economic Growth, Poverty Reduction: A Literature Review." Economics Working Paper 173. Manila: Asian Development Bank (www.adb.org/Documents/Working-Papers/2009/Economics-WP173.pdf).

5

Financial Globalization in Emerging Countries: Diversification versus Offshoring

FRANCISCO CEBALLOS, TATIANA DIDIER,
AND SERGIO L. SCHMUKLER

S tarting in the early 1990s, as developed and emerging countries became more integrated within the global financial system and especially as international transactions seemed to grow, interest in financial globalization increased substantially.[1] Since then, many have questioned the links between financial globalization and economic growth and have revisited the overall costs and benefits of financial integration.[2] In principle, financial globalization should increase access to capital and lower its costs.[3] But financial globalization may also expose

This chapter derives from the background work prepared for the World Bank flagship report, "Financial Development in Latin America and the Caribbean: The Road Ahead." The authors received very helpful comments from Augusto de la Torre, Alain Ize, Eduardo Levy Yeyati, Eswar Prasad, and Luis Servén, among many others, and from participants in presentations held by the ADBI in Tokyo, by the American University in Washington, by the Casas das Garcas in Rio de Janeiro, by the Central Bank of Brazil, by the Central Bank of Colombia and the Global Development Network Annual Meeting in Bogota, by the Chamber of Commerce in Lima, by the IMF, by the ITAM and the National Banking and Securities Commission in Mexico City, by the NIPFP-DEA in Delhi, and by the World Bank. The authors are grateful to Luciano Cohan, Juan Cuattromo, Gustavo Meza, Julian Kozlowski, Lucas Nuñez, Paula Pedro, Virginia Poggio, Andres Schneider, Patricio Valenzuela, Luis Fernando Vieira, and Gabriel Zelpo for outstanding research assistance. For help in gathering unique data, they thank the ADR team from the Bank of New York, among many others. The authors wish to thank the World Bank Latin American and the Caribbean Region, the Knowledge for Change Program (KCP), and the Development Economics vice presidency for financial support.

1. Obstfeld and Taylor (2004); Lane and Milesi-Ferreti (2007); Obstfeld (2012).
2. Rodrik (1998); Stiglitz (2002); Kose and others (2010).
3. Foerster and Karolyi (1999); Stulz (1999); Errunza and Miller (2000); Errunza (2001).

countries to foreign shocks and crises, thus raising several new macrofinancial challenges, such as the regulation and use of domestic financial markets and the conduct of macroprudential policies.[4]

Despite all the attention to financial globalization, its concept and extent have remained somewhat elusive. For example, different authors use, alternatively, net capital flows, gross capital flows, and country portfolios as measures of financial globalization.[5] Many also measure globalization through the participation of foreigners in domestic markets, while a number of other studies focus on the access of domestic firms and governments to foreign capital.[6] Moreover, while there is much discussion of increased financial globalization, little is known about whether the sharp trend of globalization that took place during the 1990s continued during the following decade or whether the nature (or type) of financial globalization has changed.[7]

In this chapter we explore two dimensions of the financial globalization process of these decades.[8] The first is *financial diversification,* that is, the cross-country holdings of foreign assets and liabilities. As home bias is reduced, domestic investors increase their investments abroad and foreigners expand their investments at home. This first dimension of globalization is determined by *who* holds the assets and liabilities in domestic and international markets. The second dimension is *financial offshoring,* that is, the use of foreign jurisdictions to conduct financial transactions. In particular, we investigate how the use of foreign markets is associated with the use of domestic markets. This second dimension of globalization is determined by *where* assets are traded, irrespective of who is trading them.

Although we study evidence from around the world, including developed countries, we concentrate our analysis on emerging countries—which are perceived to be the ones that underwent the most significant financial liberalization since the early 1990s.[9] A large part of the literature focuses on the effects of globalization on these countries—and reaches very different conclusions. Our analysis is based on a sample of countries from a selected set of emerging regions in Asia, Eastern Europe, and Latin America for which the challenges associated with the process of financial globalization are particularly relevant.

4. Dornbusch, Goldfajn, and Valdes (1995); Calvo and Reinhart (2000); Allen and Gale (2000); Reinhart and Reinhart (2009); Kawai and Lamberte (2010); Calvo (2011).

5. Lane and Milesi-Ferretti (2001, 2007); Kraay and others (2005); Devereux (2007); Gourinchas and Rey (2007); Reinhart and Reinhart (2009); Broner and others (2010).

6. Forbes (2006); Kose and others (2010); Henry (2007); Gozzi, Levine, and Schmukler (2010).

7. One exception is Levy Yeyati and Williams (2011).

8. Before the Great Depression, several emerging countries had access to international markets. But that earlier globalization period seems more restricted than the one experienced after 1990.

9. Kaminsky and Schmukler (2008).

We also analyze trends in G-7 and other developed countries.[10] Moreover, we focus on the two decades in question because the extent of financial globalization before 1990 was rather limited, especially for the broad spectrum of emerging countries.

Our findings suggest that, according to widely used de facto measures, financial diversification continued rising across emerging countries during the first decade of the 2000s when compared to the 1990s. Namely, the stock of foreign assets and liabilities (a stock measure) and capital flows by domestic and foreign agents (a gross flow measure) increased.[11] Interestingly, this trend is more accentuated in developed countries than in emerging ones. Despite starting from a higher level of financial diversification, developed countries experienced on average a greater expansion of flows as a percentage of GDP and a significantly larger increase in the stock of foreign assets and liabilities during the 2000 decade. Therefore, while the notion that emerging countries became more financially globalized during the first ten years of the 2000s seems correct, in relative terms they lagged behind the deeper globalization process observed across developed countries. Furthermore, this increased financial globalization was characterized by a two-way process that entailed a higher participation of both foreigners in local markets and domestic agents in foreign markets. Interestingly, the large expansion in cross-country holdings led by greater volumes of gross capital flows was not matched by an expansion in net capital flows.[12] Valuation effects were one of the drivers of this increase in financial diversification, especially for equity investments.

A noteworthy feature of the process of financial diversification during the first decade of the 2000s is the safer form of integration of many emerging countries, arising from the changing structure of their external assets and liabilities. More specifically, emerging countries typically became net creditors in debt assets and net debtors in equity assets. This contrasts sharply with the structure prevalent in the 1990s, when emerging countries held large debtor positions, especially in debt assets. This new structure of foreign assets and liabilities is particularly

10. The following regions (countries) are included in our sample: Asia (Indonesia, Malaysia, Philippines, South Korea, and Thailand), People's Republic of China, Eastern Europe (Croatia, Czech Republic, Hungary, Lithuania, Poland, Russian Federation, and Turkey), G-7 (Canada, France, Germany, Italy, Japan, United Kingdom, and United States), India, Latin America (Argentina, Brazil, Chile, Colombia, Mexico, Peru, and Uruguay), and other developed countries (Australia, Finland, Israel, New Zealand, Norway, Spain, and Sweden).

11. Note, however, that these measures of diversification capture only part of the financial globalization process, which also entails the ability to trade assets across countries, the ability of financial institutions to operate in different jurisdictions (most notably foreign banks operating at home), and the equalization of asset prices and returns across borders (even without actual transactions taking place). These other aspects of financial globalization are nonetheless beyond the scope of this chapter, and some of them are related to de jure measures of financial globalization.

12. Broner and others (2010).

beneficial in times of turbulence, when balance-sheet effects work in their favor. For example, during global crises the local currency value of emerging countries' foreign assets tends to increase, given that they own hard-currency debt (which appreciates vis-à-vis emerging countries' currencies), while that of their foreign liabilities shrinks, given that they owe equity to the rest of the world. As observed during the global financial crisis of 2008–09, with the collapse in economic growth and asset valuations in financial markets, the local currency value of emerging countries' equity liabilities contracted. This seems to have substantially benefited emerging countries at the expense of some developed countries, particularly the United States, and might have helped strengthen their resilience to the global financial crisis.[13]

In contrast to the widespread expansion in international financial diversification during the first decade of the 2000s, we provide evidence of more mixed patterns regarding the evolution of financial offshoring. A large expansion occurred in the 1990s, mostly because it was basically nonexistent before (at least in recent history). But the relatively large offshoring of the 1990s was not widely sustained during the following decade, as its expansion varied significantly across countries and markets. For example, capital-raising activity in foreign markets through syndicated loans expanded around the world as a percentage of GDP during the first ten years of the 2000s, especially for developed countries. On the other hand, capital-raising activity through debt and equity issues as a percentage of GDP remained somewhat stable during this period and even declined in several countries. Moreover, offshoring remains highly concentrated—that is, with not many firms participating.

Compared to domestic markets, there is also heterogeneity in the use of foreign markets. For example, in some emerging countries, and in developed countries more broadly, offshoring through corporate bonds gained in importance and foreign markets became relatively important as a source of new financing for the private sector. However, when equity markets are analyzed, this trend is seen to be limited to a much smaller set of countries, being particularly marked in People's Republic of China and in Latin America. In addition, for Latin American countries, the apparent migration to foreign equity markets by the private sector was accompanied by liquidity abroad increasing relative to domestic liquidity, suggesting a shift of equity trading to foreign markets. In contrast, public sector bond financing shifted away from foreign markets toward domestic markets for most countries in our sample, reflecting to some extent the authorities' attempts to reduce their dollar exposure and to develop their local currency public debt markets, which proved successful to some extent.

---

13. Gourinchas and Rey (2007); Lane and Milesi-Ferretti (2011); Kose and Prasad (2010); Didier, Hevia, and Schmukler (2011).

The nature of foreign financing changed too, in general toward the better across emerging countries. Mirroring changes in local bond markets is a reduction in credit risk in foreign markets through an increase in maturity and a lower degree of dollarization. For instance, foreign bond maturities at issuance were longer in the 2000 decade compared to the 1990s for both the private and public sectors in emerging countries. Moreover, some firms, as well as some governments, were able to place local currency bond issues abroad, although foreign placements typically remained almost exclusively denominated in foreign currency.

In sum, since the early 1990s there has been a broad-based increase in financial diversification through larger gross capital flows, tightening the linkages across countries. But this trend was not accompanied by a similar increase in financial offshoring through the use of foreign capital markets as a financing source or trading place.

In the rest of the chapter we discuss in more detail the diversification and offshoring dimensions of globalization, document and provide a broad overview of where emerging countries stand on commonly used and simple measures of financial diversification, and examine financial offshoring by evaluating recent trends for both the public and private sectors in absolute and relative terms (that is, the relative size of domestic and foreign capital markets for financial activities). We conclude with a discussion of possible further research on financial globalization.

The Diversification and Offshoring Dimensions

The diversification dimension of financial globalization is macroeconomic in essence. It relates to country-level capital flows and gross foreign positions in assets and liabilities—that is, domestic residents investing in foreign markets and foreigners investing at home. In theory, this process allows risk to be diversified more efficiently and provides opportunities for exploiting cross-border risk-adjusted return differentials, effectively exerting pressure to equalize returns across countries and instruments. In addition to enhancing the efficiency of resource allocation, increased financial diversification might play an important role in the development of local capital markets. It can enhance liquidity, boost research, improve the quantity and quality of information, increase transparency, and promote better corporate governance practices, thereby reducing agency problems.

Despite these positive effects, financial diversification might also have its downside. Over the years, volatile capital flows have led to more extreme booms and busts. In particular, surges in capital inflows to countries with shallow domestic financial markets and a limited menu of financial assets can generate systemic problems. Increased diversification of financial systems can also be associated with a greater exposure to external crises through the financial channel. This channel often involves international investors (common creditors) in the financial centers who propagate shocks across the various countries in their portfolios in response to changes in, for example, liquidity or asset quality.[14] Thus a crisis in one country can prompt international investors to sell off assets or to curtail lending to other countries. To the extent that these patterns characterize the behavior of foreign investors more broadly, a greater dependence on foreign financing might bring additional volatility to domestic economies by importing the fluctuations of international markets. Furthermore, because foreigners tend to provide financing in foreign currency, their involvement can lead to currency mismatches. Similarly, while domestic residents' investments abroad might help smooth their consumption, such investments may also facilitate capital flight by causing conditions at home to deteriorate (due to risk of devaluation, default, or expropriation), which, other things equal, can reduce the capital available for domestic financing.

In contrast to the macroeconomic essence of financial diversification, the offshoring dimension of globalization is mainly microeconomic and is related to the functioning of the financial sector. This dimension is based on the use by local residents of offshore (or external) markets or the use of foreign intermediaries (rather than onshore ones). Instead of issuing a stock locally, a firm might prefer to list it on a foreign exchange. The trade-offs inherent in the use of domestic and foreign markets are somewhat different in nature than those implied by the diversification dimension, and hence they entail different dynamics. A number of reasons could be behind offshoring, including access to markets with greater depth and liquidity as well as to better regulatory environments. The financial services provided offshore may also be cheaper or have specific features that make them preferable for specific transactions. Thus domestic and offshore markets may complement each other.[15] When domestic and offshore activities are complements, the correlation between financial development (understood as deeper domestic capital markets) and financial offshoring might be positive, as firms and agents use both markets for different purposes.

Nonetheless, domestic and international markets might also be substitutes, and the correlation between financial activities in these markets might turn

---

14. When leveraged investors such as banks and hedge funds face regulatory requirements, internal provisioning practices, or margin calls, they might rebalance their portfolios by selling their asset holdings in other countries. When the managers of open-end mutual funds foresee future redemptions after a shock in one country, they might raise cash by selling assets in other countries. See for example Kaminsky and Reinhart (2000); Martinez Peria, Powell, and Vladkova-Hollar (2005); and Cetorelli and Goldberg (2012) for the role of banks. Borensztein and Gelos (2003); Kaminsky, Lyons, and Schmukler (2004); Broner, Gelos, and Reinhart (2006); and Raddatz and Schmukler (2011), among others, discuss the role of mutual funds.

15. Henderson, Jegadeesh, and Weisbach (2006); Gozzi, Levine, and Schmukler (2010).

negative. An emblematic case is the use of more developed financial centers by firms and agents from emerging countries with relatively unsophisticated financial markets. Furthermore, increased offshoring may also be associated with some negative spillovers. For example, increased trading activity in foreign markets might have adverse effects on the liquidity of domestic stock markets through different channels.[16] Issuing securities abroad may shift a firm's trading volume out of the domestic market, a so-called liquidity migration effect. Moreover, it may lead to a drop in the trading and liquidity of stocks of the remaining domestic firms.[17] Because not all companies can access international markets, the negative externalities to domestic firms can be sizable. In particular, as smaller firms typically remain limited to local financing sources, such a migration can reduce not only the liquidity of the remaining firms in local markets but also their ability to raise capital, jeopardizing the intended broad-based nature of domestic capital markets.

Financial Diversification

The financial diversification dimension of financial globalization can be generally analyzed through both de jure and de facto measures. While the former is based on regulations and restrictions, including capital flow controls, the latter is related to the intensity of cross-border movements of capital. As these two types of measures are not necessarily closely correlated, some recent studies lean toward the more practical relevance of de facto measures.[18] We thus examine two commonly used de facto measures in the financial globalization literature: a stock-based one and a flow-based one.[19]

As documented in a number of studies, these de facto measures suggest an increasingly globalized world. Figure 5-1 shows the level of cross-border capital flows and the stock of cross-border assets and liabilities, scaled by GDP, for sev-

---

16. Levine and Schmukler (2007).

17. The negative effect on the remaining domestic firms might happen through two effects. The first one (negative spillovers) is linked with the increase in cost per trade at home due to fixed costs. The second effect (domestic trade diversion) follows from the fact that a firm's internationalization is related to improvements in its reputation, disclosure standards, analyst coverage, and shareholder base, which could induce investors to shift their attention away from firms trading onshore. Levine and Schmukler (2007) find empirical evidence of a significant negative effect of offshoring on domestic stock market liquidity. However, others argue instead that offshoring may enhance integration and thereby stimulate domestic trading and boost the liquidity of domestic firms. See for example Alexander, Eun, and Janakiramanan (1987); Domowitz, Glen, and Madhavan (1998); and Hargis (2000).

18. Kose and others (2010).

19. The stock of foreign assets and liabilities was compiled by Lane and Milesi-Ferretti (2007) and a flow-based one (gross capital flows by domestic and foreign residents) was compiled by Broner and others (2010).

Figure 5-1. *De Facto Financial Diversification of Countries,*
Select Countries, 1980–2007

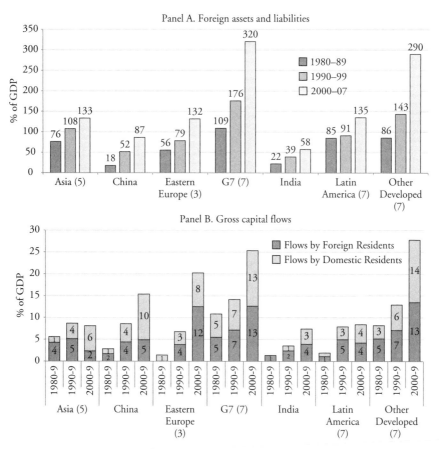

Panel A. Foreign assets and liabilities

% of GDP

1980–89
1990–99
2000–07

Asia (5) | China | Eastern Europe (3) | G7 (7) | India | Latin America (7) | Other Developed (7)

Panel B. Gross capital flows

% of GDP

Flows by Foreign Residents
Flows by Domestic Residents

Asia (5) | China | Eastern Europe (3) | G7 (7) | India | Latin America (7) | Other Developed (7)

Source: International Monetary Fund (various years); World Bank (various years); Lane and Milesi-Ferretti (2007).

eral emerging and developed regions during the 1980s, 1990s, and first decade of the 2000s. All regions witnessed an increase in financial diversification over this period, particularly during the latter decade. However, emerging regions still lag behind developed ones. The increase in financial diversification experienced by emerging countries, measured through either the stock or the flow measures, was considerably lower than that observed across developed countries. As a result, financial integration, in its diversification dimension, remains much more developed in developed countries than in emerging ones. For example, foreign assets and liabilities represented about 300 percent of GDP in developed countries in 2000–07, whereas in emerging countries they stood at less than half of that amount, around 130 percent of GDP in Asian, Eastern European, and Latin American countries.

This is a generalized process of two-way financial diversification, according to which not only have foreign residents invested more in local markets but also domestic residents have expanded their investments in foreign markets. Panel B of figure 5-1 segments capital flows by the residency of the agents completing the transaction, thus distinguishing between capital inflows by foreign residents and capital outflows by domestic residents. The figure shows that cross-border flows by both domestic and foreign residents have been on the rise during the past decades in almost all emerging and developed regions. Perhaps the only exception to this broad trend is Asia during the first decade of the 2000s, where flows by foreign residents declined significantly as a percentage of GDP, though flows by domestic residents still grew considerably.

The expansion of financial diversification, as measured by these de facto indicators, reflects not only increased volumes of gross capital flows but also positive valuation effects, stemming from the repricing of assets and liabilities. As many argue, capital gains and losses on outstanding holdings of foreign assets and liabilities can be indeed sizable.[20] Figure 5-2 illustrates these valuation effects by showing the increase between 1999 and 2007 in foreign holdings of domestic equity, scaled separately by GDP (as in figure 5-1) and by domestic market capitalization. In fact the increase in cross-border equity holdings (a component of the stock of foreign assets and liabilities in figure 5-1) is significantly smaller across all emerging regions when the growth of equity prices (proxied by market capitalization) is taken into consideration, even turning negative for Latin American countries. This suggests that the evidence of financial globalization needs to be considered with some care.

In addition to this expansion in the size of foreign assets and foreign liabilities over the past three decades, their composition evolved in a significant way. Figure 5-3 presents the changes in the different components of the stock of external liabilities (panel A) and external assets (panel B) as a share of GDP during the 1990s and the years 2000–07. When focusing on the liability side (which captures the stock of foreign investments in domestic economies), equity investments—including foreign direct investment—increased on average across emerging countries during both decades.[21] Debt investments, on the other hand, generally declined during both decades for this set of countries, with the exception of Asia in the 1990s and Eastern Europe in the first decade of the 2000s. This last trend stands in sharp contrast to that of developed countries, where debt investments greatly expanded over the same period.

---

20. See for example Lane and Milesi-Ferretti (2001, 2007); Gourinchas and Rey (2007); and Gourinchas, Govillot, and Rey (2010).

21. Even though the increases in equity investments are larger than increases in debt investments, this trend may reflect to some extent larger valuation effects, as discussed above.

Figure 5-2. *Financial Diversification, Valuation Effects,*
Select Countries, 1999–2007

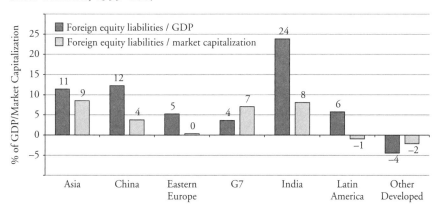

Source: World Bank (various years); Lane and Milesi-Ferretti (2007).

On the asset side (which captures the stock of foreign investments by domestic agents), emerging countries largely accumulated international reserves, a trend that has accelerated since the Asian crises of the late 1990s. This is an important feature underlying the emerging countries' improved macroeconomic and financial stances, albeit not the only one. The patterns of the other components of the stock of foreign assets are somewhat mixed. For example, Latin American countries increased their external asset positions mainly through equity investments in the first decade of the 2000s, while Eastern Europe did so through a large increase in debt investments. In the case of developed countries, debt investments capture the lion's share of the rise in their external assets during both the 1990s and the 2000 decade, though the increases in equity investments and foreign direct investment are still sizable.

These trends led to important changes in countries' overall positions as net creditors or net debtors. As discussed above, emerging countries typically experienced a decline in debt liabilities and an expansion in debt assets, especially when reserves are considered. Consequently, a number of them became net creditors with respect to the rest of the world as regards debt contracts. On the equity side, both assets and liabilities increased, albeit at different speeds. In net terms however, there has been a shift toward net debtor positions with respect to equity contracts among emerging countries; this has been increasingly so in recent years. Figure 5-4 shows the net foreign assets positions (that is, the difference between foreign assets and foreign liabilities) as a share of GDP for both equity and debt investments from 1990 to 2007. Asian and Latin American countries, together

Figure 5-3. *Structure of Financial Diversification, Select Countries, 1990–2007*

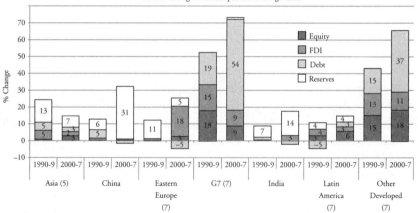

Source: World Bank (various years); Lane and Milesi-Ferretti (2007).
Note: FDI = foreign direct investment.

with India, became net creditors during the second half of the 2000 decade as regards debt contracts, while China increased its already positive position as a net creditor. At the same time, they continued deepening their net debtor stances as regards equity contracts. This stands in contrast to the mixed patterns observed in developed countries.

This evolution in the structure of countries' external assets and liabilities might play a role in avoiding the downside risks of financial globalization. For instance, when the 2008–09 global financial crisis hit emerging countries, balance-sheet effects worked in their favor. In emerging countries' not too distant past, the exchange rate nominal devaluations that typically accompanied

Figure 5-4. *Net Foreign Equity and Debt Assets, Selected Countries, 1990–2007*

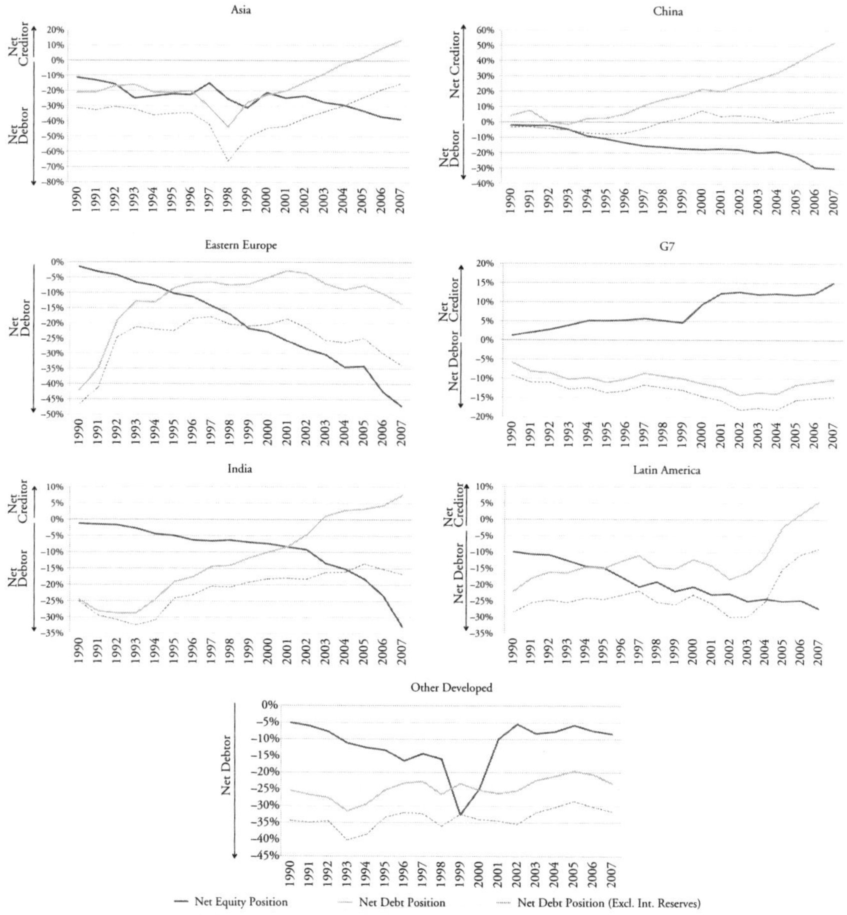

Source: World Bank (various years); Lane and Milesi-Ferretti (2007).

financial crises tended to increase the burden of foreign currency debt. In contrast, during the global financial crisis, the devaluations led to improvements in the external positions of emerging countries (when measured in local currency) due to their net creditor stances in debt contracts. Moreover, external liabilities were reduced when equity prices plummeted, thereby shrinking their net debtor equity positions. At the same time, the large pools of international reserves not only might have slowed down the appreciation of the domestic currency during the precrisis expansionary period but also might have later served as a self-insurance mechanism during the heightened turmoil period, deterring currency crises and banking panics. In fact many countries held international reserves in excess of their stock of short-term foreign liabilities. This in practice eliminated concerns about debt rollover difficulties in many emerging countries, limiting investors' incentives to attack the domestic currencies.[22] In sum, this evolution of emerging countries from a net debtor to a net creditor position, vis-à-vis the rest of the world, in terms of debt contracts—along with a reduction of foreign currency and short-term debt liabilities documented below—might have made these countries more resilient to external shocks, thus giving rise to a safer form of financial globalization.

Financial Offshoring

As the wave of financial liberalization swept the emerging world during the 1990s, financial offshoring took off, with the use of foreign markets ranging from syndicated loans to equities and bonds. Such an expansion in offshoring contrasts sharply with the lack of activity abroad during the 1980s. Nonetheless, during the first decade of the 2000s, mixed patterns emerged regarding the use of foreign markets for financial transactions by emerging countries. In fact there was a marked heterogeneity in the extent of offshoring across markets and countries.

Regarding debt contracts, somewhat opposing trends have been observed in new capital-raising activity through syndicated loans and bonds abroad across emerging countries.[23] As shown in panel A of figure 5-5, new syndicated loans continued to expand around the world over 2000–08. In contrast, as seen in panel B, the overall volume (as a percentage of GDP) of new bonds issued in foreign markets declined across a number of emerging countries, although it remained at relatively high levels. For example, bond issuance abroad fell from 3.2 to 2.4 percent of GDP a year for Asian countries and from 2.2 to 1.9 percent for Latin American countries in the first decade of the 2000s vis-à-vis the 1990s. Interestingly, this decline was concentrated on the new issuance of bonds by the private sector, as governments of countries in these two regions increased their issuance abroad as a percentage of GDP. Eastern Europe, however, stands as an exception, with bond issuance by its private sector actually expanding in foreign markets.

Mixed trends are also observed in capital-raising activity through equity issues in foreign markets as a percentage of GDP. As shown in panel C of figure 5-5, the use of foreign markets for new capital-raising equity issues greatly expanded for firms in China and Eastern Europe and, to a lesser extent, in India. On the other hand, it declined for firms in Asian and Latin American countries.

---

22. See, for example, Aizenman and Pasricha (2010); Aizenman (2011); and Frankel and Saravelos (2012).

23. For more analysis on how firms use domestic and international bond markets, see Gozzi and others (2012).

Figure 5-5. *Capital-Raising Activity in Foreign Markets, Selected Countries, 1991–2008*

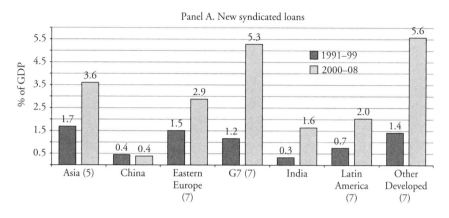

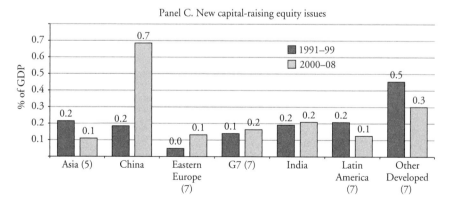

Source: World Bank (various years); Thomson Reuters' SDC platinum database.

Figure 5-6. *Foreign Bond Markets, Selected Countries, 1990–2009*

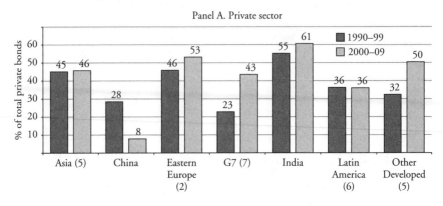

Panel A. Private sector

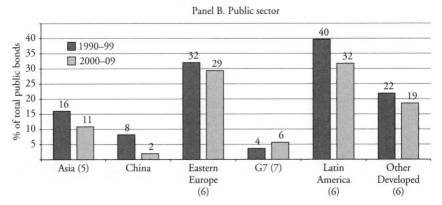

Panel B. Public sector

Source: World Bank (various years); Bank for International Settlements.

Contrasting trends are also observed across the developed world: while firms in G-7 countries increased their use of foreign markets, those in other developed countries reduced it.

Although the volume of new capital-raising activity abroad as a percentage of GDP did not show a consistent growth trend over the period 2000–08, private bond and equity financing in foreign markets still gained space relative to domestic markets in many—albeit not all—emerging regions. Panel A of figure 5-6 shows the amount outstanding of private sector bonds in foreign markets as a share of total private outstanding bonds. Bond financing in foreign markets typically increased in relevance over the period 2000–09 for emerging countries, though this increase was significantly more for developed countries. Moreover, bond financing abroad represents more than half of total bond financing by the private sector for a number of emerging countries. For example, outstanding amounts in foreign markets represented more than 50 percent of total outstanding bonds in 2000–09 for Eastern European countries and India and

Figure 5-7. *Foreign Equity Markets, Selected Countries, Various Years*

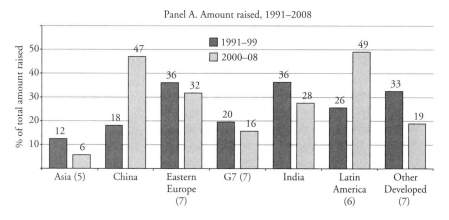

Panel A. Amount raised, 1991–2008

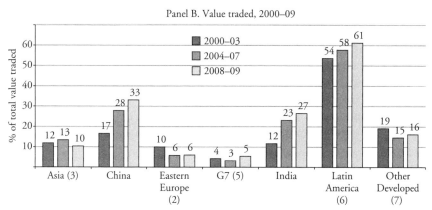

Panel B. Value traded, 2000–09

Source: Thomson Reuters' SDC platinum database; Bank of New York; Bloomberg.

about 46 percent for Asia. China however is an exception, with bonds in foreign markets representing only 8 percent of total outstanding bonds for the private sector in that period, down from 28 percent in the 1990s.

With respect to equity financing, there is more heterogeneity in the observed trends regarding the use of foreign markets relative to domestic markets. Panel A of figure 5-7 shows the ratio of equity issuance abroad to total equity issuance. Asian and Eastern European countries, along with developed ones, relied more on domestic markets for new equity issues, which already accounted for the bulk of new capital-raising issues during the 1990s. For instance, only 32 percent of the issues from Eastern European companies and 6 percent of the issues from Asian ones took place in foreign markets during 2000–08. In stark contrast, Latin America and China saw a greater degree of offshoring through equity markets during 2000–08. Equity financing abroad in these countries gained space relative to domestic markets and has come to represent almost 50 percent of total equity issues, up from about 20 percent during the 1990s.

Foreign stock issuance by emerging countries typically takes the form of cross-listings through depositary receipts (DRs), which are particularly useful to analyze the dynamics of trading activity in domestic and foreign markets. Although DRs represent ownership of stocks listed in local markets, they are traded in stock exchanges abroad, mostly in financial centers such as the New York Stock Exchange, NASDAQ, and the London Stock Exchange. Panel B of figure 5-7 shows the evolution from 2000 to 2009 of the average share of value traded abroad through DRs relative to total value traded (domestic plus abroad through DRs). A clear pattern emerges: the apparent migration to foreign equity markets by the private sector in China and Latin American countries was accompanied by increased trading abroad relative to domestic trading activity. In fact the share of trading activity abroad grew to represent the bulk of trading throughout 2000–09: 60 percent for Latin American countries and more than 30 percent for China. This trend suggests a shift of liquidity to foreign markets and a potentially diminishing role for domestic markets in light of the increased offshoring of equity markets.[24] For most other emerging regions, however, trading in foreign markets accounts for a small share of total trading activity, about 10 percent. Moreover, a stable balance in trading activity between domestic and foreign markets was maintained.

While the relevance of domestic markets in bond and equity financing relative to foreign markets declined for the private sector of many emerging countries during the first decade of the 2000s, the use of foreign bond markets by the government typically followed opposite trends. It actually increased for the public sector in most emerging countries. Public bond financing shifted toward domestic markets, though, as pointed out above, the issuance of public bonds abroad as a percentage of GDP increased during 2000–09. Panel B of figure 5-6 shows the amount outstanding of bonds in foreign markets over total public sector outstanding bonds. It is clear from this figure that the relative importance of foreign bonds decreased during 2000–09 vis-à-vis the 1990s across all emerging regions. This trend was particularly sharp among Asian and Latin American countries, consistent thus with the significant expansion of local markets for government bonds in many of these countries. Despite this declining trend, emerging countries still tend, more than developed countries, to rely on foreign markets for the placement of their debt. While across G-7 countries about 6 percent of outstanding government bonds was in foreign markets during the first ten years of the 2000s, around 30 percent was observed across Eastern Europe and Latin America.

Notwithstanding these mixed trends in the overall degree of financial offshoring, the first decade of the 2000s witnessed some interesting changes in the

---

24. See for instance Didier and Schmukler (2012a, 2012b).

Figure 5-8. *Maturity at Issuance in Foreign Bond Markets, Selected Countries, 1991–2008*

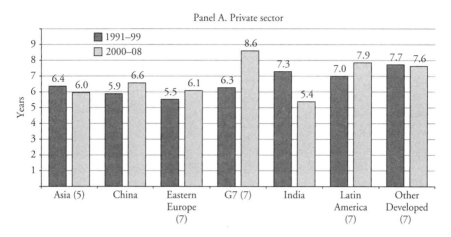

Panel A. Private sector

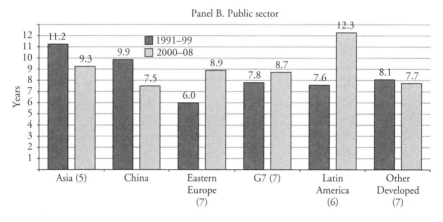

Panel B. Public sector

Source: Thomson Reuters' SDC platinum database.

nature of external bond financing across a number of emerging countries. While total bond issuance in foreign markets did not increase, on average, for these countries during this time period, a number of them changed the nature of their bond financing, apparently in a conscious effort to reduce currency and maturity mismatches following the financial crises of the 1990s.

As a consequence, the maturity profile of both public and private sector bonds in foreign markets extended through the 2000–09 period, especially for Eastern European and Latin American countries, as shown in figure 5-8.[25] For example,

25. The long maturities could also be associated with relatively short durations if most of the debt is issued at floating rates. Currently, the data do not allow us to identify such effects.

Figure 5-9. *Currency Denominations at Issuance in Foreign Bond Markets,*
Selected Countries, 1991–2008

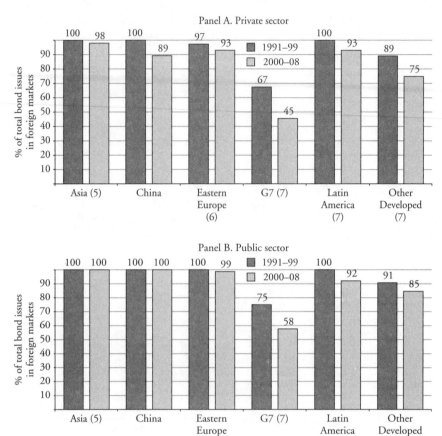

Source: Thomson Reuters' SDC platinum database.

the maturity of bonds at issuance was lengthened by about one and five years for
Latin America's private and public sectors, respectively. Asian countries however
stand out as exceptions: both public and private sector bond maturities declined
during 2000–09 relative to the 1990s.

Furthermore, many emerging countries have been able to issue bonds in
local currency in foreign markets. The private sector of most emerging regions
has succeeded in issuing some bonds in foreign markets in their own local currencies, while a few governments have also been able to do so. For example,
figure 5-9 shows that 7 percent of private sector bonds and 8 percent of public sector bonds issued abroad by Latin American countries in 2000–09 were
denominated in local currency, as opposed to a virtually nonexistent amount

Figure 5-10. *Use of Foreign Private Bond Markets, Selected Countries, 1991–2008*

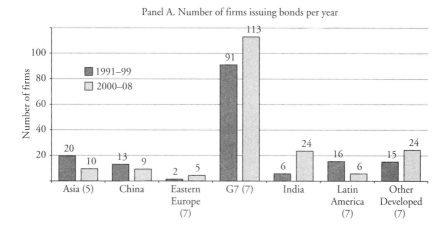

Panel A. Number of firms issuing bonds per year

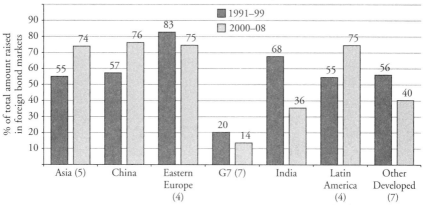

Panel B. Share of amount raised by top five bond issues

Source: Thomson Reuters' SDC platinum database.

during the 1990s. While these figures remain somewhat small, especially when compared to those of developed countries, they signal that emerging countries have started to overcome the "original sin" (generally understood as the inability to issue local currency, long-term debt in foreign markets). Clearly, these are positive strides in the long road toward a more balanced issuance pattern.

Despite all these developments, the use of foreign markets is limited to a few firms and thus remains a concern for many emerging countries, especially when contrasted with the observed patterns in developed countries. For instance, panel A of figure 5-10 clearly shows that only a small number of firms from most emerging regions actually used foreign bond markets as a source for new capital during 2000–09, typically fewer than ten firms compared to more than a hundred in the G-7 countries. Moreover, the number of firms in Asia, China, and Latin America actually declined vis-à-vis the 1990s. In addition, markets remain largely concentrated, as top issuers capture a significant fraction of the total new bond financing abroad. For instance, panel B of figure 5-10 shows that the amount raised by the largest five bond issues in foreign markets by the private sector in Asia, Eastern Europe, and Latin America represented on average about 75 percent of the total amount of bonds issued abroad during the 2000–08 period. In contrast, the largest five issues from firms of G-7 countries represented only 14 percent of the total amount raised through bonds in foreign markets. Strikingly, market concentration on issuance has in fact increased for many emerging countries. In other words, fewer and fewer firms seem to capture the bulk of the foreign market for bond financing.

As regards equity markets, the scope of offshoring also remains somewhat limited, in line with the trends observed in bond markets. As seen in figure 5-11, the number of firms using foreign equity financing on a regular basis is rather small in emerging countries when compared to developed countries. For instance, on average only two firms in Asian, Eastern European, or Latin American countries issued equity in any given year during the period 2000–08, in comparison to over fifteen firms in developed countries. Similar to the patterns observed in the use of foreign bond markets, the average number of firms raising capital in equity markets abroad did not increase for many emerging countries during the period 2000–08. In contrast, over the same period this number rose for developed countries. Equity financing in foreign markets also remained highly concentrated on a few issues. For most emerging countries, the largest five international issues represented around 90 percent of the market, though this is more in line with the levels of concentration seen in developed countries. Furthermore, the share of the total amount raised abroad by the largest five issues increased for a number of emerging countries. Finally, trading activity in foreign equity markets was also highly concentrated in a few firms (panel C of figure 5-11), with the top five firms in Latin American countries capturing more than 90 percent of the total trading activity in foreign markets. Note however that some emerging regions, such as Asia and Eastern Europe, show a reduction in trading concentration during the period.

Conclusions

The topic of financial globalization continues to receive extensive attention. In this chapter we discuss what this means for emerging countries, how much it has expanded, and to what extent its nature has shifted over time. In particular, we distinguish between two aspects of financial globalization: financial diversification (that is, the cross-country holdings of assets and liabilities) and financial offshoring (that is, the use of international financial markets by firms and

Figure 5-11. *Use of Foreign Equity Markets, Selected Countries, Various Years*

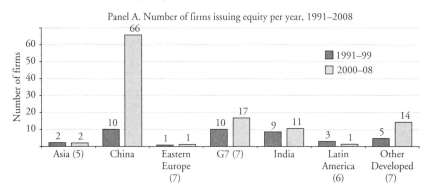

Panel A. Number of firms issuing equity per year, 1991–2008

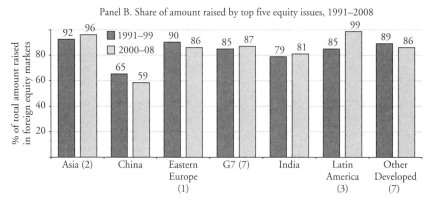

Panel B. Share of amount raised by top five equity issues, 1991–2008

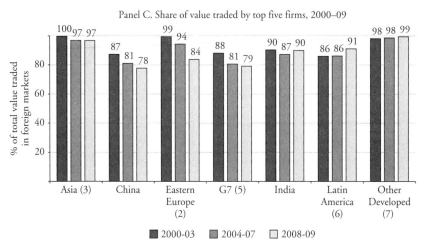

Panel C. Share of value traded by top five firms, 2000–09

Source: Thomson Reuters' SDC platinum database; Bank of New York; Bloomberg.

governments to perform their financial transactions). The former focuses on who holds the assets, the latter on where assets are transacted.

We show that, during the period 2000–09, emerging countries continued their process of financial globalization through diversification. Foreign assets and liabilities increased, as domestic residents invested more abroad and foreigners invested more at home. Moreover, the nature of the integration into the global financial system changed in several important respects. Emerging countries in particular reduced the extent of credit risk, making themselves less vulnerable to external financial shocks.

Despite this increase in diversification, the extent of offshoring did not expand as consistently across markets or across emerging countries. Whereas in the 1990s emerging countries increased their use of international markets for their financial transactions, in the following decade mixed patterns were observed. There is significant heterogeneity in the trends regarding the use of foreign markets as a percentage of GDP as well as relative to the use of domestic markets. For example, while the corporate sector of many countries increasingly used foreign debt markets, governments started using domestic debt markets more intensively. Domestic equity markets in some regions, but not in others, also gained more relevance. Furthermore, the positive developments in domestic markets in terms of the nature of financing were matched by similar developments in foreign markets.

The continuing integration of emerging countries into the global financial system poses many questions to policymakers. What are the net effects of globalization? On the one hand, it allows agents to diversify risk and tap into other investment opportunities. It also allows firms and governments to reduce the cost of capital by accessing funds that would otherwise be hard to obtain. On the other hand, globalization has several potential negative spillovers, which need to be understood in more detail (let alone netted out from the benefits). One possible negative spillover is the migration of activity to international markets, thereby reducing the financing and trading activity at home. Since not all companies can access international markets, this migration can generate negative domestic spillover effects. However, the underdevelopment of local markets is unlikely to be due to the globalization process alone.

Does financial globalization entail more risk? On the equity side, the answer appears to be negative. On the debt side, globalization might entail exchange rate risk, though in some cases it might reduce maturity risk. Hence to reduce exchange rate risk, domestic markets seem to play an important role. Moreover, what is the relation between domestic and international markets? Do domestic and international capital markets act as complements or substitutes? This chapter argues that the evidence suggests that they are complementary.

More broadly, though, what is the driver of the globalization process? Is it just a search for more and cheaper capital from segmented markets? Is it a quest for better corporate governance? The literature puts forward arguments supporting both, and some evidence suggests that the former cannot be rejected. Furthermore, because several of the trends documented in this chapter are similar across countries, what is the role for domestic policymaking given these secular forces? These questions remain unanswered and call for further research.

References

Aizenman, J. 2011. "The Impossible Trinity." In *The Encyclopedia of Financial Globalization,* edited by G. Caprio. Amsterdam: Elsevier.

Aizenman, J., and G. K. Pasricha. 2010. "Determinants of Financial Stress and Recovery during the Great Recession." Working Paper 16605. Cambridge, Mass.: National Bureau of Economic Research. Forthcoming, *International Journal of Finance and Economics.*

Alexander, G., C. Eun, and S. Janakiramanan. 1987. "Asset Pricing and Dual Listing on Foreign Capital Markets: A Note." *Journal of Finance* 42, no. 1: 151–58.

Allen, F., and D. Gale. 2000. "Bubbles and Crises." *Economic Journal* 110: 236–55.

Borensztein, E., and G. Gelos, 2003. "A Panic-Prone Pack? The Behavior of Emerging Market Mutual Funds." *IMF Staff Papers* 50, no. 1: 43–63.

Broner, F., G. Gelos, and C. Reinhart. 2006. "When in Peril, Retrench: Testing the Portfolio Channel of Contagion." *Journal of International Economics* 69, no. 1: 203–30.

Broner, F., and others. 2010. "Gross Capital Flows: Dynamics and Crises." Working Paper 1039. Bank of Spain.

Calvo, G. 2011. "Capital Inflows, Liquidity, and Bubbles." School of International and Public Affairs, Columbia University.

Calvo, G., and C. Reinhart. 2000. "When Capital Flows Come to a Sudden Stop: Consequences and Policy." In *Reforming the International Monetary and Financial System,* edited by P. B. Kenen and A. K. Swoboda. Washington: International Monetary Fund.

Cetorelli, N., and L. Goldberg. 2012. "Follow the Money: Quantifying Domestic Effects of Foreign Bank Shocks in the Great Recession." *American Economic Review: Papers and Proceedings.*

Devereux, M. 2007. "Financial Globalization and Emerging Market Portfolios." *Monetary and Economic Studies* 25: 101–30.

Didier, T., C. Hevia, and S. Schmukler. 2011. "How Resilient and Countercyclical Were Emerging Economies to the Global Financial Crisis?" Policy Research Working Paper 5637. Washington: World Bank. Forthcoming, *Journal of International Money and Finance.*

Didier, T., and S. Schmukler. 2012a. "Financial Development in Latin America: Stylized Facts and the Road Ahead." Washington: World Bank.

———. 2012b. "Financial Globalization: Some Basic Indicators for Latin America and the Caribbean." Washington: World Bank.

Domowitz, I., J. Glen, and A. Madhavan. 1998. "International Cross-Listing and Order Flow Migration: Evidence from an Emerging Market." *Journal of Finance* 53, no. 6: 2001–27.

Dornbusch, R., I. Goldfajn, and R. Valdes. 1995. "Currency Crises and Collapses." *Brookings Papers on Economic Activity,* no. 2: 219–93.

Errunza, V. 2001. "Foreign Portfolio Equity Investments, Financial Liberalization, and Economic Development." *Review of International Economics* 9: 703–26.

Errunza, V., and D. Miller. 2000. "Market Segmentation and the Cost of Capital in International Equity Markets." *Journal of Financial and Quantitative Analysis* 35: 577–600.

Foerster, S., and G. A. Karolyi. 1999. "The Effects of Market Segmentation and Investor Recognition on Asset Prices: Evidence from Foreign Stocks Listing in the United States." *Journal of Finance* 54: 981–1013.

Forbes, K. 2006. "The Microeconomic Evidence on Capital Controls: No Free Lunch in Capital Controls and Capital Flows." In *Emerging Economies: Policies, Practices, and Consequences,* edited by S. Edwards. University of Chicago Press.

Frankel, J. A., and G. Saravelos. 2012. "Can Leading Indicators Assess Country Vulnerability? Evidence from the 2008–09 Global Financial Crisis." *Journal of International Economics* 87, no. 2: 216–31.

Gourinchas, P. O., N. Govillot, and H. Rey. 2010. "Exorbitant Privilege and Exorbitant Duty." IMES Discussion Paper 10-E-20. Bank of Japan.

Gourinchas, P. O., and H. Rey. 2007. "International Financial Adjustment." *Journal of Political Economy* 115, no. 4: 665–703.

Gozzi, J. C., R. Levine, and S. Schmukler. 2010. "Patterns of International Capital Raisings." *Journal of International Economics* 80, no. 1: 45–57.

Gozzi, J. C., and others. 2012. "How Firms Use Domestic and International Corporate Bond Markets." Working Paper 17763. Cambridge, Mass.: National Bureau of Economic Research.

Hargis, K. 2000. "International Cross-Listing and Stock Market Development in Emerging Economies." *International Review of Economics and Finance* 9, no. 2: 101–22.

Henderson, B. J., N. Jegadeesh, and M. S. Weisbach. 2006. "World Markets for Raising New Capital." *Journal of Financial Economics* 82: 63–101.

Henry, P. B. 2007. "Capital Account Liberalization: Theory, Evidence, and Speculation." *Journal of Economic Literature* 45: 887–935.

International Monetary Fund. Various years. Balance-of-Payments Statistics. Washington.

Kaminsky, G., R. Lyons, and S. Schmukler. 2004. "Managers, Investors, and Crises: Mutual Fund Strategies in Emerging Markets." *Journal of International Economics* 64, no. 1: 113–34.

Kaminsky, G., and C. Reinhart. 2000. "On Contagion, Crisis and Confusion." *Journal of International Economics* 51, no. 1: 145–68.

Kaminsky, G., and S. Schmukler. 2008. "Short-Run Pain, Long-Run Gain: The Effects of Financial Liberalization." *Review of Finance* 12, no. 2: 253–92.

Kawai, M., and M. Lamberte, eds. 2010. *Managing Capital Flows: The Search for a Framework.* Cheltenham, UK: Edward Elgar.

Kose, M. A., and E. Prasad. 2010. *Emerging Markets: Resilience and Growth amid Global Turmoil.* Brookings.

Kose, M. A., and others. 2010. "Financial Globalization and Economic Policies." In *Handbook of Development Economics,* vol. 5, edited by Dani Rodrik and Mark Rosenzweig, chap. 65. Amsterdam: Elsevier.

Kraay, A., and others. 2005. "Country Portfolios." *Journal of the European Economic Association* 3: 914–45.

Lane, P. R., and G. M. Milesi-Ferretti. 2001. "The External Wealth of Nations: Measures of Foreign Assets and Liabilities for Industrial and Developing Countries." *Journal of International Economics* 55: 263–94.

———. 2007. "The External Wealth of Nations Mark II: Revised and Extended Estimates of Foreign Assets and Liabilities, 1970–2004." *Journal of International Economics* 73: 223–50.

———. 2011. "The Cross-Country Incidence of the Global Crisis." *IMF Economic Review* 59, no. 1: 77–110.

Levine, R. 2001. "International Financial Liberalization and Economic Growth." *Review of International Economics* 9: 688–702.

Levine, R., and S. Schmukler. 2007. "Migration, Liquidity Spillovers, and Trade Diversion: The Effects of Internationalization on Stock Market Activity." *Journal of Banking and Finance* 31, no. 6: 1595–612.

Levy Yeyati, E., and T. Williams. 2011. "Financial Globalization in Emerging Economies: Much Ado about Nothing?" Policy Research Working Paper 5624. Washington: World Bank.

Martinez Peria, M., A. Powell, and I. Vladkova-Hollar. 2005. "Banking on Foreigners: The Behavior of International Bank Claims on Latin America, 1985–2000." *IMF Staff Papers* 52, no. 3: 430–61.

Obstfeld, M. 2012. "Financial Flows, Financial Crises, and Global Imbalances." *Journal of International Money and Finance* 31: 469–80.

Obstfeld, M., and A. Taylor. 2004. *Global Capital Markets: Integration, Crises, and Growth.* Cambridge University Press.

Raddatz, C., and S. Schmukler. 2011. "On the International Transmission of Shocks: Micro-Evidence from Mutual Fund Portfolios." Working Paper 17358. Cambridge, Mass.: National Bureau of Economic Research. Forthcoming, *Journal of International Economics.*

Reinhart, C. M., and V. Reinhart. 2009. "Capital Flow Bonanzas: An Encompassing View of the Past and Present." In *NBER International Seminar on Macroeconomics 2008.* University of Chicago Press.

Rodrik, Dani. 1998. "Who Needs Capital-Account Convertibility?" *Essays in International Finance* 207: 55–65.

Stiglitz, J. 2002. *Globalization and Its Discontents.* New York: W. W. Norton.

Stulz, R. 1999. "Globalization of Equity Markets and the Cost of Capital." Working Paper 7021. Cambridge, Mass.: National Bureau of Economic Research.

World Bank. Various years. *World Development Indicators.* Washington.

PART III

*Strengthening
Macroeconomic
Frameworks*

6

Strengthening Macroeconomic Frameworks: The Indian Experience

SUBIR GOKARN

As we look back over the recent financial crisis with a view to drawing lessons for future policy, it is important to see it in a historical context. From this perspective, a comparison of crises over time suggests that, although the recent crisis manifested some new characteristics, some fundamental ones remained the same. The recurrence of crises reflects a basic procyclicality in the system, which is characterized by a buildup of risk taking and leverage in good times and an abrupt withdrawal from risk and an unwinding of leverage in bad times. In this sense, the patterns of asset prices in the recent crisis are reminiscent of those in previous episodes.

The overall size of the U.S. housing boom and its dynamics, particularly house prices increasing by more than 30 percent in the five years preceding the crisis and peaking six quarters before its onset, bear a remarkable resemblance to patterns observed during previous banking crises in advanced economies (Finland, 1991; Japan, 1992; Norway, 1987; Sweden, 1991; and Spain, 1977).[1] Further, the prolonged U.S. credit expansion in the run-up to the crisis is similar to earlier episodes, except that this time it was relatively concentrated in one segment, that is, the subprime mortgage market.

However, perhaps more important for the purpose of drawing lessons for future policies for both prevention and cure, there were some new dimensions with respect to the transmission and amplification of the crisis that played an important role. These new dimensions include, first, the widespread use of

---

1. Reinhart and Rogoff (2009).

complex and opaque financial instruments; second, the increased interconnectedness among financial markets, nationally and internationally, with the United
States at the forefront; third, highly leveraged financial institutions; and fourth,
the central role of the housing sector. As a result of these factors, the financial
crisis—characterized by heightened systemic risks, falling asset values, and tightening credit, business, and consumer confidence—precipitated a sharp slowing
in global economic activity.

An important aspect of the crisis is that emerging Asia as a whole proved to be
quite resilient during and after a financial crisis that became the worst economic
downturn since the Great Depression. Emerging Asia's resilience held despite
increasing trade and financial integration between advanced and emerging market economies (EMEs). In addition to the effect on GDP growth, the financial
crisis affected capital flows to EMEs through flight to safety and rising home
country bias. As in the major industrial economies, emerging Asia's governments
and central banks were quick to respond to the shock, providing the necessary fiscal and monetary stimuli. Economic activity in the large developing Asian economies rebounded in the recovery phase beginning in 2010 and registered much
higher growth rates compared with the advanced economies.

If we were to look for a distinguishing feature of the recent crisis from the
perspective of EMEs, a good place to start would be the Asian experience, characterized as it was by resilience in the face of heightened vulnerability through both
trade and financial integration. We might hypothesize that resilience as coming
from two sources: one, the overall state of the economy, particularly the financial
sector, before the crisis; and two, the nature of policy responses to the crisis. A
comparative study of Asian economies would probably reveal several common
features on both dimensions, which would then explain the region's overall resilience. However, this is beyond the scope of this chapter, whose limited objective
is to apply this perspective to India.

The Indian economy clearly felt the adverse consequences of the financial
turmoil of the advanced economies despite its financial system not having any
direct exposure to mortgage-based securities. The off-balance-sheet exposures of
Indian banks as well as other financial intermediaries were quite limited. The
impact of the crisis on India's economy came through all three channels of global
interlinkage: trade, finance, and confidence. All three affected both the financial
and the real sectors directly and indirectly, reflecting the interdependence and
integration of the two sectors.

This chapter focuses on the regulatory and prudential aspects of macroeconomic policy in India. It also describes fiscal monetary coordination in the
precrisis period, which provided a cushion for the conduct of countercyclical
policies during the crisis. It then puts in perspective the Indian policy framework dealing with capital controls and financial sector regulation. It concludes
with a discussion of some potential trade-offs that arise in the design of a

macroeconomic financial framework that might help to contain the impact of future shocks.

Impact of Financial Crisis on India

During the initial phase of the global financial crisis of 2008, it appeared that the EMEs were better positioned than the advanced economies to weather the storm. This fortunate circumstance was because of their substantial foreign exchange reserve cushions, improved policy frameworks, and generally robust banking sector and corporate balance sheets. However, any hope of these economies escaping unscathed could not be sustained after the failure of Lehman Brothers and the ensuing spike in global risk aversion. The EMEs were also adversely affected by the spillover effects of the macroeconomic turbulence generated by the global financial meltdown. Depressed consumer and investor spending in the advanced economies led to a slump in demand for EME exports, which reinforced the inflow reversal.[2] However, the effect varied, depending on these economies' level of global integration.

During the initial phase of the crisis, the impact on Indian financial markets was rather muted. However, after mid-September 2008, it increased significantly. The fact that banks dominated India's financial system and that their engagement in off-balance-sheet activities and illiquid securitized assets was negligible (given that these assets were at the heart of the crisis for advanced economies) protected India from early turmoil in international financial markets. Nonetheless, India could not remain unscathed: global developments affected its financial and real activities in the latter part of 2008–09.

The backdrop to this transmission is, of course, the steady integration of India into the global economy. Globalization in India was strengthened and reinforced in the 1990s and 2000s by seven important developments. First, trade openness (goods and services trade) increased substantially, with the trade-to-GDP ratio doubling since 1999–2000. Second, services, which were largely considered non-tradable, turned increasingly tradable mainly due to offshoring, which was led by rapid innovations in information technology (information-technology-enabled services and business process outsourcing).

Third, the trade channel of global integration is supported by migration, with the competitive edge of human resources in knowledge-based services. The rising importance of the human channel, which operates directly through remittances and indirectly through trade in goods and services, in strengthening India's global integration is reflected in the widening gap between exports and imports of goods and services and current account receipts and payments as a percentage of GDP, which increased from about 2 percent in 1990–91 to around 7 percent during 2008–09.

2. Bank for International Settlements (2010).

Fourth, India's economy became more open to external capital flows as the gross capital account-to-GDP ratio witnessed a more than threefold increase during the same period. Fifth, higher capital account openness also strengthened the integration of domestic markets with global markets, which was reflected in the stronger correlations of domestic interest rates, equity, and commodity prices with their global counterparts. These developments also facilitated the role of expectations in transmitting global shocks to the domestic economy. Sixth, even in commodity-producing sectors, global integration came through prices and not necessarily through physical trade in commodities, as global price movements have an important expectation impact on domestic prices. Seventh, greater synchronization of domestic business cycles with global cycles means that external shocks could have a greater and more rapid impact on the domestic economy.

India's financial markets—equity, money, currency markets, and credit—all came under stress from a number of directions. First, the substitution of overseas financing by domestic financing put pressure on both the money and credit markets. Second, the currency market had to deal with a reversal of capital flows as part of the global deleveraging process; simultaneously, corporations were converting the funds raised locally into foreign currency to meet their external obligations. Third, the Reserve Bank's intervention in the foreign exchange market to manage the volatility in the rupee further contributed to liquidity tightening. Fourth, Indian banks as well as corporations were finding it difficult to raise funds from external sources as a consequence of the global liquidity squeeze, and as a result pressure escalated sharply on banks for the credit requirements of corporations. Also, in their frantic search for substitute financing, corporations withdrew their investments from domestic money market mutual funds, putting redemption pressure on the mutual funds and, down the line, on nonbank financial companies (NBFCs), where mutual funds had invested a significant portion of their funds. Overall, India also witnessed large capital outflows, exchange rate depreciation, protracted contraction in merchandise exports, and a steep fall in equity prices.

All these factors contributed to a sharp deceleration in the growth of the Indian economy. It was felt that the financial channel was more pronounced due to increasing globalization. The increase in trade and the liberalization of the capital account led to more global integration of the Indian economy, which in turn made India vulnerable to global shocks. Empirically, however, it has been established that global developments affected the Indian economy mainly through financial channels.

Impact on the Financial Sector

Despite the significant easing of crude oil prices and inflationary pressures, declining exports and continued capital outflows led by the global deleveraging process and the sustained strength of the U.S. dollar against other major currencies continued to exert downward pressure on the rupee. The rupee depreciated significantly against the U.S. dollar during September and October 2008. With the rupee reaching historically low levels, the intraquarter variation (between the high and the low) rose substantially during the second quarter of 2008–09 and continued until the first quarter of 2009–10. With spot exchange rates moving in a wide range, the volatility of the exchange rates also increased during this period.

MANAGING DOLLAR AND RUPEE LIQUIDITY. With a view to maintaining orderly conditions in the foreign exchange market, the Reserve Bank announced in mid-September 2008 that it would sell foreign exchange (U.S. dollars) through agent banks to augment supply in the domestic foreign exchange market or, barring that, it would intervene directly to meet any demand-supply gaps. Despite such intervention, the rupee depreciated in October 2008. In this period, several measures were undertaken by the Reserve Bank to ease the foreign exchange liquidity situation.

A rupee-dollar swap facility for Indian banks was introduced effective on November 7, 2008, to allow these banks to manage their short-term foreign funding requirements. To fund the swaps, banks were also allowed to borrow under the liquidity adjustment facility (LAF, the Reserve Bank's overnight lending and borrowing window for the banking system) for the corresponding tenure at the prevailing repurchase rate. (The foreign exchange swap facility was originally available until June 30, 2009. It was at first extended until March 31, 2010, but was finally discontinued in October 2009.) The Reserve Bank also continued its special market operations, which were instituted in June 2008 to meet the foreign exchange requirements of public sector oil marketing companies, taking into account the then prevailing extraordinary situation in the money and foreign exchange markets. These operations were largely rupee-liquidity neutral. Finally, measures to ease foreign exchange liquidity also included those aimed at encouraging capital inflows, such as an upward adjustment of the interest rate ceiling on foreign currency deposits by nonresident Indians, substantially relaxing the external commercial borrowing regime for companies and allowing nonbanking financial companies and housing finance companies to access foreign borrowing.

In short, as the financial crisis unfolded, the Reserve Bank provided substantial dollar liquidity to curb excessive volatility in the foreign exchange market, which had a tightening impact on rupee liquidity. Such operations by the Reserve Bank in the foreign exchange market, along with transient local factors such as buildup in government balances following quarterly advance tax payments, adversely impacted domestic liquidity conditions. The call money rate moved above the repurchase rate until the end of September 2008. As a result, the weighted average daily call rate—the proximate indicator of rupee liquidity—increased sharply in the second quarter of 2008–09 and prevailed above the LAF corridor in the first half of October 2008. It reached an intrayear peak on October 10, 2008.

With receding inflationary pressures and an accelerating global crisis, the Reserve Bank switched to an expansionary regime in mid-October 2008 and announced a series of measures, including a cut of cumulative 400 basis points in the cash reserve ratio (CRR), a cut of 100 basis points in the statutory liquidity ratio (SLR), and a cut of 425 basis points (and 275 basis points) in the repurchase (and reverse repurchase) rates, respectively, to augment domestic liquidity and reduce the cost of funds to the banking system (figure 6-1). Following the reversal of capital flows and an increase in the liquidity needs of the economy, the Reserve Bank also started unwinding the outstanding balances of the market stabilization scheme (MSS), resulting in a steady release of liquidity. This scheme had been put in place earlier to create capacity to sterilize purchases of foreign exchange when capital inflows were relatively high.

Effective November 2008, the Reserve Bank also started the buyback of dated securities, issued earlier under the MSS, to augment its efforts to hasten the pace of liquidity creation. The buyback was conducted through auctions and largely dovetailed with the normal market borrowing program of the central government. The measures initiated by the Reserve Bank augmented liquidity, and the weighted average call money rate declined and mostly remained within the LAF corridor from November 3, 2008, onward. Moreover, volumes in the money market also grew from January 2009 onward, suggesting that there has not been any adverse perception of counterparty risk. Consequently, the interbank money market functioned normally in India, in contrast to those of certain advanced economies.

Figure 6-1. *Monetary Policy Response to the Global Financial Crisis, India, 2003–12*

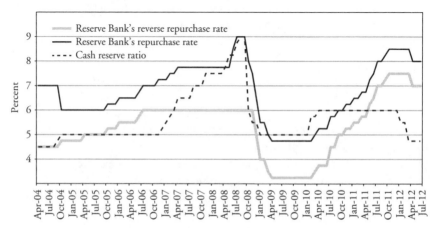

CAPITAL MARKETS AND ASSET PRICES. During the initial phase of the crisis, market capitalization of stock exchanges in East Asia and the Pacific region fell by more than 50 percent, comparable to the outcome one and a half decades earlier. Further, the decline was comparable to that of the OECD countries, which underlines the extent of global integration in transmitting shocks across markets. The Bombay Stock Exchange's (BSE) index of thirty key stocks, the Sensex, dipped by about 38 percent, to 12,860 at the end of September 2008, from a peak of 20,873 on January 8, 2008. Subsequently, it declined by a further 37 percent since the end of September 2008, to a new low of 8,160 on March 3, 2009. The decline in the Sensex from the peak to the new low was 61 percent. The volatility in Indian stock markets also increased in line with that in global stock markets since the beginning of 2008.

The macroeconomic impact of the declining stock market was evident in various ways. Household savings in equities as a share of their total savings declined. This, coupled with the decline of portfolio flows and stock prices, adversely affected the new issues of capital raised by private companies. Accordingly, the share of new capital issues in gross domestic capital formation fell.

To sum up, as Indian financial institutions—banks, mutual funds, and NBFCs—had limited international exposures in complex financial products, the Indian banking sector did not feel the heat in the first round. However, with the financial crisis deepening and beginning to spread across countries, especially after the fall of Lehman Brothers, Indian financial institutions, along with those in several other EMEs, started to face the challenges of the financial crisis in a manner somewhat different from that of their counterparts in advanced economies. The effects of the global financial crisis were felt first through the equity markets and eventually spread to the money market and the foreign exchange market. The tightening of liquidity conditions in the domestic market and the drying up of resources available from international markets, along with capital flow reversals, imposed new challenges for financial institutions in financing the productive needs of the economy.

As the impact of the crisis through the trade channel threatened to grow, the Reserve Bank initiated a spate of liquidity-easing and confidence-building measures to ensure that banks and mutual funds got ample resources to meet the demand for credit from Indian corporations. In contrast to the loss of confidence that the banking systems in advanced economies faced, the Indian banking system continued to command the confidence of the public, as was evident in the continued growth in deposits.

The monetary policy response was to introduce liquidity into the system through both conventional and unconventional measures. The conventional measures were policy rate cuts (CRR, reverse repurchases, and SLR) and open market operations. The unconventional measures were opening refinance facilities to specialized financial institutions that catered to small- and medium-size enterprises (SMEs) and to exports and clawing back prudential norms for provisioning and risk weights. Eventually, the actual or potential liquidity was Rs 5,850 billion (about 10 percent of GDP).

There are five other differences between the actions taken by the Reserve Bank of India and the central banks of many advanced countries. First, in the process of liquidity injection, the counterparties involved were banks; even liquidity measures for mutual funds, NBFCs, and housing finance companies were largely channeled through the banks. Second, there was no dilution of collateral standards, which were largely government securities, unlike the mortgage securities and commercial paper of the advanced economies. Third, despite a large liquidity injection, the Reserve Bank's balance sheet did not show an unusual increase, unlike global trends, because of the release of the earlier sterilized liquidity. Fourth, the availability and deployment of multiple instruments facilitated better sequencing of monetary and liquidity measures. Fifth, the experience in the use of procyclical provisioning norms and countercyclical regulations ahead of the global crisis helped enhance financial stability.

Impact on the Real Sector

The recent global crisis was unique in terms of its intensity and synchronization of slowdown across countries. Initially, there was widespread confidence that growth in the EMEs, particularly in Asia, would be decoupled from the problems of the advanced economies. Sound balance-of-payments positions and self-insurance provided by large international reserves accumulated from current account surpluses or private capital inflows were expected to protect them against the kind of financial shocks that had devastated the region during 1997–98. However, the region could not avoid a significant drop in growth, in large part because of a sharp contraction in exports when the financial crisis gripped the advanced world and spilled into the developing economies—and, not surprisingly, through the same channels (trade, finance, and confidence). Trade was the principal channel of transmission of deflationary impulses. In the countries where exports were growing faster than the domestic components of aggregate demand, the impact was felt through decreasing demand. In others, declines in exports impinged on economic activity by tightening the payments constraint and thereby narrowing the space for a countercyclical policy response (figure 6-2).

As indicated above, the transmission of global shocks to the real sector in India worked through four channels: trade, finance, expectations, and commodity prices. While traditionally the trade channel was the primary conduit of transmission of shocks to the real sector, financial channels have apparently become stronger over time, even as the trade channel has grown, with a rising trade-to-GDP ratio for goods and services. After the onset of the crisis, it was debated whether India, along with other EMEs, had remained unscathed and decoupled from advanced economies, which were witnessing a severe slowdown. However,

Figure 6-2. *Effect of the Global Financial Crisis on Selected Developing Asian Countries, Five Measures*

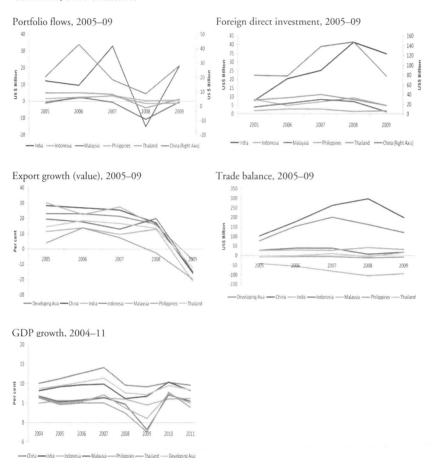

Source: World Bank (various years); International Monetary Fund (various years).

the growth of the Indian economy also slowed down from the third quarter of 2008–09, reflecting the increased business cycle synchronization of India with advanced countries and EMEs, which challenged the decoupling hypothesis, at least as far as business cycles are concerned.

Overall, the financial crisis affected the Indian economy directly through the trade channel, with export demand predominantly determined by external demand. Granger causality analysis reveals that the direction of causal relations ran from exports to GDP growth rates but not vice versa. Commodity patterns show that engineering goods were more responsive to the global economy. On the other hand, the direction of the causal relationship between the trade deficit ratio and economic growth was from the latter to the former, suggesting that import demand was driven strongly by domestic economic activity. Consequently, as import demand also contracted in tandem with domestic activity, the adverse impact of the slowdown in external demand on the balance of payments was contained.

An important lesson that policymakers took from this experience was this. To improve the prospects for exports on a more sustainable basis, the emphasis should be on both diversification, in terms of both markets and export items, and competitiveness. This had to be done without making the sector dependent on incentives like tax breaks, lower excise and customs duties on inputs used for exports, and concessional interest rates on financing for exporters, even though such incentives may be warranted in a phase of contraction in global demand as a temporary support to the export sector.

The commodity price channel operated mainly through shocks to international prices of primary commodities such as food, metals, oil, and minerals. The impact of such shocks on prices and real activity in an economy obviously depends on their weight in the consumption basket. In the past the oil price shocks—given that oil is predominantly imported—contributed significantly to inflation accelerating and growth slowing. Similarly, oil price shocks led to large fluctuations in domestic inflation. In recent periods, though food imports in the total import basket declined in significance, the global integration of food prices through the rapid financialization of commodity markets resulted in an increase in the correlation between domestic and world food price inflation. In fact, the global commodity cycle in the recent period reveals that the expansionary phase in food prices closely followed movements in global commodity price cycles (figure 6-3).

Consumption demand, though primarily driven by domestic consumption, was indirectly influenced by the external shocks. First, a slowdown in remittance inflows, which were impacted by both the slowdown in the U.S. economy and

Figure 6-3. *Growth and Inflation, India, Precrisis Period*

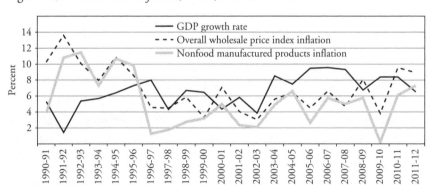

the sudden collapse of oil prices in the Middle East, seems to have affected consumption demand, as a large part of the money repatriated to India is for family maintenance. The empirical literature also suggests some relationship between private consumption demand and remittance transfers. Second, the employment impact of export-dependent and employment-intensive sectors (gems and jewelry, cotton textiles, leather goods, information-technology-enabled services, and business process outsourcing services) directly resulted in a significant loss of employment in these sectors and, hence, adversely affected consumption demand. Third, the uncertainty created by the loss of external demand and volatile global financial markets impacted the investment decisions of domestic firms, which led to overall compression in domestic investment demand.

The tightening of credit conditions in international markets reduced Indian firms' access to overseas bond markets. At the same time, access to trade credit significantly declined, with rollover problems leading to compression in import demand. Banking capital also witnessed significant outflows, which in turn led to the deterioration of domestic credit. The impact of capital inflows was reflected in a slowdown in the growth of investment demand.

The combined impact through trade, financial, and commodity prices channels was clearly reflected in growth; it decelerated with the cyclical slowdown in the first half of 2008–09 and even more so in the second half due to contagion from the global crisis. The significant deceleration in private consumption and gross domestic capital formation, along with contracting external demand, necessitated expansion in public sector demand—both consumption and investment. In fact, evidence suggests that cyclical movements in GDP growth have been mainly driven by cyclical private consumption and gross domestic capital formations.

The global financial crisis weakened the capacity of companies to invest through reduced access to financial resources, both internally and externally; further, collapsed growth prospects and heightened uncertainty severely affected the private sector's propensity to invest. All these factors led to a perceptible contraction in private investment in the economy during 2008–09. Notably, private investment behaved similarly during the past two international crises—the East Asian and dot.com crises—when the pace of private investment slowed significantly in the former and overall investment contracted in the latter. During these crises, the growth of investment in the household and public sectors also dipped substantially. These events led to a sharp fall in the growth of gross domestic capital formation. However, since, the government enhanced expenditure in infrastructure as a countercyclical measure, the pace of incremental public investment did not witness a sharp decline. At the same time, household investment accelerated sharply. Since gross domestic capital formation is powered by private investment, the steep contraction in private investment led to a sharp deceleration in its growth (figure 6-4).

Figure 6-4. *Components of Aggregate Demand, India*

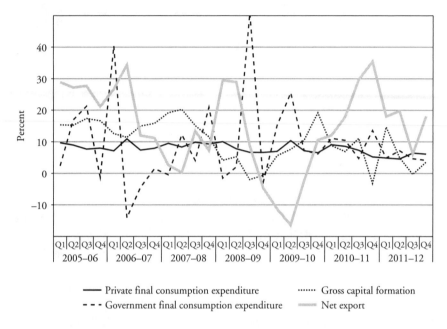

The impact on the industrial and services sectors was amplified in the second half of 2008–09, with an overall contraction in merchandise exports and a deceleration in the growth of services exports—along with shattered confidence—reinforcing the adverse affects stemming from the financial channel. Further, growth deceleration was more severe in the industrial sector than in the services sector, as manufacturing exports, which contribute a large part of industrial sector demand, contracted sharply on the back of a sharp fall in the spending of the advanced economies on consumer durables. However, services sector growth continued to decelerate during 2009–10, whereas industrial growth revived significantly (figure 6-5), perhaps reflecting the persistence of the trade channel on this set of activities.

The government of India and the Reserve Bank of India responded to the growth slowdown with fiscal and monetary policy measures. While the Reserve Bank undertook calibrated policy measures to improve both domestic and foreign exchange liquidity in the system, the government implemented counter-cyclical fiscal stimulus measures to support aggregate demand. Both monetary and fiscal policy measures appear to have brought the desired results, as manifested by the recovery in growth in 2009–10 and 2010–11.

Broadly speaking, in most Asian countries, the first response to the global financial crisis was to safeguard the safety and soundness of their financial systems, including their banking systems. Unlike in the 1997 crisis, no country

Figure 6-5. *Sectoral Growth Dynamics, India*

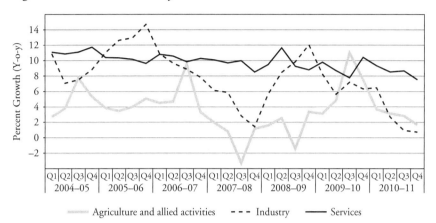

resorted to control over capital outflows, neither for residents nor for foreigners. Instead, several measures were announced to boost confidence and increase the resilience of the financial system to shocks. Indonesia, Republic of Korea, Malaysia, the Philippines, and Thailand expanded deposit insurance. With the stabilization of capital flows in the last quarter of 2008, monetary authorities in almost all countries started to cut policy rates, including countries with relatively high inflation, such as Turkey, in order to stimulate domestic demand. In India, Indonesia, and Korea central banks not only provided liquidity support to financial institutions in local currency but also used international reserves to lend in foreign currency in order to offset the reduction in external financing, notably to exporters. Moreover, as capital flows recovered, currency interventions were no longer sterilized, unlike in the period before the outbreak of the crisis.

The countercyclical fiscal response was unprecedented, not only for the region but also in the developing world as a whole. The fiscal package in fifteen developing economies in East, South, and Central Asia amounted to 7.5 percent of 2008 GDP, almost three times the average level in the G-7 major industrial countries.[3] The People's Republic of China introduced the largest fiscal package, close to US$600 billion, but in terms of share of GDP some smaller countries implemented even bigger packages; for instance, the Thai fiscal stimulus package amounted to some 17 percent of GDP. compared to 13 percent in China.

Despite substantial declines in net capital inflows (US$107 billion in 2007–08 to US$7.2 billion in 2008–09), the external sector of the economy showed resilience; the reserve loss (excluding valuation) was only US$20 billion during 2008–09. For the year as a whole, the current account deficit widened to

3. Akyuz (2010).

2.3 percent of GDP in 2008–09, from 1.3 percent of GDP in 2007–08. The significance of maintaining comfortable foreign exchange reserves, even with a largely flexible exchange rate regime, became evident during the year when the severest of external shocks could be managed without any exceptional measures to modulate specific transactions in the current and capital accounts.

Macroeconomic and Macroprudential Policy Responses

India's ability to weather the recent crisis can be largely attributed to its banking sector policies of past decades. Recognizing the procyclical behavior of the financial system, India adopted a countercyclical approach, while designing regulatory policies in the larger interest of financial stability. In addition, a number of measures taken by the Reserve Bank helped in mitigating the impact of the crisis on the banking sector and put the economy back on a recovery path. These measures include crisis management measures, prudential regulatory measures, and measures initiated for charting the future of banking sector development.

Crisis Management Measures

Since the deepening of the global financial crisis in September 2008, financial markets in India experienced an unusual tightening of liquidity. The foreign exchange market also came under pressure. To deal with the tightened liquidity situation, the Reserve Bank reintroduced a second LAF window, this one on a daily basis. Further, as a temporary measure, banks were allowed access to additional liquidity support under the LAF (up to 1 percent of their net demand and time liabilities from their SLR portfolio), and they could seek a waiver of the usual penal interest. In order to increase inflows of foreign deposits, the Reserve Bank increased interest rate ceilings on nonresident deposits. Further expanding the liquidity provision beyond the banking system, to alleviate liquidity stress faced by mutual funds, a fourteen-day special repurchase facility was instituted, and banks were allowed temporary use of SLR securities for collateral purposes exclusively for this purpose.

Further, there were reductions in repurchase and reverse repurchase rates as well in the CRR in order to step up liquidity in the banking system. The SLR, too, was brought down. Additionally, banks were permitted to borrow funds from their overseas branches and correspondent banks. The systemically important NBFCs were permitted to raise short-term foreign currency borrowings. The government announced the setting up of a special purpose vehicle for addressing the temporary liquidity constraints of this group of intermediaries.

Prudential Regulatory Measures

A number of measures to strengthen the prudential regulatory framework were also implemented. The provisioning requirements for all types of standard assets were reduced, except in the case of direct advances to the agricultural and SME sectors, which had a lower provisioning requirement to begin with. But from a longer term perspective on financial stability, these were seen to be temporary. In December 2009 banks were advised to raise their provisioning coverage ratio by the end of September 2010, from 40 percent to 70 percent of the nonperforming advances. In April 2011 banks were further advised to transfer the surplus provisions into an account styled as a countercyclical capital buffer. The objective was to ensure that banks built up a good cushion of provisions to face macroeconomic shocks in the future. In addition to this, in May 2011 specific provision requirements on certain categories of nonperforming assets were enhanced to strengthen the financial soundness of the banking sector.

In the aftermath of the crisis, the Reserve Bank differentially modified the provisioning requirements and the loan-to-value ratio in order to limit exposure to various sensitive sectors. Further, risk weights on banks' exposures to all unrated claims on corporations, claims secured by commercial real estate, and claims on NBFCs were reduced to 100 percent from 150 percent. The Reserve Bank has also been vigilant about banks' involvement in securitized assets. The guidelines issued in 2006 prohibited originators from booking profits up front at the time of securitization. Banks are required to maintain a minimum capital of 9 percent on credit enhancements and to disallow the release of credit enhancement during the life of the credit-enhanced transaction. Hence Indian banks did not have the same incentive to securitize their loans as other economies had.

CAPITAL ADEQUACY. Further, some reforms aimed at ensuring banking sector stability in the medium to long term are also under way. Learning lessons from the crisis, the Basel Committee on Banking Supervision has come out with an enhanced Basel II framework (commonly known as Basel III), which proposes higher quantity and quality of capital and stronger liquidity standards. Indian banks are not expected to have major problems in adjusting to the new capital rules in terms of either quantity or quality. However, some challenges may materialize, given the significant government ownership of banks. If the current ownership pattern is to be maintained, the government will have to divert funds from some other use in order to enhance the banks' capital. As to countercyclical capital buffers, notwithstanding the concerns about calibrating the buffers, the Reserve Bank's prescription of higher capital adequacy and sector-specific countercyclical provisioning to risk weight measures is expected to limit the procyclical behavior of the banking sector.

LEVERAGE. Yet another measure proposed under the enhanced Basel II is a minimum tier-1 leverage ratio of 3 percent to contain the leverage on banks' balance sheets. Estimates for India, however, show that the leverage in the banking system has been quite moderate. Banks are not expected to have any major problem in meeting the leverage ratio requirement, as their tier-1 capital is comfortably placed at over 9 percent and they have limited derivative positions.

LIQUIDITY. The Basel Committee also prescribes revision of the definition of liquid assets so that they remain liquid in periods of stress. It prescribes two major ratios: a liquidity coverage ratio, to ensure that a bank maintains an adequate level of unencumbered, high-quality assets that can be converted into cash to meet its liquidity needs for a thirty-day time horizon; and a net stable funding ratio, to promote medium- and long-term funding of banks' assets and activities. A minimum amount of liquid assets are available at Indian banks at any point, on account of the mandatory CRR and SLR. Further, excess SLR securities (over and above the statutory minimum of 23 percent) are expected to provide a liquidity buffer, as they facilitate borrowings from the Reserve Bank's LAF window and from collateralized segments of the money market. Moreover, as most Indian banks follow a retail business model, their dependence on short-term or overnight wholesale funding is limited.

The Reserve Bank plans to broadly adhere to the internationally agreed-on phase-in period (beginning January 1, 2013) for implementation of the Basel III framework. The Reserve Bank is studying the Basel III reform measures for preparing appropriate guidelines for implementation. It is taking steps to disseminate information on Basel III to help banks prepare for the smooth implementation of the framework.

SECURITIZATION. As securitization was at the heart of the recent global financial turmoil, the originate-to-distribute model of securitization was reexamined from many angles in the aftermath of the crisis. It was proposed to further strengthen the regulations for securitization by stipulating a minimum lock-in period of one year for bank loans before these loans are securitized. It has also been proposed to lay down minimum retention criteria for the originators at 10 percent of the pool of assets being securitized as another measure to achieve the same objective.

Fiscal and Monetary Policy Coordination

In retrospect, the relationship between monetary and fiscal policies in India highlights the typical situation in a developing country, where fiscal policy dominance in the process of achieving macroeconomic objectives often necessitates a subservient monetary policy. The basic approach is to ensure that monetary and fiscal policies work in harmony to achieve common objectives. However, during the 1990s there was greater focus on improving the monetary-fiscal interface in order to provide the flexibility necessary to monetary management. The following discussion highlights the evolution of the monetary-fiscal interface over the past decades and the efforts to strengthen the positive linkages through fiscal rules.

Easing the Fiscal Constraint on Monetary Policy

Since the reforms of the early 1990s, the statutory preemptive ratios for earmarking the banking resources for government and also for parking banking reserves with the Reserve Bank of India were brought down, interest rates were deregulated, and the automatic monetization of fiscal deficits was phased out. With the government's recourse to the Reserve Bank becoming more disciplined, a phase of reduced monetization by the Reserve Bank and high bond financing of deficits began. This phase naturally required the development of a government securities market and active public debt management by the Reserve Bank to ward off upward pressure on interest rates.

Concomitantly, the Reserve Bank activated its indirect instruments of monetary policy, and open market operations were used to address new emerging sources of monetization (in the form of capital inflows), as the Indian economy was opened and the foreign exchange market was deregulated. Accordingly, while net Reserve Bank credit to the government declined, net foreign assets gained in prominence as a source of money creation. With control of monetary aggregates becoming difficult in the wake of capital flow volatility (which was acting as an autonomous source) and prospects of financial innovations making money demand unstable, the Reserve Bank in 1998–99 switched to monetary policy formulation through a multiple-indicator approach, monitoring an array of real and financial indicators. Monetary policy progressively put greater emphasis on interest rate channels, augmenting its instruments in June 2000 through the introduction of the LAF, which sought to bridge banks' liquidity mismatches based on their market bids for repurchases in government securities.

Fiscal Discipline and Monetary Policy

Although reductions in the central government's fiscal deficit GDP ratio during the first half of the 1990s were reversed during the second half, the net Reserve Bank's credit to the government continued to decline, eventually turning into surplus by the end of the decade. Nonetheless, the emergence of government dissavings and the need to benchmark practices to international standards and codes generated an urgency to introduce rule-based fiscal discipline. Accordingly, the Fiscal Responsibility and Budget Management (FRBM) Act was passed in August 2003 and operationalized in July 2004, whereby the central government planned to eliminate its revenue deficit and reduce its fiscal deficit to 3 percent of GDP by 2008–09. The FRBM Act embodies the spirit of intergenerational equity and long-term macroeconomic stability. It also prohibits (since 2006–07) the central government from borrowing from the Reserve Bank, except through ways and means advances for bridging temporary differences in receipts and payments. However, the Reserve Bank can buy and sell government securities in the secondary market.

Although relieved of fiscal dominance through direct monetization, monetary policy faced new challenges emerging from liquidity overhang resulting from strong capital flows. The Reserve Bank responded through a policy mix of sterilization through open market operations, prepayment of external debt, and liberalization of foreign exchange market transactions. Another challenge was the maintenance of sizable surplus cash balances by the central government after August 2003, enabled by an increase in Treasury bills and a debt swap scheme for state governments, while its recourse to ways and means advances was virtually absent.

This buildup of cash balances led to an unintended tightening of monetary conditions, which might or might not be consistent with ongoing monetary policy. Further, as capital inflows surged, the Reserve Bank took increased recourse to open market operations, whereby government securities were offloaded from its portfolio and excess liquidity absorbed for sterilizing the monetary impact of capital flows. With the depletion of its government securities portfolio, the Reserve Bank had to progressively use LAF as an instrument for sterilizing capital flows instead of outright sales through open market operations. The MSS became operative in April 1, 2004, when injections of primary liquidity on account of increases in the Reserve Bank's foreign exchange reserves were absorbed by the issuance of central government securities. The money raised by the government through these issuances was maintained and operated by the Reserve Bank in a separate account solely for the redemption and buyback of the issuances.

Driven by continued rule-based fiscal correction, the combined fiscal deficit to GDP ratio of the central government and the state government was reduced from 8.5 percent in 2003–04 to 4.1 percent in 2007–08, thereby meeting the FRBM targets in advance. The combined debt-to-GDP ratio also declined, from 85.9 percent to 71.4 percent, during the same period. The fiscal consolidation strategy was essentially revenue led, as the central government's gross tax-to-GDP ratio rose from 9 percent to almost 12 percent during the same period. As the environment was rapidly changing under the rule-based fiscal policy and increased domestic and global financial integration, financial stability assumed policy priority for the Reserve Bank.

In particular, the Reserve Bank recognized the importance of complementarity between macroeconomic and financial stability. Accordingly, a policy-induced shift from uncollateralized to collateralized segments in the money market occurred by restricting activity in the call money market to banks and primary dealers only, while LAF operations were fine-tuned for the smooth management of liquidity conditions. Monetary policy also became sensitive to the inflationary pressures emerging from the firming up of international oil prices, even though the headline inflation rates remained subdued in light of government restriction of full pass-through to the prices of petroleum products. The

Reserve Bank continued to favor fuller pass-through in view of the overhang and the impact of higher international oil prices on the underrecoveries of oil companies. While the government adopted a policy of issuing oil bonds in lieu of subsidies to these companies, its adverse implications on the fiscal situation were being widely acknowledged despite not being captured in the revenue deficits of the government.

Further, the Reserve Bank began monitoring the aggregate demand pressures embodied in rising bank credit, high asset prices, and above-trend growth in monetary aggregates, as well as the global risks stemming from larger macro-economic imbalances and higher oil prices. These observations affected policy preemptively so as to contain inflationary expectations during 2004–07, as the Indian economy was migrating to a higher growth path. This risk-sensitive approach was adopted in view of the unprecedented expansion in bank credit and an upturn in asset prices, particularly in housing and real estate. In this context, to supplement monetary measures—and to protect the banking system from a possible asset bubble without undermining growth—other prudential measures were initiated, such as enhanced provisioning requirements and risk weights in specific sectors and select supervisory reviews. Thus improving fiscal conditions and increasing the independence of the Reserve Bank (allowing it to respond preemptively not only to underlying inflationary pressures but also to spurts in asset prices with monetary and prudential tools) sustained high economic growth. Overall, the rule-based fiscal policy pursued under the FRBM Act helped to ease fiscal dominance and thus contributed to overall improvement in monetary management (figures 6-6 and 6-7).

Figure 6-6. *Combined Deficit, Government Sector, India*

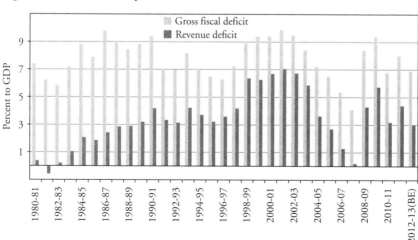

Figure 6-7. *Debt of the Government Sector, India*

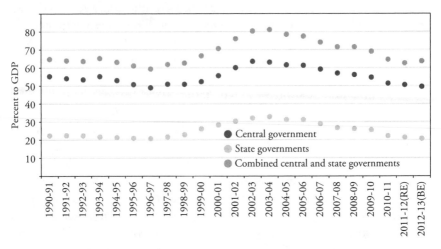

Fiscal-Monetary Coordination

Monetary and fiscal policies acted in coordination to minimize the impact of the global crisis on the Indian economy. The Reserve Bank swiftly switched away from the tight monetary stance adopted earlier. By March 2009, as wholesale inflation began to decline and consumer inflation moderated, the Reserve Bank sharply reduced both its CRR and its repurchase rate by 400 basis points and adopted several measures, including nonconventional means, to augment domestic and foreign exchange liquidity. India's fiscal policy was already in an expansionary mode before the crisis. The announcement of a rural employment guarantee, payouts to government employees recommended by the Sixth Pay Commission, and additional subsidies for food and fertilizer acted as automatic stabilizers. Additionally, the government launched three stimulus packages between December 2008 and February 2009.

The distinguishing feature of India's monetary policy responses to the global financial crisis is the role of the Reserve Bank. In contrast to the policy responses of other central banks, the Reserve Bank of India brooked no compromise in terms of counterparty dealings and collateral standards, while supplying liquidity to the financial system. The Reserve Bank met the funding needs of nonbanks primarily through banks, and that only against the eligible collateral of government securities, unlike the mortgage securities and commercial paper issued by the advanced economies. Moreover, the balance sheet did not expand, as in the advanced countries, because of the release of earlier sterilized liquidity through an MSS, an instrument that was used earlier to sterilize the monetary impact of large capital flows. More important, the availability and deployment of multiple instruments facilitated better sequencing of monetary and liquidity measures. For instance, with liquidity management being an integral part of monetary policy even during normal times the scaling up of such operations in response to the crisis did not create major frictions in the market. That is, the Reserve Bank clearly communicated with the market, which helped reduce the moral hazard problem.

Fiscal consolidation progressed up to 2007–08 in consonance with the mandated path under the rule-based framework in respect to both the central government and the state governments. Credible progress toward fiscal consolidation during the precrisis period provided fiscal space for undertaking expansionary fiscal policy during the period of crisis. A resilient feature of its public debt that seems to have protected India from the global financial crisis is that most of it is held domestically, which implies that the government's fiscal deficit is financed through household savings. The three stimulus packages were largely provided by a reduction in indirect taxes (excise and customs) and some incentives to the export sector.[4] To support the recovery, the extraordinary fiscal stance adopted during 2008–09 in response to the global crisis was sustained during 2009–10.

As a result, revenue deficit and gross fiscal deficit as a percentage of GDP were higher than in 2008–09. The fiscal stimulus was estimated at 2.3 percent of GDP for 2008–09 and 1.5 percent for 2009–10.[5] The government ensured quality of fiscal policy by better targeting of expenditure to spur aggregate demand and to add to capacity creation through an increased focus on social and physical infrastructure. It is evident from the fact that, during 2009–10, capital expenditure increased by about 25.0 percent vis-à-vis revenue expenditure of 14.9 percent. The stimulus thus contributed to a faster recovery, while also aiming at improving distribution of the benefits of growth. These measures led to a deviation in 2008–09 and 2009–10 from the fiscal consolidation path mandated under the FRBM Act. Even though the central government's GFD-to-GDP ratio of 2.5 percent in 2007–08 was lower than the FRBM target of 3.0 percent set for 2008–09, it shot up sharply to 6.0 percent in 2008–09 and subsequently to 6.4 percent in 2009–10. Accordingly, the government had to invoke the emergency provisions of the FRBM Act to seek relaxation from fiscal targets.

Fiscal expansionary measures in the wake of the crisis necessitated a marked scaling up of market borrowing programs of both central and state governments. Growth in combined gross market borrowings increased sharply, to 71 percent and 43 percent in 2008–09 and 2009–10, respectively. The enhanced market borrowings posed a challenge for the Reserve Bank to minimize any disruptive pressures on the government securities market. Accordingly, the Reserve Bank

4. The first fiscal stimulus package was introduced in December 2008, the second in January 2009, and third in February 2009.
5. Based on revised GDP estimates.

had to continuously review and adapt its debt management strategy, in consultation with the central government, in response to the evolving economic conditions. Therefore, the government's market borrowing program was conducted in a nondisruptive manner, without any conflict with its monetary management function. Higher government borrowings could raise interest rates by pushing up yields on government securities, which entail the risk of conflicting with the low interest rate stance that may be pursued by the monetary authority in the face of an economic slowdown.

During 2009–10 some policy measures adopted by the Reserve Bank are noteworthy. The market borrowing program was front-loaded, taking advantage of the usual slackness of credit offtake from banks during the first half of the year. Similarly, MSS securities were desequestered to meet a part of the borrowing requirements. The Reserve Bank also resorted to active liquidity management by way of unwinding MSS securities and purchasing securities through a preannounced calendar of open market operations in order to reduce uncertainty and infuse confidence in the market. The Reserve Bank also continued with the policy of passive consolidation of dated securities during 2009–10. Even though the high fiscal deficit and inflationary expectations led to some pressure on medium to long-term yields, the Reserve Bank, through active liquidity management operations and by shortening the maturity profile, was able to deal with this pressure. In fact, the overall weighted average yield on central government securities was lower in 2009–10 than in 2008–09.

To sum up, the accommodative monetary policy stance of the Reserve Bank, besides ensuring nondisruptive financing of fiscal plans, created an overall liquidity and interest rate condition that was conducive to growth. Stability in the domestic financial system not only boosted the overall business confidence, it ensured availability of resources from banks, nonbanks, and markets to meet the financing needs of the recovery. Thus while the magnitude of the crisis was global in nature, the domestic monetary and fiscal policy responses were adapted to domestic growth outlook, inflation conditions, and financial stability considerations.

With signs of economic recovery strengthening, the government recommitted to the path of fiscal consolidation in 2010–11, outlining a partial exit from the stimulus measures undertaken earlier. Fiscal developments during 2010–11 were characterized by buoyancy in tax revenues and by more than anticipated collections from 3G and BWA spectrum auctions, which were used by the government to increase allocations for rural infrastructure and other priority areas. On balance, the government was able to achieve a less than the budgeted GFD-GDP ratio, at 4.9 percent in 2010–11, thereby achieving a reduction of 1.6 percentage points over the previous year. Moving forward, the government expects to reduce the GFD-GDP ratio to 3.5 percent by 2013–14, which is higher than the path indicated by the Thirteenth Finance Commission. This reflects withholding of a complete rollback of indirect taxes due to inflationary concerns, the recognition of the nonavailability of one-off nontax revenues, and a rescheduling of its disinvestment plans.

The postcrisis challenge for fiscal monetary coordination is that the fiscal deficit of the government has remained elevated since 2008–09. Strong signs of fiscal consolidation, which will shift the balance of aggregate demand from public to private and from consumption to capital formation, are critical to create the space for lowering the policy rate without the risk of resurgent inflation. In the absence of credible fiscal consolidation, the Reserve Bank will be constrained from lowering the policy rate in response to decelerating private consumption and investment spending.

The global financial crisis brought to light the importance of coordination between monetary and fiscal authorities to address the impact of macroeconomic shocks. Coordination became critical to foster the recovery and to calibrate an exit. While the monetary policy initiated the exit process on the back of emerging inflationary concerns in the economy, the fiscal policy calibrated the exit from the expansionary stance adopted during the crisis. Such a policy mix is likely to help in maintaining a balance between growth and price stability. Furthermore, the newly formed Financial Stability and Development Council, comprising the government, the Reserve Bank, and other financial sector regulatory bodies, is likely to provide a platform for information sharing for systemic risk assessment and coordination in respect to regulatory issues. Going forward, the establishment of the Debt Management Office by the central government is also likely to facilitate debt management, distinct from monetary management. These institutional reforms, providing greater functional autonomy to both arenas, make monetary fiscal coordination even more critical during a period of economic and financial stress.

Evaluation of Existing Policy Frameworks: Macroeconomic and Regulatory Policies

The major uncertainty that continues even after the crisis is determining what can ensure financial stability. It is argued that, while there is considerable agreement in principle that a new framework for financial stability is needed, there is still no consensus on what this framework should look like and how it should operate.[6] Suggestions to make macroeconomic policies more sensitive to financial stability include better regulation and supervision (including Basel III and macroprudential measures), strengthening domestic institutions, and more effective global coordination and cooperation aim at enhancing the architecture for financial stability. But gaps remain in almost every major area of this architecture. For example, how monetary policy can prevent asset bubbles and excessive

6. Caruana (2010).

leverage is still being debated; a consensus that monetary policy must lean against the wind won't be of much help unless there is consensus on how.

The second gray area is fiscal exit in advanced economies. While the precrisis consensus was for fiscal policy to play only a secondary role, since the crisis fiscal activism has been unprecedented, with large increases in debt levels, which may conflict with monetary policy sooner or later. Even if a return to fiscal consolidation becomes the consensus, how and when that could happen will be uncertain. Any options—whether reduced expenditure or higher taxes—could weaken growth, and to depend on the recovery to benefit from revenue buoyancy could only further delay consolidation. The third uncertainty is about future reforms in the financial sector and about the approach to financial innovations. The right balance between innovations and regulations could again be a consensus, but country practices would differ widely. If the procyclical behavior of the financial system has to be curbed, that will involve a sacrifice of growth. The stability and growth trade-off will leave scope for discretion to policymakers.

In the sphere of macroeconomic policy consensus, two major limitations have generally been recognized. One is the excessive focus by central banks on inflation targeting versus inflation objectives, assuming low and stable inflation as the single most important contribution that a central bank could do for the economy, including growth and financial stability (ignoring thereby asset price bubbles and excessive use of leverage). Second is the presumption that markets function efficiently in a sound macropolicy environment and, more important, the perception that financial crises could be an emerging market phenomenon.

The third dimension was more or less largely ignored: the risk of weakness or stress in one systemically important financial institution spreading fast to cause a financial crisis in an integrated financial system in which the interconnected spillovers are hard to identify. Macroprudential policies to stem risks from the procyclical behavior of the financial system were missing in the precrisis phase. In contrast to the experience of the advanced economies, the Reserve Bank's regulatory and supervisory policies have always been oriented toward systemic stability. The Indian banking system remained largely sound and resilient to shocks, as indicated by various stress tests. The high level of leverage in developed countries, which was one of the causal factors behind the global financial crisis, continues to remain low in India. The regulatory and supervisory structure of the Reserve Bank was further strengthened during the year. The important policy decisions for commercial banks include strengthening countercyclical provisioning norms, avoiding excessive leverage in the housing loan segment, and supporting credit to microfinance institutions.

Significantly, in the aftermath of the global financial crisis, the mandate of central banks in some countries is being widened, to include systemic regulation and macroprudential supervision. In India regulation and supervision have long been the most crucial function of the Reserve Bank. The Reserve Bank currently has the mandate to regulate banks as well as NBFCs and has conducted its regulatory and supervisory functions with the objective of maintaining systemic financial stability as well as preventing the failure of individual entities. Strong prudential regulations were adopted by the Reserve Bank much ahead of the outbreak of the crisis. The Indian financial system still remains largely bank oriented, on the belief that a resilient banking system is crucial in maintaining systemic stability.

An important change in precrisis consensus of importance to EMEs is in the sphere of management of capital flows. Recommendations for open capital accounts and polar exchange rate policies (either fixed or flexible) seem to have changed since the crisis. Intermediate exchange rate regimes and the use of soft capital controls could become new norms, as far as developing and emerging economies are concerned. But global norms on how to deal with both surges and sudden stops in capital flows—in terms of instruments and the timing of their use—could be necessary to relieve uncertainty in the minds of international investors about the discretionary policy response of countries in managing capital flows.

From the perspective of EMEs, the recent debate on the legitimacy of capital controls has brought to the fore the apparent disconnect between theory and practice in addressing the issue. The theoretical conventional wisdom was that capital controls of any kind are suboptimal because they are market distorting. Governments using them are only redistributing income and welfare from one domestic stakeholder to another. In other words, they generate a zero-sum outcome in the best of circumstances. Under more realistic assumptions, by reducing efficiency in capital allocation, they may even lead to a negative-sum outcome.

The Indian experience provides some important insights. India has been hailed by proponents of the conventional wisdom in recent years for having jettisoned day-to-day management of capital inflows and, significantly, the exchange rate. The long-stated policy position that foreign exchange intervention is only done in situations of excessive volatility has been a reality since early 2007. The movement of the rupee in the period since then testifies to this. It has been by far the most volatile of major EME currencies and is now perceived by markets to be a virtually free-floating currency.

However, India does maintain significant capital controls. These are mostly focused on the quantity, tenure, and pricing of debt inflows. The pecking order of capital inflows puts foreign direct investment at the top of the list, for obvious reasons. Then follows foreign institutional investment in equities, in which the investor bears both market and exchange rate risk. Debt flows are the least preferred; within this category, short-term flows are less preferred than long-term ones. Admittedly, trade credits, on which there is no restriction below durations of six months, are being used to bypass restrictions on short-term borrowing, requiring a review of the policy framework. But this apart, the Indian approach to capital account management can be usefully viewed in terms of a distinction between strategic and tactical controls. Strategic controls are essentially the ones that India uses. Some kinds of inflow are deemed less desirable, and quantity or price controls are imposed on them.

Once the pecking order and the accompanying controls are decided, all other flows are unfettered, and stakeholders fully bear all associated risks, including exchange rate risk. To enable them to do this more efficiently, a range of market instruments for hedging purposes is being gradually introduced. In essence, strategic controls define the boundaries of the playing field, providing stakeholders with the assurance that no further restrictions will be imposed on them and that they are free to exploit opportunities for both earning returns and managing risks. In this context, reform, or liberalization, could be taken to mean the periodic redefinition of both the pecking order itself and the accompanying reforms.

Tactical controls are measures that introduce barriers into the playing field itself. When countries use them, they introduce a new element of uncertainty into the calculations of both foreign and domestic stakeholders. Return and risk considerations must now take into account the likelihood of capital controls being introduced in specific circumstances and withdrawn in others. Even in the absence of explicit controls, foreign exchange intervention with the objective of reducing exchange rate volatility influences the return-risk calculations of investors. The ongoing debate on the desirability and merits of capital controls will become more constructive if the distinction between strategic and tactical controls is recognized. Countries must first decide the pecking order of capital flows and what they will do to enforce it. For any country, this will emerge from a combination of factors related to external vulnerability and tolerance for risk.

Research clearly has a role in distinguishing between superior and inferior options for strategic controls, depending on country characteristics and objectives. Tactical controls, on the other hand, are essentially emergency responses to intense pressure and will largely depend on country circumstances: what the pressures are, what instruments are immediately available, and which of them is likely to have the quickest impact. While a set of differentiating conditions may eventually emerge, a deeper understanding of country experiences than currently exists is probably necessary.

For the past few years, the exchange rate regime in India has been what might be best described as a bounded float. There are virtually no restrictions on foreign direct investment (except for limits on specific sectors) and on portfolio investment in equities. However, there are restrictions on debt inflows, driven by considerations of external stability. These limits relate to quantity, tenure, and pricing. Short-term debt is the least preferred, because it is seen as most vulnerable to sudden reversals, while long-term debt, despite risk concerns, is seen as contributing to the resource flow into infrastructure and so is viewed more favorably. These controls on debt might be viewed as structural or strategic capital controls; they are altered relatively infrequently in response to changing macroeconomic conditions and not with a view to impacting the daily movement of the exchange rate.

While India does not target the level of exchange rate, nor does it have a fixed band for nominal or real exchange rates to guide interventions, the capital account management framework helps in the bounded float. If volatility increases, appropriate tools, including those in the realm of capital account management, are used. Within these overall boundaries, the exchange rate is determined by daily variations in demand and supply. In the recent episode of depreciation, as indicated earlier, a sharp fall in capital inflows led to a drying up of supply, while demand on account of the current account deficit continued unabated, leading to the outcome we saw.

There has been a long-standing debate on the merits and demerits of this exchange rate policy, which has returned to center stage in the wake of recent developments. It is important to point out that the different policy responses across EMEs to the volatility in capital inflows were largely the outcome of their exchange rate policy framework. Countries that orient their exchange rate regimes to export competitiveness typically have current account surpluses. This is a characteristic of the Asian EMEs, and in this sense India is a significant exception to the Asian rule. These surpluses are reflected in a buildup of foreign exchange reserves, which may be further enhanced by large inflows of capital and the further accumulation of reserves to prevent currency appreciation, which undermines competitiveness in the short run.

In the current global context, when capital inflows stop, reserves built up from current account surpluses provide the capacity to manage exchange rates in the face of external pressure. India has large reserves, but because it has a current account deficit, the reserves are essentially counterbalanced against its external liability position. In an extreme scenario, if there is a large outflow of capital, the adequacy of reserves will be judged by the economy's ability to finance the current account deficit and, over and above that, meet short-term claims without any disruption or loss of confidence. In light of this, the value and use of reserves in the Indian context must be viewed somewhat differently than in the context of a structurally current account surplus economy. Reserves essentially provide assurance to external counterparties that India has the capacity to meet its obligations.

Three Balancing Acts

The 2008–09 financial crisis has been analyzed extensively, and multiple lessons have been drawn for the entire range of stakeholders, from policymakers and regulators to individual investors and bank depositors. It is relatively difficult to add to this list from the account of impacts and policy responses provided in this chapter. Nonetheless, some general characterization of the experience in terms of the broad issues raised here is necessary. I attempt to do this in terms of three balancing acts that I believe were critical to both limiting the impact of the crisis on economies like India's and maintaining a degree of stability in the event of future shocks. Descriptions of the three balancing acts—prudent and innovative, global and domestic, and aggregate and composite—follow.

Prudent and Innovative

Under normal circumstances, there is always an uncomfortable trade-off between prudential regulation and the pressing need for financial development to service the needs of the real economy. Financial innovation that promises to reduce the costs of capital or the availability of funds for new and potentially risky activities is, clearly, something that all economies have benefited from in various growth phases. Prudential regulation, either of the banking system or of the financial markets, has generally been viewed as a hindrance. However, the recent crisis demonstrates that aggressive innovation not accompanied by appropriate prudence—whether by way of appropriate measurement of risks or by way of adequate provision of financial buffers—can cause serious damage to the financial system.

This may be severe enough to at least temporarily render it incapable of meeting even the most basic requirements of financial services by the real sector. Financial shocks quickly translate into real shocks under these circumstances, and attempts to rescue the system through capital infusions may simply end up repairing damaged balance sheets rather than enhancing the capacity of the system to intermediate funds. The tortoise and the hare analogy may be appropriate here, with a prudent regulatory approach that puts a great weight on the riskiness of innovations contributing to the long-run stability (hence, productivity) of the financial system.

Global and Domestic

The global policy response to the crisis was a perfect mix of magnitude, timing, and coordination. In all likelihood, the global economy would have been far worse off in the absence of this response. However, as subsequent developments suggest, the impact of the common response was quite differentiated in terms of outcomes. A logical explanation for this is that the conditions created by the crisis were actually different across economies, with some having to deal with an intense vicious circle of real and financial sector interactions. In countries in which the real impact was modest, like India, the strength of the policy response, while completely understandable and justifiable under the circumstances, may have actually complicated the management of the postcrisis recovery.

As described above, India began to experience an inflation spurt in the very early stages of the postcrisis recovery, to which the very large infusion of liquidity and the strong fiscal stimulus may have contributed. In hindsight, domestic conditions might have facilitated recovery with less aggressive policy responses. The implication is that policymakers should not downplay domestic conditions, either strengths or weaknesses, when responding to a global shock. The policy response needs to be calibrated to find the balance between global and domestic factors. This argument also suggests that, while a common and coordinated global response to a crisis may be appropriate, for that response to be effective in each country, the magnitude and timing may need to take account of domestic conditions.

Aggregate and Composite

After the crisis, monetary and fiscal stimulus measures combined to generate the forces of recovery across the world. However, since private spending declined as a result of the crisis, more so in some economies than in others, the policy response to the crisis effected a significant shift in the composition of aggregate demand across the global economy. Public spending rose to compensate for falling private spending. Attempts to normalize the balance led to a striking difference in outcomes between the advanced and the emerging economies.

In the advanced economies, concerns about excessive fiscal commitments led to aggressive consolidation in a situation, in which private spending was apparently yet to fully recover. This may be a contributory factor to the rather disappointing way in which the recovery has unfolded in these economies. By contrast, emerging economies had to deal with inflationary pressures, using monetary instruments to which public spending is relatively insensitive. As a result, monetary transmission is both diluted and falls disproportionately on investment spending, raising concerns about capacity creation and medium-term growth performance. India is among the fast-growing emerging markets that has the right balance between consumption and investment in aggregate demand. It does not face the problems of overinvestment or excessive leveraged consumption. In the high-growth phase, before the global financial crisis, leveraged consumption did increase—but from a rather low base.

Investment, on the other hand, rose faster. Government consumption rose on the back of a large fiscal stimulus. In 2010–11, rebalancing took away from government consumption in favor of private consumption, but investment declined sharply in the second half of the year. There is now a need to maintain a long-term balance between consumption and investment by rebalancing demand from consumption to investment. For this, there is a need to step up savings. The implication is that the policy mix must take into account the potential complications that a large shift in the composition of demand may create once the immediate crisis has abated.

References

Akyuz, Yilmaz. 2010. "The Global Economic Crisis and Asian Developing Countries: Impact, Policy Response, and Medium-Term Prospects." Third World Network. Penang.

Bank for International Settlements. 2010. *Annual Report, 2008–09.*

Caruana, Jaime. 2010. "Macroprudential Policy: Working Towards a New Consensus." Remarks, BIS/IMF Institute conference, Washington, April 23.

International Monetary Fund. Various years. *Direction of Trade Statistics.*

Reinhart, Carmen, and Kenneth S. Rogoff. 2009. *This Time Is Different: Eight Centuries of Financial Folly* (Princeton University Press).

Reserve Bank of India. 2010. "Global Financial Crisis and the Indian Economy: Report on Currency and Finance, 2008–09."

World Bank. Various years. *World Development Indicators.*

7

The Macroprudential Policy Framework from an Asian Perspective

KIYOHIKO G. NISHIMURA

I n this chapter I take up several key issues relating to macroeconomic policy frameworks, explicitly taking account of financial markets, or macroprudential policies, especially from an Asian perspective. In particular, I ask the following two questions: What methods should we employ to detect intolerable accumulation of risks in the financial system? And how should we maintain financial stability in the short run while improving efficiency in credit intermediation functions to support long-term economic growth?

I am seeking practical, best-practice answers to these questions, rather than optimum solutions based on a particular theory.[1] This practical and somewhat atheoretical approach is warranted, since we are still very much short of having a satisfactory macroeconomic theory that deals adequately with complex and sometimes violent financial markets, although there has emerged a sizable literature on the relationship between macroeconomic activity and financial markets.

Before trying to answer these inherently difficult questions, it is worth looking back to the evolution of both the current financial crisis in the United States and Europe and that in Japan two decades ago. Although much attention has been focused on financial excess as typified by excessive leveraging in financial institutions, I emphasize the importance of the underlying changes in fundamentals,

---

1. Clark and Large (2011) present ten questions in framing appropriate macroprudential policy, crystallizing its fundamental and practical problems. In the chapter, I touch on only those that I think are most relevant from the Asian perspective.

especially demographic factors such as population aging. The latter has particularly important implications for the future in Asia. The basic message here is that many of Asia's growing economies may face problems in the near future similar to those of developed countries, and it is thus of the utmost importance to implement appropriate macroprudential policy now.

Financial Crises and Fundamentals

Although three years have passed since the so-called Lehman shock, we are still in the process of soul-searching: pursuing a better understanding of its causes and the appropriate policy response to it. Since Japan and a number of Asian economies already experienced their own financial crises in the 1990s, we Asians may be in a position to compare them and draw the necessary lessons. Indeed, there are many similarities between the recent crisis in the United States and the eurozone, on the one hand, and Japan's financial crisis since the 1990s, on the other. In the case of both the U.S.-eurozone crisis and the bubble era in Japan, risks were accumulated, particularly in real-estate-related sectors, during the period of high growth and low inflation.[2]

The recent literature on financial crises focuses mostly on explaining how bubbles develop and how they influence economic activity through leveraging in financial markets.[3] Here the measures of economywide financial activity, such as deviation from the long-run trend of the credit-to-GDP ratio, are informative and possible guides for macroprudential policy.

Demographic Factors

I would like to emphasize a sometimes overlooked background factor, and that is demographic change in the form of population aging. Indeed, the bubble-and-burst phenomenon and the subsequent financial crises seem to coincide roughly with the turning point of population pyramids in Japan, the United States, and Europe. There are some telling figures on the inverse dependency ratio, which indicates how many people of working age it takes to provide for one dependent person.[4] The Japanese ratio peaked around 1990, and it was in the very

2. The period is known as the "Great Moderation" in the U.S. case.
3. European Central Bank (2010) and Basel Committee on Banking Supervision (2011) provide a concise survey of models with macrofinancial linkage proliferating recently in this literature. Bianchi (2010), Jeanne and Korinek (2010a, 2010b), and Stein (2011) focus on the credit externalities and pave the way for exploring the effects of macroprudential measures. In particular, Bianchi (2010) and Jeanne and Korinek (2010b) study financial crises in open economies, aiming to provide macroprudential remedial measures. However, there is unfortunately relatively little from an Asian perspective. Exceptions include Hattori, Shin, and Takahashi (2010) and Hahm, Shin, and Shin (2011).
4. I take these figures from Nishimura (2011b), which contains more figures about other European countries, both core and periphery.

Figure 7-1. *Ratio of Working-Age Population to Rest of Population, Japan and the United States, 1950–2050*

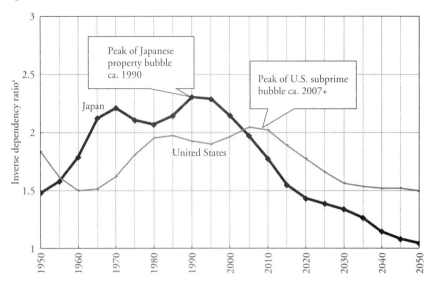

Source: United Nations (2010).
a. The inverse dependency ratio is the number of working-age people to one dependent person.

next year, 1991, that the Japanese bubble peaked. The peak of the U.S. ratio was between 2005 and 2010, and the peak of the U.S. subprime bubble was 2007 (figure 7-1). The economically troubled countries of the eurozone have a similar pattern to those of Japan and the United States. The ratios for Ireland and Spain have almost the same time profile; they peaked around 2005, which corresponds to the peak of their property bubbles (figure 7-2). The ratio for Greece and Portugal peaked around 2000. The significant point is that several financial crises all coincide with the turning point in these demographic dynamics.

Asset Price Bubbles

The life-cycle theory—or more precisely speaking, the overlapping-generation model—suggests that demographic change is one of the most forceful drivers of asset prices. After all, assets are a means of saving for the young and dissaving for the old, and thus the numbers of the young and the old determine the demand and supply for these assets.[5]

The recent history of crisis seems to confirm this line of reasoning. In figure 7-3 real land prices in Japan (national average, for all purposes) are juxtaposed

---

5. Empirical evidence suggests strongly that this is the case. See Takáts (2010) for property prices and Liu and Spiegel (2011) for equity prices. For a readable account of this issue, see "Economics Focus: Bringing Down the House," *The Economist,* September 24, 2011, p. 94.

Figure 7-2. *Ratio of Working-Age Population to Rest of Population,
Four Periphery Europe Countries, 1950–2050*

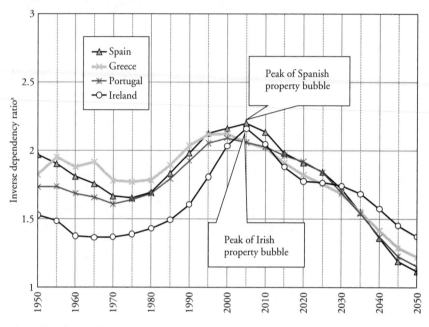

Source: United Nations (2010).
a. The inverse dependency ratio is the number of working-age people to one dependent person.

Figure 7-3. *Age of Population and Property Prices, Japan, 1955–2030*

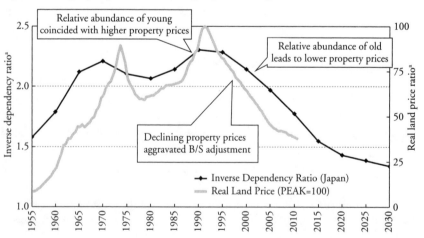

Source: United Nations (2010); Japan Real Estate Institute; Japan Ministry of Internal Affairs and Communications.
a. The inverse dependency ratio is the number of working-age people to one dependent person. The real land price
is measured against a peak of 100 in March 1991.

Figure 7-4. *Age of Population and Property Prices, United States, 1955–2030*

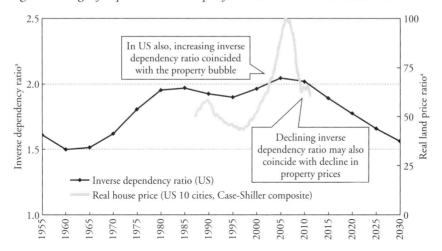

Source: United Nations (2010); U.S. Bureau of Labor Statistics.
a. The inverse dependency ratio is the number of working-age people to one dependent person. The real land price is measured against a peak of 100 in December 2005.

with the country's inverse dependency ratio from 1955 to 2010. This figure shows, first, that the relative abundance of young people coincided with sharply higher property prices. Second, in contrast, the relative abundance of old people seems to be leading to lower property prices. In the United States, also, an increasing reverse dependency ratio coincided with the property bubble (figure 7-4). After the bubble burst in 2007, property prices seem to have followed the long-run movement of the inverse dependency ratio, although it would be premature to draw any conclusions from this at the moment. We see a similar pattern in the Irish and Spanish experience (figures 7-5 and 7-6).

I am not suggesting that this demographic factor is the sole cause of the asset bubbles that led to the crises. There may be other factors, as for example in the case of Greece and Portugal, which experienced bubbles in their public sectors rather than in asset prices—but still faced a crisis. Likewise, other countries underwent similar demographic changes and yet did not fall into crisis. I only point out that a favorable demographic background (increasing the inverse dependency ratio) might be fertile ground for the excessive optimism that led economic agents in many countries to take a highly leveraged position to boost their returns.[6] In other words, asset bubbles might dance over the long-run tide

6. Nishimura and Ozaki (2006, 2011) provide a decision-theoretic foundation of excessive optimism and pessimism, showing that seemingly irrational excessive optimism and pessimism can be analyzed in the framework of rationality. See also Bracha and Brown (2010).

Figure 7-5. *Age of Population and Property Prices, Ireland, 1955–2030*

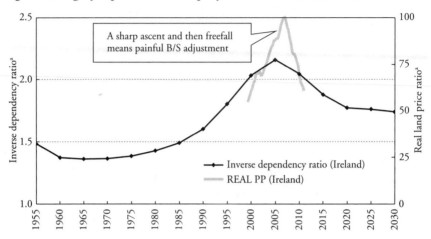

Source: United Nations (2010); OECD; Bank for International Settlements.
a. The inverse dependency ratio is the number of working-age people to one dependent person. The real land price is measured against a peak of 100 in December 2006.

Figure 7-6. *Age of Population and Property Prices, Spain, 1955–2030*

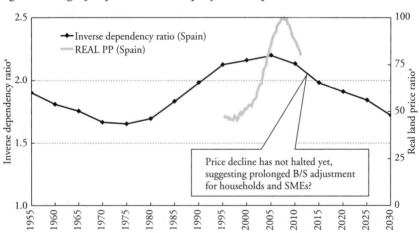

Source: United Nations (2010); OECD; Bank for International Settlements.
a. The inverse dependency ratio is the number of working-age people to one dependent person. The real land price is measured against a peak of 100 in September 2007.

of demographic change.[7] By the same token, the eventual sharp reversal of the ratio made resolution of accumulated financial excesses particularly difficult, resulting in the prolonged and severe balance-sheet adjustment that followed the crisis—and that is still under way.

Aftermath

To determine the effect of balance-sheet adjustments after the bursting of a bubble, let me first clarify who leveraged during the bubble periods. In Japan it was the corporate sector, whose loans-to-GDP ratio increased by 29 percentage points in the ten years before the bubble burst in 1991. In the United States it was the household sector, whose ratio of housing loans to disposable income jumped by 39 percentage points in the ten years before the bubble burst in 2007. These sectors were interest sensitive and thus constituted the transmission gears of the ordinary monetary transmission mechanism in the periods before the bubbles burst. However, after the bubbles burst, these leveraged sectors became insensitive to policy rate reduction because of the acute balance-sheet adjustments. This led to a breakdown in the ordinary monetary transmission mechanism. It should be noted here that declining property prices greatly aggravated the balance-sheet adjustments of Japanese corporations and U.S. households.[8]

In looking to the future, I would like to emphasize that balance-sheet adjustments after the bubbles burst in Japan, the United States, and the eurozone, whether private or public, must be carried out *at a time when the population is aging.* This acute balance-sheet adjustment is unprecedented in the modern history of economic growth.

Where Does Asia Stand?

Asian economies and financial systems weathered the recent financial crisis relatively well. Their recovery since 2009 has been markedly rapid, and emerging Asia is now a growth engine of the global economy. The fiscal situation of emerging Asia is also far more favorable than that of many developed countries. Furthermore, with the exception of Japan, Asian economies have not yet faced serious problems with population aging.

Nonetheless, I would like to point out potential future issues and the absolute necessity of a prudent approach now. Figure 7-7 shows the inverse dependency ratios for the People's Republic of China juxtaposed with those for Japan and the United States. The Chinese ratio seems still to be rising rapidly, but it will peak

7. One possibility is to incorporate the bubble, as formulated in Martin and Ventura (2010), into the detailed, overlapping-generation framework of Braun, Ikeda, and Joines (2009) extended to the multicountry framework, to calibrate the bubble-bust and subsequent balance-sheet problems, both national and international. See also Aoki and Nikolov (2011).

8. See Nishimura (2011c) for more detail on this balance-sheet adjustment.

Figure 7-7. *Ratio of Working-Age Population to Rest of Population, People's Republic of China, Japan, and the United States, 1950–2050*

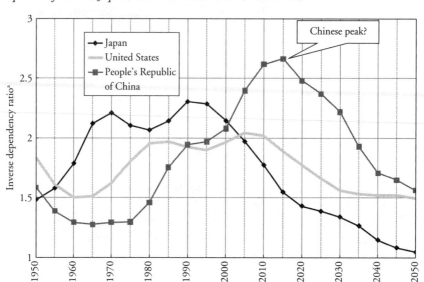

Source: United Nations (2010).
a. The inverse dependency ratio is the number of working-age people to one dependent person.

a bit later than in Euro-American countries. The peak will be around 2010–15, after which it will decline as rapidly as it is now rising. The inverse dependency ratios of many other Asian countries have a quite similar time profile to that of China, and some are even more pronounced (figure 7-8).

Macroprudential Policy: Three Dos and One Don't

The recent financial crisis, as well as the "Great Moderation" leading up to the crisis, brought to bitter recognition the gap between macroeconomic and microprudential policies. Thus macroprudential policy has come into the spotlight as something that would fill this gap. However, we are still very much short of having a satisfactory macroeconomic theory that deals adequately with complex and sometimes violent financial markets. Consequently, the very definition of macroprudential policy remains elusive, even four years after the crisis.

How are we to draw the lines between macroeconomic, macroprudential, and microprudential policies? What indicators are useful in detecting risks? What should be the tools of macroprudential policy? Should capital controls also be considered a macroprudential policy tool? How are we to achieve appropriate burden sharing among monetary, macroprudential, and microprudential policies in order to maintain financial stability?

Figure 7-8. *Ratio of Working-Age Population to Rest of Population, Seven Asian Countries, 1950–2050*

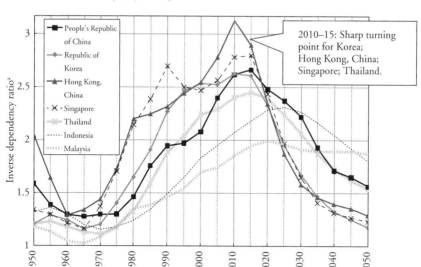

Source: United Nations (2010).
a. The inverse dependency ratio is the number of working-age people to one dependent person.

Since we do not yet have a satisfactory theory to give clear-cut answers to these questions, I take a more pragmatic approach and propose three dos and one don't for prospective macroprudential policies.

Do Detect Risks in Advance

To avoid another crisis and subsequent stagnation, it is critically important for policymakers to detect undue risk accumulation. Information propagation always plays a critical role in the inception and transmission of a systemic crisis. Thus information and intelligence—or more precisely speaking, market intelligence—are of the utmost importance both for risk detection and for crisis management. Here both bottom-up and top-down approaches are absolutely necessary.

The history of financial crises provides clear evidence that systemic crisis is often ignited by the bankruptcy not of large firms but of relatively small firms, such as Sanyo Securities in Japan (1997) and Northern Rock in the United Kingdom (2007) (figure 7-9). This reveals one crucial aspect of financial intermediation, that is, information. Since financial transactions are a collection of information flows, the failure of a small financial institution may cause an immediate marketwide liquidity crisis, or a run, if the failure gives rise to widespread fear or uncertainty in the market.

Figure 7-9. *Assets, Sanyo Securities and Northern Rock*

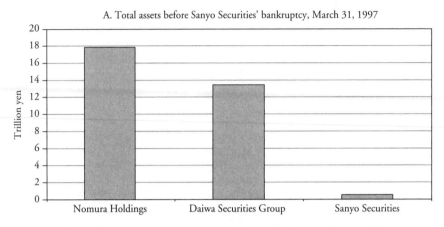

A. Total assets before Sanyo Securities' bankruptcy, March 31, 1997

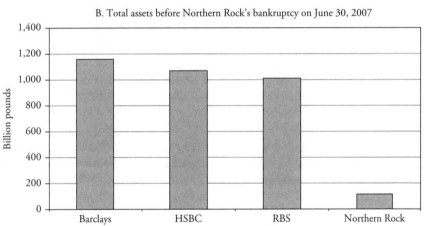

B. Total assets before Northern Rock's bankruptcy on June 30, 2007

Source: Bloomberg.

Thus in terms of both risk detection and crisis prevention, market intelligence obtained through face-to-face contacts and dialogue with market participants is critically important. In this regard, most Asian central banks can boast of their grip on individual institutions' activities and microeconomic information of the market. Nonetheless, the increased sophistication and innovation of financial services makes risk detection increasingly difficult. In some cases, financial institutions themselves do not seem fully aware of the risks associated with their investments and transactions, especially those related to structured products and derivatives. Any complacency in terms of risk detection could itself be another source of risk, and authorities should encourage market participants to continuously improve their risk-management skills. Painstaking information gathering, continuous updating, and open-minded risk assessment are all about market intelligence.

In this regard, macroprudential measures—such as information exchange through the publication of the Financial Stability Report (FSR)—have the potential to provide new ways of using information and market intelligence. Macroprudential policies can be effective only if they facilitate dialogue and coordination between market participants and authorities and also between macroeconomic and microeconomic policies.

I therefore turn now to macroeconomic risks and excesses and the indicators used to detect them. In most cases of bubble and burst, the large gyrations of financial markets and the economy are driven by psychological swings: economic entities are likely to become excessively optimistic in bubble periods and excessively pessimistic when those bubbles burst. In economic boom periods, such as Japan's bubble era and the Great Moderation, the coexistence of high growth and low inflation may lead to the illusion of productivity growth and an expectation of continued low interest rates. Such optimism is likely to induce a euphoric view of asset prices and an underestimation of risks. One the other hand, in a prolonged downturn, economic entities become excessively pessimistic, leading to further deterioration of the economy, and thus their pessimism becomes self-fulfilling. In order to avoid an excessive accumulation of these risks, it is critically important to detect any such extreme optimism or pessimism behind the developments indicated by various financial data.

For such purposes, we should carefully avoid becoming a hostage to any particular form of reasoning or theory. Although indicators such as credit-to-GDP ratio and the deviation of real estate prices from the trends may provide useful information, we do not have any decisive indicators in this respect. The theory I perused earlier is valuable in explaining what has happened before but is not so helpful in providing an indication of what will happen in the future. Every crisis may take a different form. Excessive reliance on specific indicators might cause us to miss important risks or misidentify nonexistent risks. Moreover, we should take into account a variant of Goodhart's law: If a central bank announces its intention to focus on specific indicators in order to take action to discourage risk taking, market participants might try to take risks without influencing these indicators, and these indicators might eventually lose their information value.[9] This problem would be further intensified if we focus on a narrower range of indicators.

Thus it would be wise for policymakers to monitor impartially a variety of indicators. Moreover, we need to make full use of market intelligence in order

9. See Goodhart (1975), for the original account, and Goodhart and Tsomocos (2011), for its most recent application.

to interpret various data comprehensively, since price data themselves may not indicate whether they are in line with fundamentals or driven by euphoria.

Let me now explain the various efforts made by the Bank of Japan in this field. The bank executes both on-site examinations and off-site daily monitoring of a wide range of financial institutions, including securities firms. Through such activities, the bank, making full use of market intelligence, tries to identify any signs of risk accumulation. The bank also maintains close dialogue with market participants, such as the counterparties of market operations.

Moreover, the Bank of Japan makes a regular comprehensive risk assessment of the overall financial system, analyzing both macroeconomic data and micro-economic information. It publishes its assessment on financial stability in its semiannual financial system report. Moreover, the bank's assessments of the risks in the financial system are useful inputs to the decisionmaking of monetary policy in the two-perspectives framework (discussed later).

The Bank of Japan is also making efforts to exploit wide-ranging data, use macroeconomic stress testing, and establish econometric models incorporating the financial sector. Such efforts are in line with those of other central banks. In addition, the Bank of Japan's economists have devised an innovative system of financial cycle indexes (FCIXs), which are designed to be early warning indicators.[10] These FCIXs are not based on a particular theory but on the age-old analytic tradition of economic trends and cycles. Although the jury is still out on their performance, the FCIXs seem to be promising: they predicted Japan's financial crisis and warned of the recent financial crisis about a year in advance (figure 7-10).

From my viewpoint, FCIXs would be useful tools for macroprudential policies, since they could provide early warning signals of excessive optimism or pessimism. Indeed, one of the most difficult challenges for macroprudential policy is how to spot excessive optimism or pessimism, especially because we do not yet have a credible theoretical framework that can be applied for such purposes. In this regard, the FCIX approach may be atheoretical in the sense that it does not depend on a particular economic theory, but this is an advantage in light of the unsatisfactory state of theory. Owing to their strengths as indicators, FCIXs would contribute to effective monitoring of the financial system as a whole from the macroprudential perspective.

Do Avoid Procyclicality

Another aspect of macroprudential policy is as a means to counter procyclicality. After detecting undue risk accumulation, policymakers would be required to check further accumulation of risks and to discourage risk taking. On the other hand, if policymakers find that market participants have become excessively risk-

---

10. See appendix 7A for a detailed explanation of FCIXs.

Figure 7-10. *Financial Cycle Indexes, Japan, 1985–2010*[a]

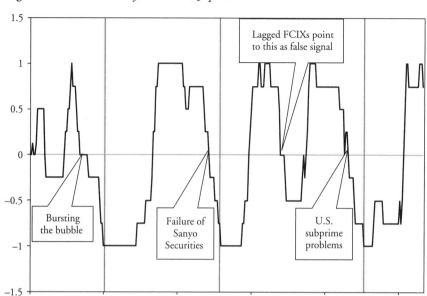

Source: Bank of Japan calculations.
a. Type D forecast real-time leading index; index = 0 → turning point. From left to right, the vertical lines indicate the bursting of the bubble, the failure of Sanyo Securities, and the surfacing of the U.S. subprime problem.

averse, they would be called upon to restore confidence in the market. The basic principles are simple: Don't be so lenient when things are booming, and don't be so restrictive when things turn sour. Here, coordination of monetary and macroprudential policy is necessary—and very effective.

In this regard, the Bank of Japan is making use of a two-perspectives framework in its conduct of monetary policy. The framework involves a two-step policy consideration: policy should be guided by the most probable scenario for the future course of the economy (first perspective), but at the same time it should incorporate "remote risk factors" that might affect the economy adversely if they happen to materialize, even though they may not be in the main scenario (second perspective).[11] The latter clearly includes systemic financial risks. Thus when it contemplates monetary policy, the bank examines a broad range of information—not only conventional indicators, such as inflation, but also financial information and market intelligence about risk accumulation. The bank assesses such information in a comprehensive manner and communicates to the public its assessment of these tail risks.

11. See Nishimura (2007) for clarification.

Figure 7-11. *World's Deepest Tsunami Breakwater at Kamaishi Port, Japan*

Source: Kamaishi Port Office, Guinness World Records.

Figure 7-12. *Tsunami Stone, Aneyoshi, Japan*

Source: *Yomiuri Shimbun.*

Needless to say, there can be other styles of communication, such as conveying central banks' risk assessment in terms of changes in their inflation forecasts over a long horizon within their inflation-targeting frameworks. There is no clear-cut answer as to the most suitable communication strategy, since the appropriate style of communication depends upon the economic and financial structure of the particular jurisdiction. However, there is an apparent need for financial risk assessment and its communication to the general public, beyond conventional inflation assessment.

On the issue of the new regulatory framework and procyclicality, one of the regular agenda items of recent international debates is how to address procyclicality in financial regulation. The Basel Committee has tried to address this issue in Basel III, which incorporates a capital conservation buffer and countercyclical buffer.

Here implementation is the key. Should banks conceive of the capital conservation buffer as a part of the minimum capital requirement and maintain the buffer regardless of the phase of the cycle, the introduction of the buffer might result in the banking sector holding more capital than is optimal from the intertemporal viewpoint.[12] In order for Basel III to be an optimal regulatory framework, not only from a static but also from a dynamic perspective, it should be implemented appropriately and accompanied by adequate supervision. This is all the more true for the countercyclical capital buffer.

In a similar vein, we should be aware of the possible side effects of a newly introduced systemically important financial institutions (SIFI) framework. Capital surcharges for "additional loss absorbency" in the SIFI framework may lead to the risk that SIFIs keep more capital than optimal on an intertemporal basis, which may cause more acute credit contraction in the midst of a recession. Moreover, there is the confounding factor of possible deposit concentration in SIFIs. In the midst of Japan's financial crisis, we experienced a substantial shift of deposits from small banks to money center banks. If a SIFI framework and the capital surcharge make people believe that SIFIs are much safer than non-SIFIs, a SIFI framework might even accelerate the shift of deposits in a stressed situation, but the surcharge might discourage SIFIs from fully implementing the credit intermediation functions formerly performed by non-SIFIs. Here again, implementation is the key. We should carefully examine various aspects of newly introduced regulatory frameworks and cautiously implement them, in order that these regulations will actually counter procyclicality as expected.

---

12. This is exactly the reason that Basel III differentiates the capital conservation buffer from the minimum capital requirement. The capital conservation buffer and accompanying regulations, such as restraining dividends, are designed to be used in a countercyclical way. Otherwise, there is no rationale to distinguish between the capital conservation buffer and the minimum capital requirement.

Do Avoid Unintended Cross-Border Impacts

We are now tackling the difficult issue of implementing new regulations for crisis prevention when economic and financial conditions are still fragile and financial markets are globally integrated. Policymakers should be extremely careful to avoid any unintended cross-border consequences when introducing a new rule, especially in terms of possible negative impacts on overseas markets.

One example of this kind of problems is the Volcker rule of the Dodd-Frank Act. It is intended to restrict proprietary trading by banking entities for the purpose of short-term gain, whose fundamental reasoning I fully agree with. However, depending on how related regulation is written and how the regulation is actually implemented, the rule could have significant implications for important market-making activities as well as for market liquidity. Thus U.S. government bonds and most other U.S. agency obligations are exempt from the rule. However, the act does not explicitly exempt the government obligations of other countries, including Japan, Canada, and European countries, even though market liquidity is no less important for the securities of non-U.S. governments.

Thus "prudent" implementation is absolutely necessary for prudential measures, such as those in the Dodd-Frank Act, to avoid unintended and potentially hazardous effects on other countries' financial markets. Needless to say, we should not expect any law to be a perfect solution in this difficult environment, and well-articulated guidance by the authorities and well-balanced implementation of the law is of utmost importance in this regard.

Don't Harm Long-Term Efficiency

That having been said, let me elaborate one *don't* of macroprudential policy, especially from a long-term perspective.

Since there is no clear definition of macroprudential policies or of their policy tools, any policy tool could be justified as a part of that policy. Thus we have to be careful of the danger of making macroprudential policy "a new excuse for an old addiction," which often leads to long-term inefficiency. Indeed, most of the tools often referred to as macroprudential policy tools, such as ceilings on loan-to-value (LTV) and debt-to-income (DTI) ratios in property markets and capital controls in foreign exchange markets, cannot be free from the risk of distorting asset allocation, which leads to inefficiency in the long run. Thus policymakers should be required to examine carefully the consequences of each macroprudential policy action from the long-run perspective. Long-run consequences often develop in a relatively short period of time, when addiction continues.

It is important to design the SIFI framework in a manner compatible with incentives. One of the root causes of the recent crisis was excessive risk taking. If the SIFI framework encourages SIFIs to pursue further the yield-searching, originate-to-distribute, model due to the need to downsize balance sheets while maintaining their return on equity, the effect might rather be to destabilize the financial system. In this regard, I would like to reiterate that the SIFI framework should be a comprehensive package of effective regulation and supervision sustainable in the long run.

Furthermore, SIFI regulation will be counterproductive if it hinders SIFIs' core financial intermediation. Since the demand for financial services is largely determined by the needs of the real economy, any additional regulation imposed on SIFIs will reduce their financial functions to some extent, or the financial intermediation performed by SIFIs will be replaced by similar services offered by other entities. Thus should there be a significant difference between the regulatory burden imposed on SIFIs and that on non-SIFIs, financial transactions might shift to less regulated entities, and the risk underlying the financial system as a whole might therefore heighten. Shadow banking is a typical problem of this kind.

Asia should be well aware of these problems. First, emerging Asia is now at the center of global economic growth. To sustain such growth, the need for fund intermediation is also likely to increase. Hence should new financial regulations hinder the core financial function at a global level, the negative impact on the real economy could be all the more serious. Second, some emerging Asian economies, where asset price hikes threaten to create bubbles, have already adopted macroprudential tools, such as lowering the LTV and DTI ratios of real estate–related loans. Accordingly, these countries should examine the costs and benefits of their macroprudential policy actions and devise appropriate and timely exit policies to avoid long-term inefficiency.

Macroprudential Measures and a False Sense of Security

The recent financial crisis (the so-called financial tsunami), and the tragic great earthquake in northern Japan (with its gigantic real tsunami), show vividly that tail risks may materialize in our lifetime, and thus they are not really tail risks. Policy frameworks anticipating only "ordinary" shocks within the usual economic cycles may not be very effective in mitigating the impact of such tail events when they actually materialize. The recent financial crisis in particular has forced policymakers to review their own policy frameworks and to examine how they could identify tail risks and deal with tail events.

Nonetheless, at this juncture we do not have fully reliable indicators for detecting tail risks nor panaceas against the maladies that accompany these tail events. We have to bear in mind that, no matter how intellectually inspiring policymakers may find this new tool, macroprudential policy can never be a substitute for appropriate macroeconomic policy or for effective financial supervision. Japan's experience of its bubble economy is a good example. Japan learned just how difficult it is to control asset prices solely with macroprudential tools such as an administrative ceiling on bank loans to the real estate sector.[13]

Thus in detecting tail risks and tackling tail events, we have to avoid any complacency or false sense of security in our macroprudential policy framework. If we mistakenly believe that we could discover excessive risk accumulation through observing specific indicators, or that macroprudential policies could be mightily effective in achieving financial stability, such complacency could itself become another source of instability.

Let me illustrate the importance of avoiding a false sense of security by telling you the story of the world's deepest tsunami breakwater at Kamaishi port in northern Japan (see figure 7-11). At 1,960 meters long and 63 meters deep, it was celebrated as the deepest breakwater in the world by Guinness World Records when it was completed in March 2009. Exactly two years later, it was shattered by the force of a tsunami equivalent to the impact of 250 jumbo jets flying at 1,000 kilometers an hour—the very apotheosis of a real tail event.

With hindsight, we cannot deny that this seemingly indestructible tsunami breakwater, and other facilities to ward off possible tsunami threats, gave us a sense of security. It might have led us to underestimate the magnitude of a tail event of a tsunami and thus to ignore the antique stone inscriptions warning of the devastation of tsunamis (figure 7-12). Hundreds of these so-called tsunami stones, some more than six centuries old, dot the coast of Japan. We now know the true cost of relying on this false sense of security.

Appendix 7A: The Financial Cycle Indexes

The financial cycle indexes (FCIXs) developed by K. Kamada and K. Nasu are used to monitor financial stability from the macroprudential perspective.[14] They are designed specifically as an alternative to the early warning indicator introduced by G. L. Kaminsky and C. M. Reinhart.[15]

Kamada and Nasu focus on the Juglar cycle—a cycle with a duration of seven to eleven years—included in financial time series, according to the result of analyzing the data compiled by L. Laeven and F. Valencia.[16] The Juglar cycle is extracted from the original time series by the HP filter-based band-pass filter.[17]

---

13. I explain the inadequacy of macroprudential policy in Japan in Nishimura (2011a).
14. Kamada and Nasu (2011).
15. Kaminsky and Reinhart (1999).
16. Laeven and Valencia (2010).
17. The OECD (2008) adopted the HP-based band-pass filter in place of the phase average trend (PAT) method to construct its composite leading indicators. The PAT is a traditional method of trend detection originally developed by the NBER and is calculated as follows: Deviations from a seventy-five-month centered moving average are first calculated; then the obtained series is divided into expansion and contraction phases and the average is calculated for each phase; a three-phase centered moving average is calculated, and these averages are interpolated.

This filter consists of two HP filters with different smoothness parameters, specifically $\underline{\lambda}$ and $\bar{\lambda}$ as defined below:

$$\underline{\lambda} = \left\{ 2\sin\left(\frac{\pi}{7f}\right) \right\}^{-4} \text{ to extract cycles lasting longer than seven years;}$$

$$\bar{\lambda} = \left\{ 2\sin\left(\frac{\pi}{11f}\right) \right\}^{-4} \text{ to extract cycles lasting longer than eleven years.}$$

In both of the above, f is the parameter used to adjust the formulas for the frequency of an original time series. The Juglar cycle lasting seven to eleven years is given by the difference between the two HP trends obtained above. The two financial crises are used to categorize data into leading and lagging indicators.

—January 1990: the triple sell-off in the yen, equity, and bond markets, which is considered the beginning of the bursting of the asset-price bubble; and

—November 1997: the bankruptcy of Sanyo Securities, which is considered the start of a series of financial institution bankruptcies.

Data are considered a leading indicator if the Juglar cycle extracted turns down before the above two crises; they are considered a lagging indicator if the extracted Juglar cycle turns down after the two crises.

FCIXs comprise leading and lagging indexes. Kamada and Nasu propose three types of index: types D, C, and B. Here we explain the type-D leading FCIX, which is a diffusion index and constructed as follows:

$$D_t = \frac{1}{N}\sum_{i=1}^{N} I\left(\Delta b_{i,t}\right),$$

where b denotes the Juglar cycle extracted from a leading indicator; Δb its first difference; N the number of leading indicators; and $I(X)$ the index function, which takes on $+1$ if X is positive and -1 if X is negative. The type-D lagging FCIX is obtained in a similar fashion.

FCIXs may not be very sensitive to a revival of financial activity, because they are designed to detect signs of financial crisis. As the father of business cycle analysis, Arthur Spiethoff, pointed out, the timing of recoveries is often ambiguous, compared with that of crises.

The Japanese FCIXs are constructed only from monthly, quarterly, and semi-annual financial data that can be traced back at least to the mid-1980s. Kamada and Nasu have found eight leading indicators: stock prices of the banking, real estate, and construction sectors; the lending attitude of financial institutions; the financial positions of firms; current profit levels of firms; housing loans; and commodity prices. Some of the leading indicators are affected by global shocks and enable the leading FCIX to detect financial crises prevailing in overseas economies.

In contrast, Kamada and Nasu have found eleven lagging indicators: corporate debt; household debt; lending interest rates; changes in interest rates on loans; the two monetary aggregates, M2 and M3; deposits; land prices nationwide and in large urban areas; as well as three- and nine-year government bond yields. The leading indicators cover mainly balance-sheet information, so that the lagging FCIX reflects domestic financial conditions.

In the scheme of Kamada and Nasu, a possible financial crisis is warned of when the leading FCIX falls to the zero point. This simple scheme successfully forecast the BNP Paribas shock about one year ahead of its occurrence in August 2007. However, this result should be interpreted with caution, since the index fails to take into consideration the uncertainty caused by real-time estimation problems.[18] Figure 7-10 plots the predicted type-D leading FCIX. It forecasts three financial crises successfully, falling to zero in May 1988 (nineteen months before the triple sell-off), in February 1997 (eight months before the bankruptcy of Sanyo Securities), and in June 2006 (fourteen months before the BNP Paribas shock).

The predicted leading FCIX takes positive values during November 1999 to December 2001, reflecting the IT bubble. However, no crisis was observed in Japan during this period. To avoid a potential false alert, it is possible to discern such an economic lull. The lagging index is useful for this purpose. The lagging index (not shown here) indicates that Japan remained in a contraction phase during the period November 1999 through April 2004, suggesting that the revival of the leading index during the period November 1999 through December 2001 might be indicative of an economic lull.

Some caveats are in order here. First, although FCIXs make it possible to detect signs of impending financial crises, they do not enable one to identify the source, type, or size of the crisis. Second, FCIXs do not make obvious the optimal policy measures that should be undertaken. With the help of FCIXs, policymakers must monitor financial institutions carefully and devise policy measures appropriate for the economic and financial conditions.

18. FCIXs are not immune to real-time estimation problems, such as the end-of-sample and lagged-data-publication problems, which may cause serious delay in warning signals. As a solution, Kamada and Nasu (2011) propose to predict the Juglar cycle's turning point, where the growth rate falls to zero, by an inflection point, where acceleration falls to zero in real-time data. This is an application of the well-known rule of thumb: acceleration drops before velocity does.

References

Aoki, K., and K. Nikolov. 2011. "Bubbles, Banks, and Financial Stability." Paper prepared for the 2011 International Conference, Bank of Japan.

Basel Committee on Banking Supervision. 2011. "The Transmission Channels between the Financial and Real Sectors: A Critical Survey of the Literature." Working Paper 18.

Bianchi, J. 2010. "Credit Externalities: Macroeconomic Effects and Policy Implications." *American Economic Review* 100, no. 2: 398–402.

Bracha, A., and D. J. Brown. 2010. "Affective Decision-Making: A Theory of Optimism-Bias." Discussion Paper 1759. Cowles Foundation, Yale University.

Braun, R. A., D. Ikeda, and D. H. Joines. 2009. "The Saving Rate in Japan: Why It Has Fallen and Why It Will Remain Low." *International Economic Review* 50, no. 1: 291–321.

Clark, A., and A. Large. 2011. "Macroprudential Policy: Addressing the Things We Don't Know." Occasional Paper 83. Group of Thirty.

European Central Bank. 2010. *Financial Stability Report.* December.

Goodhart, C. A. E. 1975. "Monetary Relationships: A View from Threadneedle Street." In *Papers in Monetary Economics,* vol. 1. Reserve Bank of Australia.

Goodhart, C. A. E., and D. P. Tsomocos. 2011. "The Role of Default in Macroeconomics." Discussion Paper 2011-E-23. Institute for Monetary and Economic Studies, Bank of Japan.

Hahm, J.-H., H. S. Shin, and K. Shin. 2011. "Non-Core Bank Liabilities and Financial Vulnerability." Department of Economics, Princeton University.

Hattori, Masazumi, Hyun Song Shin, and W. Takahashi. 2010. "A Financial System Perspective on Japan's Experience in the 1980s." Paper prepared for the 2009 Bank of Japan International Conference, Princeton University. Revised.

Jeanne, O., and A. Korinek. 2010a. "Managing Credit Booms and Busts: A Pigouvian Taxation Approach." Working Paper 16377. Cambridge, Mass.: National Bureau of Economic Research.

———. 2010b. "Excessive Volatility in Capital Flows: A Pigouvian Taxation Approach." *American Economic Review* 100, no. 2: 403–07.

Kamada, K., and K. Nasu. 2011. "The Financial Cycle Indexes for Early Warning Exercise." Working Paper 11-E-1. Bank of Japan.

Kaminsky, G. L., and C. M. Reinhart. 1999. "The Twin Crises: The Causes of Banking and Balance-of-Payments Problems." *American Economic Review* 89, no. 3: 473–500.

Laeven, L., and F. Valencia. 2010. "Resolution of Banking Crises: The Good, the Bad, and the Ugly." Working Paper WP/10/146. International Monetary Fund.

Liu, Z., and M. M. Spiegel. 2011. "Boomer Retirement: Headwinds for U.S. Equity Markets?" *Economic Letter* 2011–26. Federal Reserve Bank of San Francisco.

Martin, A., and J. Ventura. 2010. "Theoretical Notes on Bubbles and the Current Crisis." Working Paper. Centre de Recerca en Economia Internacional.

Nishimura, K. G. 2007. "The New Policy Framework of the Bank of Japan: Central Banking in an Uncertain World." *Asian Economic Papers* 6, no. 3: 132–43.

———. 2011a. "Macroprudential Lessons from the Financial Crises: A Practitioner's View." In *Asian Perspectives on Financial Sector Reforms and Regulation,* edited by M. Kawai and E. Prasad. Brookings.

———. 2011b. "Population Ageing, Macroeconomic Crisis, and Policy Challenges." Speech. Seventy-Fifth Anniversary Conference of Keynes' General Theory. University of Cambridge.

———. 2011c. "This Time May Truly Be Different: Balance Sheet Adjustment under Population Ageing." Speech. American Economic Association Annual Meeting, Denver.

Nishimura, K. G., and H. Ozaki. 2006. "An Axiomatic Approach to ε-contamination." *Economic Theory* 27: 333–40.

———. 2011. "ε-exuberance: An Axiomatic Approach." Keio University.

OECD. 2008. *OECD System of Composite Leading Indicators.*

Stein, J. 2011. "Monetary Policy as Financial-Stability Regulation." *Quarterly Journal of Economics.*

Takáts, Elöd. 2010. "Ageing and Asset Prices." Working Paper 318. Bank for International Settlements.

United Nations. 2010. *World Population Prospects: The 2010 Revision Population Database.*

8

Emergence in the Postcrisis World: Widening Asymmetries between Advanced and Emerging Economies

MEHMET YÖRÜKOĞLU

From a so-called Great Moderation to a savings glut during the last two decades, the world economy witnessed a very rapidly changing economic landscape. Globalization, emergence, and rapid technological change were the most important drivers of this change. Globalization increased productivity all over the world, helped to improve welfare tremendously in both advanced and developing countries, and has been one of the important factors shaping the Great Moderation era. Financial markets and goods markets became increasingly interconnected, as individuals and firms kept diversifying their financial portfolios to avoid idiosyncratic risks, without caring about increasing systemic risks resulting from this increased interconnectedness.

Since individuals and firms were more and more able to diversify their idiosyncratic risks at a seemingly smaller cost, false confidence and excess risk appetite were created. Distribution of shocks for financial portfolios has dramatically changed; more frequent adverse shocks were avoided by diversification at the expense of low-frequency tail shocks, created by the increased interconnectedness—which was totally ignored at the individual level. At the aggregate level, however, sentiments were against more regulation, and financial deregulation was more fashionable because of sustained growth and lack of volatility.

In the goods market, the twin of this was more and more specialization of production. On the one hand, increased global trade and specialization increased productivity and the variety of goods available to consumers, increasing their welfare immensely. On the other hand, the increased interconnectedness and specialization made the world more sensitive and vulnerable to global shocks. This is why some export-driven economies were affected so severely by the crisis during its initial phase.

The emergence process, which is a strong implication of the neoclassical growth model, started to take place only in the last two decades. The convergence process was seen as a *process of miracle,* as in the Nobel Laureate Robert Lucas's seminal work "Making a Miracle."[1] Japan and later the Republic of Korea were the best examples of making economic miracles. But during this early wave of emergence only around 200 million people emerged together, roughly around 4 percent of the total world population. However, in the last two decades, the emergence process became much more common. In terms of the effect that it has on the global economy, this wave has an incomparably stronger impact. In this wave, around 4 billion people are emerging together, or more than 60 percent of the world population (in such countries as People's Republic of China, India, Indonesia, Brazil, Mexico, and Turkey). This huge emergence wave has far-reaching implications. Since there is such a difference between the consumption baskets of consumers in advanced and emerging economies (EMEs), the fast growth of the incomes of EME consumers puts significant pressure on relative prices globally. The consumption basket of EME consumers is dominated by commodities, food, and energy. Therefore relative prices of these items have a tendency to increase during the convergence process.

This rapid change in the world economic landscape is likely to continue at a faster pace after the global financial crises. The first reason for faster convergence after the crisis is households, firms, and governments in advanced economies being in excess debt. These agents' borrowing is constrained now; they cannot borrow to increase their consumption and investment and, on the contrary, have to deleverage. The demographics also limit consumption growth in advanced economies. Therefore total consumption in advanced economies will grow only slowly for a long period of time.

The second reason for faster convergence after the crisis is related to changing global risk perceptions. Credit rating agencies and overall risk perceptions about EMEs have been quite backward looking. Because of this approach, the global investment flow to EMEs has not been at the pace that it would be if credit rating agencies had been more forward looking up to the crisis. This is in fact one of the reasons that advanced economies like the United States felt the pressure of the savings glut so strongly on the way to the crisis. A study by Morgan Stanley shows that the optimal share of emerging economy assets in the global portfolios should be around 30 percent, much more than the current level of 10 percent. It is expected that in the coming years this gap will be filled at a pace of 2 percent a

---

1. "Making a Miracle" appears as a chapter in Lucas (2002).

year. This means that around US$500 billion of extra capital will flow to EMEs each year. As a third reason for more rapid convergence, the global financial crisis is likely to speed up the shift of production from advanced economies to EMEs. The tension between efficient producers and inefficient producers in the Schumpeterian theory of the creative destruction of recessions can be applied to the global economic landscape.

That globalization, emergence, and rapid technological changes will have stronger impacts on the global economic landscape after the global financial crisis has important implications on macroeconomic policy for EMEs. Increasing growth and inflation differentials between advanced economies and EMEs under an environment of abundant liquidity make inflation targeting insufficient to maintain price stability and financial stability at the same time. To maintain price stability without accumulating financial instability risks, the inflation targeting framework should be supported with a strong macroprudential framework and with more disciplined fiscal policies. Many EMEs, including Turkey, started to use macroprudential tools more actively after the global financial crisis.

In this chapter I argue that, after the global financial crisis, the asymmetries between advanced and emerging economies and the imbalances created due to these asymmetries may be even larger than before. In the second section I go over the Turkish experience on employing macroprudential and liquidity policies after the global financial crisis. In the third section I argue that the inflation and growth differential between advanced and emerging economies will be larger after the crisis. I discuss a new channel, which creates an inflation gap between advanced and emerging economies; this might be viewed as the new goods' bias in inflation measurement. I develop a North-South model of this new goods' bias. After parameterizing the model, I quantify the impacts of the bias.

Global Financial Crisis and Emerging Market Economies: Issues and Consequences

The global financial crisis had important impacts on the real economy and the financial markets of EMEs. Partially driven by trade linkages, at the initial phase of the crisis, EME output—as measured from peak to trough—showed substantial decline, with considerable variation across countries and subgroups.[2] On the other hand, the impacts on financial markets were characterized by a collapse in asset prices and private credit growth, an increase in risk premium, and exchange rate depreciation; all were closely linked with the reversal in capital flows and global deleveraging. However, soon after this short initial phase, EMEs started to grow again, significantly supporting overall world economic growth.

---

2. See Kose and Prasad (2010) for further details on country and subgroup variations among EMEs.

The increased importance of trade linkages due to globalization was the most important channel through which the EMEs were affected. The specialization of EMEs' export bundles made this external demand shock act as a strong sectoral shock. Since the export bundle is very specialized, and is much different from the domestic consumers' average consumption basket, a negative external demand shock becomes very hard for domestic demand to absorb. This creates a sectoral shock, necessitating a reallocation of factors of production between export-oriented sectors and sectors dominated by domestic demand. However this is a slow and costly process. The reallocation of factors of production takes time, initially creating significant excess capacity in export-oriented sectors. Capacity utilization rates in export-oriented sectors decrease, and unemployment increases for a substantial period of time. A negative sectoral shock compared to an overall balanced negative shock, which affects all sectors similarly, creates more underutilization of capacity and disproportionally more unemployment, since it requires sectoral reallocation, which happens only very slowly.

The Turkish experience is a good example of this process. Between 2002 and 2008 the average yearly growth rate of Turkish imports and exports was more than 25 percent a year. During the same period Turkish exports and imports measured in U.S. dollars almost tripled. The Turkish economy used to be more of a closed economy, but in less than a decade international trade became an important factor. The change in the sectoral composition of exports is even more dramatic. Before 2002 textile, yarn, and food-related sectors dominated Turkish exports, whereas by 2008 sectors like automobiles and parts, electrical machinery and appliances, and industrial machinery started to be more important. This reflects the rapid transformation of Turkish production and exports. The Turkish production sector rapidly climbed the technology ladder in that period.

However, this outstanding success also increased the sensitivity of Turkish exports' external demand to global business cycles. The sectors that have become more dominant are demand-sensitive sectors, like investment and durable goods. It is estimated that if overall demand goes down by 1 percent, the demand for textile and food products goes down around 1 to 2 percent, whereas the demand for durable goods, including automobiles, goes down as much as 4 or 5 percent. The Turkish export sector has specialized further since then. For instance, its average 2002 export bundle was much closer to its average 2008 domestic consumption bundle. When external demand for Turkish export products shrinks, the specialization in the export bundle leads to a sectoral shock, as opposed to an overall demand shock in the economy.

Studies show that sectoral shocks negatively effect resource utilization, since they require significant resource reallocation between sectors. Therefore after a sectoral shock, capacity reallocation and unemployment are disproportionately negatively effected. As a result, the Turkish unemployment rate rapidly increased in the early phases of the global financial crisis. Unemployment was at 10.3 percent in September 2008 and 16.1 percent in February 2009. Partly due to tax reductions implemented in certain sectors and seasonality factors, unemployment began to fall; by July 2009 it was 12.8 percent. This was 2.9 percentage points more than July 2008.

Monetary Policy Measures to Cope with the Crisis

Just before the crisis, the Turkish economy had been hit by strong idiosyncratic inflationary shocks mainly due to prices of unprocessed food in addition to global commodity and energy price shocks. Therefore, Turkey entered the global financial crisis with moderately high inflation and high real and nominal policy rates. The economy had already slowed down for country-specific conjectural reasons, and because of a tight monetary policy. As domestic and external demand fell, and the crisis began to deepen, inflation expectations rapidly declined.

Significantly declining commodity and energy prices also put strong downward pressure on inflation. Seeing that these factors would support the inflation outlook and that the output gap would remain significantly negative for a long time, the Central Bank cut the main policy rate by 1,025 basis points (from 16.75 percent) to help out the real and the financial sector. Although central banks globally were cutting their policy rates significantly, the cuts by the Turkish Central Bank were the highest among both the OECD countries and EMEs. The cuts were quite successful, rapidly inducing market rates (including deposit and credit rates) to fall and short- and long-term real interest rates to approach record low levels.

Furthermore, swift measures were taken regarding foreign exchange and money and credit markets to sustain the recovery. First, as the crisis hit the EMEs by October 2008, one of the measures that the Turkish Central Bank took was to terminate foreign exchange (FX) market intervention and provide the necessary FX liquidity in the market. Additionally, by the end of October 2008 the bank provided additional FX liquidity to alleviate the possibility of price fluctuations as market liquidity tightened. The bank also resumed its intermediary functions related to foreign exchange deposits and gradually increased the transaction limits of banks in the FX deposit market. Furthermore, to help out the banking sector and to increase the FX liquidity of the banks, the required reserve ratio for FX liabilities of banks and other financial houses was lowered by 2 percent by the end of 2008.

Important measures for the Turkish lira market were also taken. First, in the money market, to reduce the potential volatility in overnight rates, the bank tightened the gap between borrowing and lending rates by 1 percent. Second, after October 2008, to reduce tension in money markets and eliminate volatility in overnight rates, the bank started to inject more excess liquidity. On the other hand, the well-functioning credit market was also an important component of crisis prevention. To this end, as the probability of a permanent liquidity shortage started to increase, the bank started three-month repurchase auctions and reduced the Turkish lira required reserve ratio by 1 percent.

With the help of the strong measures mentioned above, the economy began a very fast recovery in the second quarter of 2010. Largely due to rapidly declining credit interest rates and tax incentives, private consumption acted as the major driving force of the recovery process; however investment demand was relatively weak at the earlier stage of recovery. In a typical recovery, one would expect investment demand to lead the recovery; however, this was not the case, at least at the initial phase, mainly because of high global uncertainty. The global economic outlook—particularly in the main trading partners in the euro area—also delayed the recovery of external demand. However, an increase in product market diversification and relocation led to a gradual increase in total exports at later periods.

As FX liquidity improved and international capital flows revived, the Turkish lira started to appreciate. To this end, the Central Bank began in August 2009 to intervene in the FX market to build up reserves. However, as the surge in capital inflows increased in mid-2010, the bank decided to alter the method of FX buying auctions, to be effective October 4, 2010. This policy aimed to benefit from capital inflows more effectively, with a view to strengthening FX reserves and to enhancing resilience against sudden reversal in flows. In addition, due to improvement in the FX market and the acceleration of private credit growth, the FX required reserve ratio was also increased to the precrisis level of 11 percent.

Furthermore, several measures are being taken that target the Turkish lira market. First, technical interest rate adjustment and a corridor system are being implemented for efficient liquidity management. With this policy, a certain deviation of overnight market rates from the policy rate is allowed. This policy also lengthens the maturity of Turkish lira transactions. Second, the Central Bank started to use the one-week repurchase auction interest rate rather than the overnight borrowing rate as its policy rate while maintaining the monetary policy stance.

As credit growth accelerated and the surge in capital flows increased, the required reserve ratios were increased gradually. Additionally, the remuneration of reserves was also terminated to increase the effectiveness of this policy tool.[3] Therefore, the changes in the required reserve are expected to increase the effectiveness of the policy mix of a lower policy rate (as discussed below) and a wider interest corridor. Besides, to enhance financial stability, the required reserve ratio for termination liabilities is differentiated in favor of termination liability depos-

3. For further details, see Central Bank of the Republic of Turkey (2010).

its with longer maturities. Therefore, this policy is meant to both slow the acceleration in credit growth and reduce the maturity mismatches and related risk by lengthening the maturity of liabilities.

Postcrisis Era: Need for Macroprudential Policies

The postcrisis era for EMEs, including Turkey, can be divided into two phases. The initial phase starts around the beginning of 2010, when emerging economies started to exhibit a very strong recovery from the negative effects of the global financial crisis, and ends with the intensified eurozone sovereign debt crisis, in August 2011. As of April 2012 we are still in the second phase. Both of these phases strongly called for the extensive use of macroprudential policies appropriate for each phase to ease the pressure on monetary policy and to prevent the risk of accumulating financial instability due to increasing global imbalances. Turkey is a good case study, where macroprudential tools are used symmetrically in both phases.

The first phase started at the beginning of 2010 and ran until August 2011, when the eurozone sovereign debt crisis hit the global economy. With the major central banks' provision of abundant liquidity, for EME policymakers (in countries with high growth potential but structural capital deficits), the first phase was challenging. In this phase, EMEs returned to their precrisis high growth performance. By the second quarter of 2010, Turkish output exceeded its precrisis level. With the debt crisis evolving in some European economies and with the slowdown of growth in the third quarter, the domestic and external demand divergence became more pronounced. In particular, the import of goods and services had rallied, but total exports had been steady. It was clear by mid-2010 that the Turkish economy was heading toward a big current account deficit, in a global environment with uncertainties about the sustainability of capital inflows.

There was no problem in financing a high current account deficit, because the global liquidity was abundant, the global risk appetite was strong, and the fundamentals of the economy—especially that of the banking and financial sector—were sound. However, in this global environment, EMEs mostly attracted short-term capital inflows. Especially in the Turkish case, nominal interest rates (including the policy rate and the rates in the financial markets)—although they were at historically low levels—were still quite attractive, especially for short-term foreign investors, given the near-zero nominal returns in global financial markets. With the motivation of appreciating emerging country currencies (and with further appreciation expectations), these relatively high nominal returns were attractive for short-term investors. Therefore, the composition of capital inflows rapidly tilted toward short-term flows, and although there was no problem with the quantity, the quality of financing the current account deficit deteriorated rapidly and significantly.

Figure 8-1. *Current Account Deficit and Credit, Turkey, 2004–10*

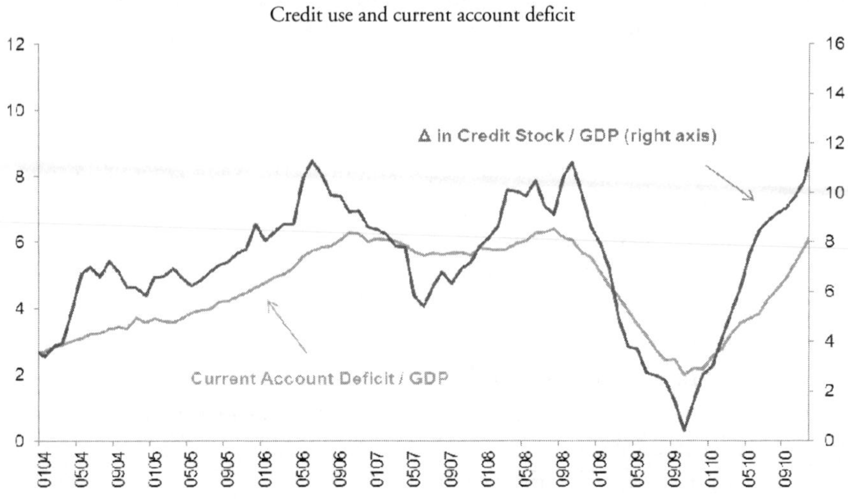

Credit use and current account deficit

Source: Central Bank of the Republic of Turkey.

For capital-hungry EMEs with high growth potential, the unbalancing effect of abundant global liquidity was not limited to its worsening effect in the quality and composition of capital inflows. It had a strong direct effect in increasing the current account deficit through rapid credit growth, which fueled domestic demand. Especially in Turkey, with the help of this extra liquidity, the banking sector, with high growth potential and high profitability, was very eager to provide credit-hungry economic agents with easy credit. The rapidly improving nonperforming loans ratio also made banks more comfortable in their lending decisions. As a result, credit in the banking sector increased rapidly. In general, the effect of credit growth on the current account balance may not be that clear, but for an economy growing above trend, with a significant savings gap, and with credit-hungry agents, one would expect fast credit growth to further fuel the current account deficit. Figure 8-1 clearly demonstrates the relationship between credit use and the current account deficit.

Another unbalancing effect of abundant global liquidity was the appreciation pressure that excessive short-term capital inflows were creating on Turkish lira. The unbalancing effect of this pressure is most observable in EMEs with an already high current account deficit. The extra appreciation pressure through this channel hurt the competitiveness of domestic production and exports, at the same time giving incentive for import consumption. The appreciation of the Turkish lira in this phase is observable in figure 8-2, which plots the consumer price index (CPI) and the producer price index based on real effective exchange rates.

Figure 8-2. *Real Exchange Rates, Consumer Price Index, and Producer Price Index, Turkey, 2003–12*

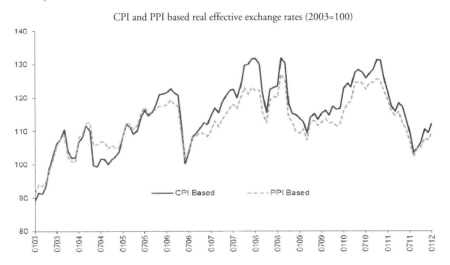

Source: Central Bank of the Republic of Turkey.

The widening of the current account deficit is the outcome of two main forces. The first one is the extensive borrowing opportunities due to excessive liquidity and low interest rate. These induce demand for domestically produced and imported goods. Second, the appreciation of the real exchange rate, which further triggers import demand, also undermines export performance. In addition, the capital transactions that finance the current account deficit are also an important source of vulnerability. Foreign direct investment (FDI) once financed the current account deficit. The uncertainties of today's international economic outlook changed that, so that the more recent wave of capital inflows is mainly in the form of portfolio investment and, to some extent, in bank loans. Although FDI is considered a stable form of capital flow, portfolio flows are likely to have sudden reversals and to be susceptible to informational problems and herding behaviors.[4] Therefore, by being financed by capital inflows, the current account deficit and its linkage with financial stability calls for an optimal policy mix by the central bank.

In this context, an increase in policy rates suppresses credit demand; hence it could reduce the current account deficit through the credit channel. However, such a policy would increase the domestic and foreign interest rate differential and thus feed further capital inflows—and therefore the appreciation of the domestic currency. This in turn leads to further deterioration of the current account deficit. Although the net effect remains ambiguous and requires

---

4. See for example Calvo and Mendoza (2000).

an empirical examination, still increasing the policy rate does not seem to be a plausible option to curb the current account deficit. Therefore, macroprudential instruments to restrain the momentum in credit growth and a gradual reduction in the policy rate to limit the trend in exchange rate appreciation could be an optimal policy mix.

Clearly, in this first phase of the postcrisis era, the problem for Turkish authorities was to slow down credit growth and the current account deficit, at the same time improving the quality of financing of the current account deficit by discouraging short-term capital inflows. Moreover, since there was no sign of heating in the economy, and because the supply side of the economy was very strong as well, this balancing was done in an environment of relatively benign inflation, without slowing down the economy abruptly with a tight monetary policy. Furthermore, the policy was such that no further short-term capital inflows were attracted, which would have put excessive appreciation pressure on the lira through a tight monetary policy and high nominal interest rates. What was needed was a rebalancing of the economy through a slowdown in credit growth and an undoing of the unnatural appreciation pressure that abundant global liquidity was creating on the lira.

On the policy side, therefore, the problem was that the policy rate appropriate for price stability did not match the policy rate that would ensure financial stability. Extra policy tools were needed to achieve both at the same time. In this respect, the addition of other policy instruments are warranted to maintain financial stability; these include required reserves and liquidity management facilities and such other measures targeting credit growth as loan-to-value caps and regulation of the size and composition of bank balance sheets.

It is necessary to clarify the context of policies for financial stability and the elements that the Central Bank is considering monitoring. As found in previous studies, the countries with a more leveraged domestic financial system suffered larger output loss during the crisis.[5] In addition, the maturity and currency mismatches have been the triggering factors behind the banking crisis, particularly in Latin America. Given the scale of the economy, lower bank loans and lower household liabilities with less FX risk exposure helped the Turkish economy to be more resilient during the global financial crisis. Therefore, sustaining household debt and bank leverage at moderate levels is an important component of financial stability. However, maturity mismatches have been widening, as firms' external debt and government debt securities' maturity got longer, while deposit maturity is getting shorter. The other elements of policies for financial stability include the FX position of the public and private sectors and FX risk management using futures and option markets instruments.

5. Berkmen and others (2009).

Financial Stability Outcomes: An Evaluation of the Two Phases

The two phases of Turkey's response to the global financial crisis are described here.

FIRST PHASE. The divergence of domestic and external balances, surge in capital inflows, credit growth, widening current account deficit, and real and nominal appreciation of the Turkish lira became apparent in the last quarter of 2010. These domestic and external conditions set up a difficult dilemma for economic policy, and maintaining financial stability became an essential requirement for sustained price stability. In this context, particularly after mid-November, the Central Bank started to use a new policy mix—a lower policy rate, a wider interest rate corridor, and higher reserve requirements—to solve the policy dilemma. To give incentive to increase the maturity of the deposits in the banking sector, reserve requirement ratios were differentiated across maturities. Longer maturities became subject to lower reserve requirement ratios.

The policy mix after mid-December was implemented by raising required reserves on Turkish lira liabilities to 9.5 percent on average, with a significant differential between the rates on short-term and long-term liabilities.[6] In addition, the policy rate was reduced by 75 basis points, the interest rate corridor was widened by 50 basis points, and daily FX purchases were reduced to US$50 million for 2011.

The widening of the interest rate corridor led to a substantial deviation of the overnight interest rate from the policy rate and to an increase in volatility of overnight rates. This policy also affected short-term rates on swap transactions and on their volatility. Besides the increase in volatilities, the initial impact of the interest rate and of the required reserve policy changes could also be observed from a marginal increase in maturities of swap transactions, Turkish lira repurchase transactions, the maturity composition of deposits, and a steepening yield curve (without any significant change in inflation expectations).

Daily FX purchases—with a further increase in required reserves and a lower policy rate and interest rate corridor—affected the nominal and real exchange rates. The effect of these policies can be seen in figure 8-3, which shows how the Turkish lira vis-à-vis the U.S. dollar started to depreciate and to diverge from other emerging market currencies. In contrast to sterilized FX intervention with open market operations, FX interventions paired with an increase in reserve requirements and other market liquidity measures are expected to have an immediate impact on the real exchange rate. This argument is supported

6. In mid-December the required reserve ratios were adjusted for maturity, with a lower rate for liabilities with a longer maturity. In late January 2011 the required reserve ratio was raised to 12 percent for demand deposits, to 10 percent for one month, to 9 percent for deposits with one to under three months' maturity (and other lira liabilities, including repurchase transactions), to 7 percent for three to under six months, to 6 percent for six to under twelve months, and to 5 percent for deposits of one year and longer.

Figure 8-3. *Exchange Rates, Turkish Lira and Other Emerging Market Currencies, 2010–12*[a]

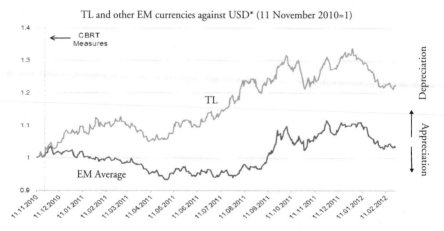

TL and other EM currencies against USD* (11 November 2010=1)

Source: Central Bank of the Republic of Turkey; Bloomberg.
a. Emerging markets included are Brazil, Chile, Czech Republic, Hungary, Mexico, Poland, South Africa, Indonesia, Republic of Korea, and Colombia.

by Carmen Reinhart and Vincent Reinhart, in a framework that extends the seminal overshooting model of Rudiger Dornbusch.[7] The theoretical findings in Reinhart and Reinhart are supported by evidence from Latin American and Asian countries during the 1990s, when these economies experienced substantial and volatile international capital flows.

The initial impact of the new policy mix on the maturity of debt instruments, credit growth, the exchange rate, and the yield curve is in line with the Central Bank's projections. In the initial phase of the post-Lehman era, the policy rate was reduced and the interest rate corridor was widened, whereas the range of required reserve ratios was widened, differentiating across maturities, with the weighted average of the ratio increasing from 5 percent to around 15 percent. The Central Bank also stopped paying interest on reserves, which made the reserve requirement policies more effective. The effect of the policy mix on exchange rates is plotted in figure 8-4. Between October 2010 and August 2011 (when the eurozone sovereign debt crisis surfaced), the Turkish lira depreciated by around 20 percent. Given the strong appreciation pressure that was put on emerging economy currencies by abundant global liquidity and strong short-term capital inflows, and the large current account deficit that the Turkish economy was experiencing, this gradual depreciation of the lira was a healthy development. As a result, the CPI and the producer price index rebalanced in this period.

7. Reinhart and Reinhart (1999); Dornbusch (1976).

Figure 8-4. *Policy Mix and Credit, Turkey, 2007–12*

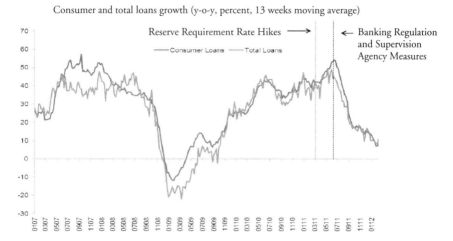

Source: Central Bank of the Republic of Turkey.

Consumer loans and total loans growth were around 45 percent (year on year) before the measures were instituted; they dropped gradually to around 15 percent by early 2012. Especially given the contribution of rapid credit growth to domestic and internal demand imbalance that the economy has been suffering from, the moderation in credit growth was a very healthy development as well.

As a result of the slowdown in credit growth and the value of the Turkish lira coming more in line with fundamentals, domestic demand started to moderate, showing signs of a significant rebalancing. The slowdown in final domestic demand is illustrated in figure 8-5. With moderating domestic demand and a more competitive Turkish lira, a rebalancing in exports and imports started to become more evident by the third quarter of 2011. Mainly because of rising energy and commodity prices, terms of trade developments in this period did not help the rebalancing, but the rebalancing in real exports and real imports has been quite strong.

A current account deficit measure excluding energy was close to balance by the first quarter of 2012. In this period increasing energy prices significantly slowed the improvement in the current account balance by putting a strong upward pressure on inflation. As a result of incentives put in place for longer maturity through differentiated required reserve ratios (although the average maturity is still too low), the maturity of deposits started to increase significantly. Also, with the help of macroprudential policies and increased uncertainty in the short-term interest rate due to the corridor system, the quality of financing of the current account deficit improved significantly. Short-term capital inflows

Figure 8-5. *Domestic Demand, Turkey, 2005–11*

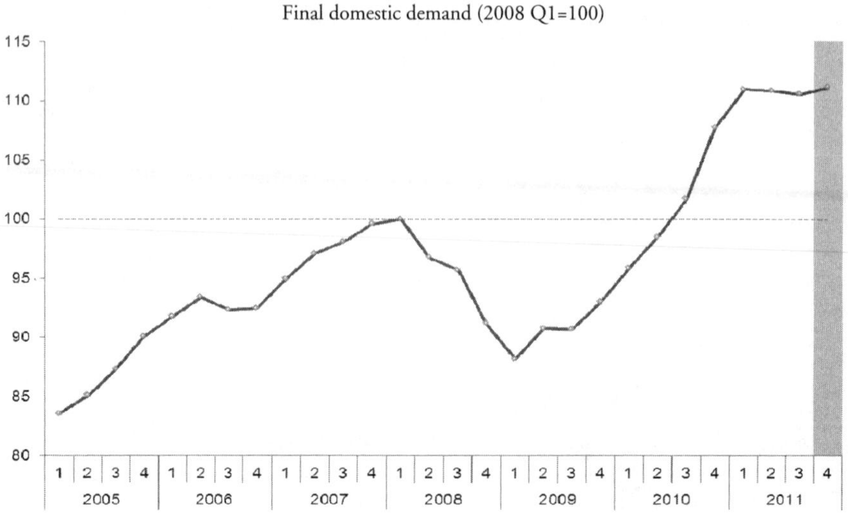

Final domestic demand (2008 Q1=100)

Source: Central Bank of the Republic of Turkey.

started to moderate, and foreign direct investment and long-term capital inflows started to increase again.

In summary, as a result of the macroprudential measures taken and the policy mix used, it was evident by the third quarter of 2011 that a significant rebalancing was under way in the Turkish economy. During this rebalancing, in August 2011, the eurozone sovereign debt crisis erupted, which changed the global economic environment almost totally for emerging economies.

SECOND PHASE. The Central Bank's response in this phase has been almost the opposite of its policies in phase one. With the economy on the path to achieving a successful rebalancing, financial stability concerns were alleviated, while price stability became the most important issue. The eurozone sovereign debt crisis affected global growth expectations negatively and decreased risk appetite significantly. As a result of increasing demand for dollar liquidity and the flight to quality, short-term capital inflows to emerging economies decreased, causing an overall depreciation of all currencies against the U.S. dollar.

For the Turkish economy, the pass-through from the weaker Turkish lira was already putting upward pressure on core inflation, which rose from around 3 percent in the last quarter of 2010 to around 7.5 percent by the end of 2011. Increases in prices for unprocessed food and tax increases on tobacco also significantly contributed to a rise in headline inflation. By the end of 2011 headline inflation rose to 10.45 percent, whereas the contribution of the exchange rate and import price pass-through, unprocessed food prices, and tax increases in

Figure 8-6. *Unit Labor Cost, Turkey, 2005–11*[a]

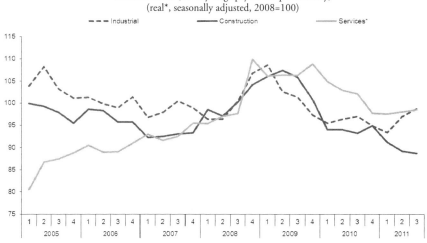

Unit labor cost (Hourly wage payments/ productivity)
(real*, seasonally adjusted, 2008=100)

Source: Central Bank of the Republic of Turkey.
a. Unit labor cost is hourly wage divided by productivity.

tobacco prices were 5 percent, 2 percent, and 1.1 percent, respectively. In other words, around 8.1 percent of 10.45 percent of the 2011 year-end inflation was due to these three factors.

Although economic growth was significantly above potential in 2011 (8.5 percent), there were no signs of overheating. With strong employment growth and investment, capacity utilization was below potential. Turkish economy grew at rates significantly above the potential (9 percent in 2010 and 8.5 percent in 2011). Credit growth boomed in 2010, and the supply side of the economy was also very strong, offsetting the potential of inflationary pressure from demand. That there was no significant cost-side pressure on inflation can also be seen in declining unit labor costs in 2010 and 2011 (figure 8-6). In summary, with no apparent signs of overheating, the target inflation was due to one-time temporary factors, and the Central Bank communicated that it would tighten its policy if it saw any threat of second-round effects on inflation. As a result, unlike earlier episodes of inflationary shocks, this time medium-term inflation expectations were well anchored, with no signs of deterioration (figure 8-7). Nevertheless, it is clear that maintaining expectations in the rest of 2012 would be a challenge, given that the base effects of the inflationary shocks received in 2011 will be in the year-on-year headline inflation numbers almost until the last quarter of 2012.

After the eurozone sovereign debt crisis, capital inflows to EMEs decreased significantly. This put significant depreciation pressure on their currencies. For most EMEs with currencies under strong valuation pressure in the earlier phase,

Figure 8-7. *Inflation Expectations, Twelve Months and Twenty-Four Months, Turkey, 2008–12*

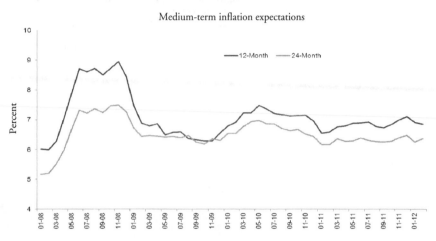

Source: Central Bank of the Republic of Turkey.

this was in fact a welcome development. This was clearly not the case for the Turkish lira, though, since at that point (according to different measures of the real effective exchange rate), it was not overvalued at all. As important, the volatility of capital flows also increased, increasing the volatility of the value of EME currencies.

Using the same set of tools, in this phase the Central Bank took measures in the opposite direction. To provide the necessary FX liquidity and to ease the undue depreciation pressure on the lira, the Central Bank started to sell FX through auctions. Given the high levels of current account deficit and the increased volatility in capital inflows, that the Central Bank was ready to provide the extra FX liquidity, when needed, had a strong reassuring effect on economic agents. Another important step that significantly decreased the volatility of the value of the lira was widening the interest rate corridor by shifting the upper band upward. A wider interest rate corridor of the North enabled the Central Bank to tighten up temporarily and significantly when there was stress in FX markets. This proved to be a very effective tool to undo the negative effects of increased FX market volatility. Indeed, in this phase, with these policies in effect, the volatility of the lira with respect to other EME currencies declined significantly.

The policy trade-off here is increased short-term interest rate volatility versus significantly decreased FX volatility. Higher short-term interest rate volatility leads to higher levels of long-term interest rates due to the extra uncertainty introduced; however, it does not lead to an increase in the volatility of long-term interest rates. After this tighter policy (through a wider interest rate corridor) started, bank loan rates increased significantly. Actually, the increase in the bank lending rates induced by this policy were so significant that the Central Bank could deliver the necessary tightening through the wider corridor without a need to increase the policy rate.

Also in the second phase, the Central Bank took measures to increase the liquidity positions of the banking sector. The Central Bank significantly cut the FX and the required reserve lira ratios on banks to help out the liquidity positions of the banks under this environment of increased liquidity needs.

In summary, after the eurozone sovereign debt crisis, while strengthening its policies for a more balanced economy, the Turkish Central Bank took measures to ensure a soft landing, following an above-potential growth for two consecutive years. The indicators up to now show that a soft landing to a more balanced economy will be achieved. However, due to increasing energy prices and imports, converging to a healthy level of current account balance will take some time. The Central Bank's measures to mitigate undue pressures on the value of the Turkish lira have made it one of the least volatile EME currencies.

As stated earlier, besides the interest rate policy, the Central Bank's policy mix consists of macroprudential policy and liquidity policy. The liquidity policy is made up of the interest rate corridor and the funding strategy. It is designed to undo the unbalancing impacts of such global conjectural forces as quantitative easing and the crisis environment. Since the imbalance is due to global conjectural forces, when these forces fade away, these extra liquidity policies will not be needed. However, emerging economies like Turkey need macroprudential policy and its tools because of structural reasons. The underlying factors of these structural reasons include globalization and the convergence process, which will continue for a long time. These factors create persistent growth and inflation differentials between advanced and emerging economies. In the rest of the chapter I argue that these structural forces will be even stronger after the global financial crisis, which will make policymaking in EMEs even more difficult. These structural forces manifest themselves as strong appreciation pressures on EME currencies, rapid credit growth, and current account imbalances. To cope with these forces, EME authorities will need to employ macroprudential policies and fiscal policies to ease the increasing pressures on monetary policy.

Increasing Growth and Inflation Differentials between Advanced and Emerging Economies in the Postcrisis Era

In the last decade we have seen significant and persistent differentials in inflation, policy interest rates (real and nominal), and growth rates between advanced and emerging economies. These differentials are likely to be even larger after the crisis, which may further fuel global imbalances. Why are these differentials important and how do they fuel global imbalances?

Growth differential is a healthy outcome of the emergence and convergence process, which immensely increases the welfare of people in both emerging and advanced economies. However, if precautions are not taken, persistent growth differentials may lead to asset price bubbles, unsustainable current account deficits, and exchange rate misalignments. Faster growth, as long as growth is supply driven, is not inflationary. The relative strength of supply and demand changes across emerging economies. In export-driven economies like China, supply factors may be dominant. But in economies with rapid credit growth, strong domestic consumption demand may put upward pressure on the current account deficit and inflation. The growth differential in annual terms between advanced and emerging economies has been around 4 percent since 2002. This implies roughly twenty years of half-life convergence. In other words, at this pace we can expect the income gap between advanced and emerging economies to halve in roughly every twenty years.

Persistent inflation differentials may accumulate financial instability risks. Central banks with persistently higher inflation will continuously struggle to reduce the inflation level, resulting in higher real and nominal policy rates and potential exchange rate appreciations. During the global financial crisis, core inflation dropped in both advanced and emerging economies. The drop was more significant for the emerging economies, so that the differential in core inflation between advanced and emerging economies decreased. However, with the rapid recovery after the crisis the differential is back to its precrisis level.

There was a remarkably constant average policy rate differential of around 6 percent between advanced and emerging economies from 2007 to 2011. Although the initial policy response of emerging economies to the global financial crisis was toward tightening, the policy response of the advanced economies was toward easing. Emerging economies started to ease later, following the advanced economies.

The growth differential between advanced and emerging economies is a consequence of the convergence process. However it is harder to explain the persistent inflation differential between advanced and emerging economies. Consider an inflation-targeting central bank following an implicit Taylor rule. From the perspective of such a central bank, having a growth performance close to the growth potential of the country and having an inflation level close to the preferred level (target level) of inflation are both normal. Therefore, if a country has no problem with growth but has difficulty in achieving the desired level of inflation, the central bank of the country should be more concerned about achieving its inflation target at the cost of having a little less growth. Thus if the central banks of advanced and emerging economies follow an inflation-targeting framework with an implicit Taylor-rule-like policy function, and these two groups of countries have similar preferences regarding growth and inflation, it is contradictory that one of these groups has persistently higher growth and higher inflation as the other group. Simply, emerging economy central banks should have traded more abundant good (growth) with the scarce one (lower inflation).

Then the question becomes, Why do emerging economies persistently have significantly higher inflation than advanced economies, given that they are relatively more successful in creating growth? Why don't they simply give up some growth for lower inflation? One answer to this question may be that emerging economies might benefit from the Great Moderation era at a later stage. But the fact that this constant differential has been persistent for almost a decade now raises a demand for an explanation. I believe that CPI differences between advanced and emerging economies are the main driver of this persistent differential. Compared with advanced economies' consumer baskets, emerging economies' consumer baskets contain more food, energy, and commodities. This puts an upward pressure on the price of these components and, therefore, an upward pressure on inflation.

In the rest of the chapter, I go over another important difference between the CPI baskets of advanced and emerging economies. I call this the new goods' bias. New goods, which are usually technology intensive, constantly flood the economy. Innovative new goods and their introduction to the market usually involve significant fixed costs, like research and development costs. Because of these costs and other factors (such as the higher monopoly power of the innovator firm initially, learning by doing, and further cost-reducing technological improvements), the price of a new good rapidly declines following its introduction. Since prices are high initially, richer consumers start to consume the new good; as its price declines, the new good diffuses to the general population. Similarly at the country level: a successful new good becomes a part of the CPI basket of the richer countries early on; only later does it become part of the CPI basket of the poorer countries.

As the drop in the price of a new good flattens out, in richer countries the disinflationary pressure of the introduction of the new good will be significantly larger than in poorer countries. As the pace of innovation of new goods increases, this inflation wedge increases. Similarly, as the price of a new good declines faster initially, its diffusion will be faster, and the disinflationary impact in the rich country will be large. Hence the disinflationary wedge between rich countries and poor countries will be large. In the next section I develop a North-South model of this disinflationary wedge.

Inflation Wedge between Advanced and Developing Economies: New Goods' Bias

Studies show that the importance for growth of both innovation and the introduction of new goods has been increasing. The introduction of new goods creates bias in inflation measurement mainly through two channels. First, the introduction of a new good increases the welfare of consumers, which is not captured in inflation measures. Second, after this introduction, the price of the new good declines rapidly due to learning by doing, technological progress, and competition. However, many of these new goods will never be significant enough to become part of the consumer basket used to measure inflation. For these goods, decline in their prices after introduction will not be captured by the measured inflation. Even for the new goods that will eventually become significant enough to enter the CPI basket, it will take time.

Again, up to the point when the new good becomes a part of the CPI basket, the decline in prices will not be captured despite the fact that a significant portion of price declines of the goods in their life cycle occur during this phase. Here there is an asymmetry between advanced and developing economies. Income level and the diffusion of new goods are positively related. In other words, new goods diffuse faster among high-income groups. If we extend this across countries, a successful new good, since it diffuses more rapidly in high-income countries, becomes a part of high-income countries' CPI basket earlier. Therefore a large fraction of the total price decline in the life cycle of this new good is accounted for by high-income countries. Thus new goods' bias in inflation measurement is likely to be more important in developing countries.

In the last decade, both the speed of innovation and introduction and the pace of price decline after introduction have increased significantly. Both of these factors increase the importance of the new goods' bias in inflation measurement. Figure 8-8 exhibits the pace of diffusion of significant new products over 120 years. As the figure demonstrates, the speed of diffusion of new products has increased through time. It took more than 70 years for the telephone to reach around a 50 percent penetration rate, whereas Internet access reached a similar penetration level in just 10 years. The most important factor behind the increase of speed of diffusion is the faster price decline rate of new products.

Figure 8-9 plots diffusion half-lives for new products. The time it takes a new product to penetrate half of the population has shrunk tremendously since 1860. The trend change in the figure after the information technology revolution is noticeable. These new products diffused much more rapidly compared to earlier new products. This was mainly because of their rapid price decline. The below-trend diffusion of the half-life of automobiles is also remarkable. That was mainly again due to the rapid price decline of automobiles, particularly after Ford's Model T.

To understand how the introduction of a new product affects inflation measurement—and how it may create a wedge in inflation measurement between advanced economies and EMEs—consider the price profile of a new product (figure 8-10). The figure gives the new product's price decline curve after its introduction to the market. The new product is considered, eventually, to be significant enough to become a part of the CPI basket in both types of economy. The good is introduced to the market at point A. At point B, it becomes part of the advanced economy's CPI basket. At point C, it becomes part of the

Figure 8-8. *Diffusion of New Goods, 1880–2000*

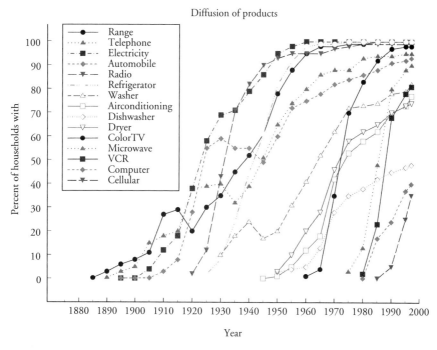

Figure 8-9. *Half-Lives of New Goods, 1860–2000*

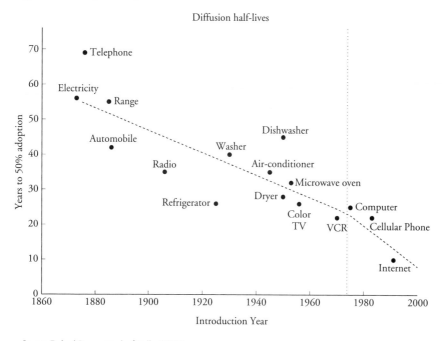

Figure 8-10. *Price Profile of a New Good*[a]

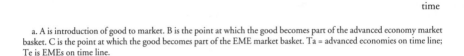

a. A is introduction of good to market. B is the point at which the good becomes part of the advanced economy market basket. C is the point at which the good becomes part of the EME market basket. Ta = advanced economies on time line; Te is EMEs on time line.

EME's CPI basket. Points Ta and Te represent the moments when this good becomes a part of the advanced economy CPI basket and of the EME CPI basket, respectively.

The decline in price between points A and B will not be taken into account in inflation measurements in the advanced country, whereas the price decline after point B will be taken into account. However, for the EME, the price decline up to point C will be ignored by inflation measurements. The time gap between Ta and Te will crucially depend on the per capita income difference between these two countries. It will also depend on the average price decline rate between these two points. The bigger the income difference, the larger the time gap will be. A higher average price decline rate between these two points will shorten the time gap. Theoretically, the new good's bias, ceteris paribus, will create some inflation wedge between advanced and emerging economies. But will this wedge be quantitatively significant? To answer this question, I present a simple two-country, North-South model.

The Model

Consider a two-country, North-South, model. Let labor be the only input of production, and let's assume it is immobile between the countries. The production function in both countries is given by $F(l) = A_i l$, where A_i is the productivity level in country i. The productivity level in the South is just a $\lambda < 1$

fraction of the productivity level of the North, that is, $A_s = \lambda A_N$. Every period, new varieties of goods are invented exogenously and costlessly, so that the total number of goods available grows at some constant rate. A new variety is initially expensive, but through time (due to technological improvements, learning by doing, and increasing competition, which are not modeled explicitly here), the price of a variety declines. For simplicity, let the price profile during the life of a product be exogenously given. Let the price of a variety of age t be given by $p_t = 1 + p_0 e^{-\rho t}$, where p_0, $\rho > 0$. Therefore the price of a new variety is $1 + p_0$ at age zero, but through time its price asymptotically converges to one at a declining rate.

Let the number of goods available at time t be given by $N_t = N_0 e^{\gamma t}$. The productivity levels in both countries grow at rate γ; hence the productivity gap between the countries as a ratio remains constant. If an individual consumes a certain variety, his consumption level is fixed at level $\bar{c}$. So he may either consume $\bar{c}$ amount of a variety or may not consume any amount of that product. Individuals' utility function is given by

$$U(c) = \log\left(\int_0^{N_t} c_i^\theta di\right)^{\frac{1}{\theta}},$$

where c_i is the individual's consumption of the ith variety, and it is either zero or $\bar{c}$. Individuals' lifetime utility maximization problem is standard. Consider the equilibrium where the number of varieties available is such that individuals in the North barely consume all varieties. Since the productivity and income levels in the South is a λ fraction of the North's ($Y_s = \lambda Y_N$), the total consumption of the South and the North will read

$$\bar{c} N_0 e^{\gamma t} = \lambda \bar{c} N_0 e^{\gamma(t-\tau)}.$$

All varieties at the margin give the same amount of extra utility; however the newer varieties are more expensive. The agents in the South will consume the cheapest varieties they can afford, so that the threshold variety can be solved from the equation

$$\bar{c} N_0 e^{\gamma t} = \lambda \bar{c} N_0 e^{\gamma(t-\tau)},$$

yielding

$$\tau = -\frac{\ln \lambda}{\gamma}.$$

Therefore the consumers in the South consume all varieties up to age τ.

In each country there is a monetary authority, which supplies money in the country's own currency. Let the amount of currency in each country be denoted by M^i. Let μ^i denote money supply growth rate in country i. Now let's calculate the inflation of different varieties. Let the inflation level of age τ variety in country i be Π_τ^i. Hence,

$$\Pi_\tau^i = \mu^i - \gamma + \frac{\frac{dp_\tau}{d\tau}}{p_\tau} = \mu_i - \gamma - \frac{p_0 \rho e^{-\rho t}}{1 + p_0 e^{-\rho t}}.$$

Inflation in each country will be given by

$$\Pi^i = \int_{-\infty}^{x_i} s_j^i \Pi_j^i \, dj,$$

where s_j^i is the share of the jth variety in the basket of the ith country. The share of the jth variety in the basket of the ith country is given by

$$s_j^i = \frac{n_j p_j}{\int_{-\infty}^{x_i} n_k p_k \, dk},$$

where n_j is the number of varieties of age j. Therefore $n_j = \dfrac{dN_j}{dj} = \gamma N_0 e^{-\gamma \tau}$.

Here, $\displaystyle \int_{-\infty}^{x_i} n_k p_k \, dk = \int_{-\infty}^{x_i} \left[\gamma N_0 e^{-\gamma j} \left(1 + p_0 e^{-\rho j} \right) \right] dj = N_0 \left(e^{-\gamma \tau} + \frac{\gamma p_0}{\gamma + \rho} e^{-(\gamma + \rho)\tau} \right).$

Therefore, plugging these in the inflation equation will yield

$$\Pi^i = \mu^i - \gamma + \int_{-\infty}^{x_i} \frac{\gamma N_0 e^{-\gamma j} \left(1 + p_0 e^{-\rho j} \right)}{N_0 \left(e^{-\gamma \tau} + \dfrac{\gamma p_0}{\gamma + \rho} e^{-(\gamma+\rho)\tau} \right)} \frac{-p_0 \rho e^{-\rho j}}{\left(1 + p_0 e^{-\rho j} \right)} \, dj,$$

and

$$\Pi^\tau = \mu^i - \gamma - \frac{\gamma p_0 \rho e^{-\rho \tau}}{\gamma + \rho + \gamma p_0 e^{-\rho \tau}}.$$

Consider a country that starts to consume the frontier good with time lag τ. Let the disinflation pressure that introduction of new goods creates in such a country be denoted by $\overline{\Pi}^\tau$. Then it is clear that

$$\overline{\Pi}^\tau = \frac{\gamma p_0 \rho e^{-\rho \tau}}{\gamma + \rho + \gamma p_0 e^{-\rho \tau}}.$$

Assume that the monetary authorities in both countries have a common preferred inflation level Π^*, so that they increase the money supply to achieve the inflation level of Π^*. Therefore,

$$\mu^i = \Pi^* + \gamma - \frac{\gamma p_0 \rho e^{-\rho\tau}}{\gamma + \rho + \gamma p_0 e^{-\rho\tau}}.$$

The disinflation pressure from the new goods is larger in the North than in the South. It is clear that the disinflation pressure is decreasing with the time lag τ:

$$\frac{d\overline{\Pi}^\tau}{d\tau} = \frac{\left(-\rho^2 \gamma p_0 e^{-\rho\tau}\right)\left(\gamma + \rho + \gamma p_0 e^{-\rho\tau}\right) - \left(-\rho\gamma p_0 e^{-\rho\tau}\right)\left(\gamma p_0 \rho e^{-\rho\tau}\right)}{\left(\gamma + \rho + \gamma p_0 e^{-\rho\tau}\right)^2}$$

$$\Rightarrow = \frac{\left(-\rho^2 \gamma p_0 e^{-\rho\tau}\right)\left(\gamma + \rho\right)}{\left(\gamma + \rho + \gamma p_0 e^{-\rho\tau}\right)^2} < 0.$$

I argue in the first section of this chapter that in the last couple of decades, because of information technology and globalization, the pace of innovation of new goods has increased. Also, the price profile of new goods became steeper, declining very rapidly after introduction, yielding a more rapid diffusion. In the following, I show that in this model, as the growth rate of the number of goods increases, disinflation pressure increases:

$$\frac{d\overline{\Pi}^\tau}{d\gamma} = \frac{\left(\rho p_0 e^{-\rho\tau}\right)\left(\gamma + \rho + \gamma p_0 e^{-\rho\tau}\right) - \left(1 + p_0 e^{-\rho\tau}\right)\left(\gamma p_0 \rho e^{-\rho\tau}\right)}{\left(\gamma + \rho + \gamma p_0 e^{-\rho\tau}\right)^2}$$

$$\Rightarrow = \frac{\rho^2 p_0 e^{-\rho\tau}}{\left(\gamma + \rho + \gamma p_0 e^{-\rho\tau}\right)^2} > 0.$$

Next I show that, as the price profile of new goods becomes steeper, for the North (where $\tau = 0$), the disinflationary contribution of new goods increases. First, in general,

$$\frac{d\overline{\Pi}^\tau}{d\rho} = \frac{\gamma p_0 e^{-\rho\tau}\left(1 - \rho\tau\right)\left(\gamma + \rho + \gamma p_0 e^{-\rho\tau}\right) - \left(1 - \gamma\tau p_0 e^{-\rho\tau}\right)\left(\rho\gamma p_0 e^{-\rho\tau}\right)}{\left(\gamma + \rho + \gamma p_0 e^{-\rho\tau}\right)^2}$$

$$\Rightarrow = \frac{\gamma\left(1 + p_0 e^{-\rho\tau}\right) - \rho\tau\left(\gamma - \rho\right)}{\left(\gamma + \rho + \gamma p_0 e^{-\rho\tau}\right)^2}.$$

For the North, $\tau = 0$ and

$$\frac{d\overline{\Pi}^0}{d\rho} = \frac{\gamma\left(1 + p_0\right)}{\left(\gamma + \rho + \gamma p_0\right)^2} > 0.$$

However for the South the effect of a steeper price profile on the disinflationary contribution is not clear. Up to some level of income gap with the North and lag level, the effect is still positive, but for larger income gaps and corresponding lag levels the effect is actually negative. Hence there is a cut-off level of lag, τ, which solves

$$\gamma\left(1 + p_0 e^{-\rho\tau}\right) - \rho\tau(\gamma - \rho) = 0,$$

around which the change in the contribution changes sign.

Next I show that new goods' eventual price decline potential, p_0, also positively affects the inflationary contribution of new goods. Hence,

$$\frac{d\overline{\Pi}^{\tau}}{d\rho} = \frac{\left(\rho\gamma e^{-\rho\tau}\right)\left(\gamma + \rho + \gamma p_0 e^{-\rho\tau}\right) - \left(\gamma e^{-\rho\tau}\right)\left(\gamma p_0 \rho e^{-\rho\tau}\right)}{\left(\gamma + \rho + \gamma p_0 e^{-\rho\tau}\right)^2}$$

$$\Rightarrow = \frac{\left(\rho\gamma e^{-\rho\tau}\right)\left(\gamma + \rho\right)}{\left(\gamma + \rho + \gamma p_0 e^{-\rho\tau}\right)^2} > 0.$$

It is of interest to know how disinflationary pressure from the introduction of new goods, $\overline{\Pi}^{0} - \overline{\Pi}^{\tau}$, changes between the North and the South for a given lag, as the model parameters change. First,

$$\overline{\Pi}^{0} - \overline{\Pi}^{\tau} = \frac{\gamma p_0 \rho}{\gamma + \rho + \gamma p_0} - \frac{\gamma p_0 \rho e^{-\rho\tau}}{\gamma + \rho + \gamma p_0 e^{-\rho\tau}} = \frac{\left(1 - e^{-\rho\tau}\right)\left(\gamma^2 p_0 \rho + \gamma p_0 \rho^2 + \gamma^2 p_0^2 \rho\right)}{\left(\gamma + \rho + \gamma p_0\right)\left(\gamma + \rho + \gamma p_0 e^{-\rho\tau}\right)}.$$

It can easily be shown that

$$\frac{d\left(\overline{\Pi}^{0} - \overline{\Pi}^{\tau}\right)}{d\gamma} > 0, \text{ and } \frac{d\left(\overline{\Pi}^{0} - \overline{\Pi}^{\tau}\right)}{d\rho} > 0.$$

That is, the differential between disinflationary contribution of new goods to the North and the South increases with the pace of new goods' innovation, γ, and the steepness of the price decline, ρ.

Let e_n denote the nominal exchange rate between these two countries. The goods are freely tradable between the countries without any frictions, so that the law of one price holds for the goods that are consumed in both countries. Then, if the age-τ variety is consumed in both countries, $p_\tau^S = e_n p_\tau^N$, so that the price of age-τ good in the South is equal to the price of age-τ good in the North when the price in the North is expressed in the northern currency. Here e_n denotes the nominal exchange rate between the countries. Taking the derivative of both sides of this equation with respect to time yields,

$$\frac{dp_\tau^S}{dt} = \frac{de_n}{dt} + \frac{dp_\tau^N}{dt}.$$

Plugging the equation into

$$\mu^S - \gamma - p_0 \rho e^{-\rho\tau} = \frac{de_n}{dt} + \mu^N - \gamma - p_0 \rho e^{-\rho\tau}$$

yields

$$\frac{de_n}{dt} = \mu^S - \mu^N = \frac{\gamma p_0 \rho e^{-\rho\tau}}{\gamma + \rho + \gamma p_0 e^{-\rho\tau}} - \frac{\gamma p_0 \rho}{\gamma + \rho + \gamma p_0}$$

$$\Rightarrow = \frac{\left(1 - e^{-\rho\tau}\right)\left(\gamma + p_0 \rho + \gamma p_0 \rho^2 + \gamma^2 p_0^2 \rho\right)}{\left(\gamma + \rho + \gamma p_0\right)\left(\gamma + \rho + \gamma p_0 e^{-\rho\tau}\right)}.$$

Therefore the change in the nominal exchange rate between the countries' currencies is given by

$$\frac{de_n}{dt} = \frac{\left(1 - e^{-\rho\tau}\right)\left(\gamma^2 p_0 \rho + \gamma p_0 \rho^2 + \gamma^2 p_0^2 \rho\right)}{\left(\gamma + \rho + \gamma p_0\right)\left(\gamma + \rho + \gamma p_0 e^{-\rho\tau}\right)} > 0.$$

Therefore the nominal exchange rate increases, and the Southern currency appreciates at the rate $\frac{de_n}{dt}$.

The real exchange rate between the currencies, $e_r = e_n + \Pi^S - \Pi^N$, also increases at the same rate:

$$\frac{de_r}{dt} = \frac{de_n}{dt} + \Pi^S - \Pi^N = \frac{de_n}{dt} + \Pi^* - \Pi^*$$

$$\Rightarrow = \frac{\left(1 - e^{-\rho\tau}\right)\left(\gamma^2 p_0 \rho + \gamma p_0 \rho^2 + \gamma^2 p_0^2 \rho\right)}{\left(\gamma + \rho + \gamma p_0\right)\left(\gamma + \rho + \gamma p_0 e^{-\rho\tau}\right)}.$$

In summary, the price decline of new goods puts downward pressure on inflation in the North. Since at the point when the new goods diffuse to the South the price decline of the good relatively flattens out, it does not create a similar downward pressure on inflation in the South. Since goods are freely tradable between countries, and the monetary authorities of both countries target the same level of inflation (Π^*), and increase the money supply accordingly, in equilibrium, the value of the Southern currency appreciates. Notice that both the nominal and the real exchange rate of the South appreciate by the same amount. The only way, in this model, the authorities of the South can get rid of the nominal and real appreciation is to target a higher inflation level compared to the North, so that

$$\Pi^*_s = \Pi^*_N + \frac{\left(1 - e^{-\rho\tau}\right)\left(\gamma^2 p_0 \rho + \gamma p_0 \rho^2 + \gamma^2 p_0^2 \rho\right)}{\left(\gamma + \rho + \gamma p_0\right)\left(\gamma + \rho + \gamma p_0 e^{-\rho\tau}\right)}.$$

The Parameterization of the Model

Reasonable parameter values can show how significant these effects can be. The parameter values of the model are γ, p_0, ρ, λ. The parameters that determine the price profile of a new good p_0 and ρ can be calibrated using historical data on the evolution of prices of new innovations. Here I simply use the data of one of the most economically significant innovations in economic history, automobiles. Automobiles were invented and introduced to the market in the late nineteenth century. After that point, the production of automobiles grew very rapidly. Due to productivity improvements, the price of automobiles declined very significantly. In 1910 the average price of an automobile was around $2,500 (in 1929 U.S. dollars), whereas in 1920, just after a decade, the average price of an automobile dropped to below $900 (figure 8-11).

The diffusion of automobiles was very fast (figure 8-12). In 1910 diffusion was less than 2 percent, whereas in 1930 diffusion was more than 75 percent. Automobile price data show that p_0 and ρ give the best fit: $p_{1910+t} = 1 + p_0 e^{-\rho t}$, with $p_0 = 2.5$ and $\rho = 0.3$. As can be seen in figure 8-13, the functional form with this parameterization yields a quite nice fit to the actual data. For the growth rate of the number of new goods I use $\gamma = 0.02$ for the benchmark economy. Figure 8-14 exhibits the disinflationary contribution from new goods for different levels of Southern income as a fraction of Northern income. For the benchmark parameterization, the disinflationary pressure from the innovation of new goods is more than 4 percent. However for the Southern economy, even with 60 percent of Northern income, the disinflationary contribution of the diffusion of new goods is close to zero.

As an example, let's take the United States and Turkey as the North and South countries, respectively. Given that Turkey has around 30 percent of U.S. income, the differential of disinflationary contribution between the United States and Turkey is around 4 percent (table 8-1).

Figure 8-11. *Price Profile of the Automobile, 1910–40*

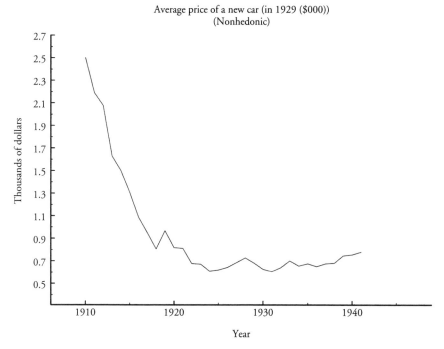

Average price of a new car (in 1929 ($000))
(Nonhedonic)

Source: U.S. Bureau of the Census (1975).

Figure 8-12. *Diffusion of the Automobile, 1910–50*

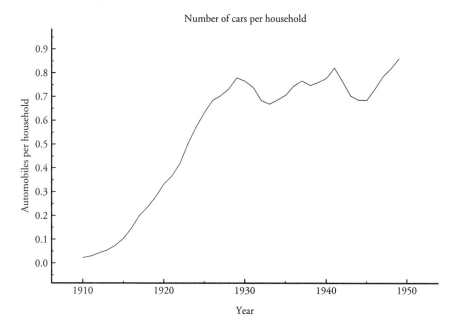

Number of cars per household

Source: U.S. Bureau of the Census (1975).

Figure 8-13. *Price Profile after Innovation, the Automobile, 1900–35*

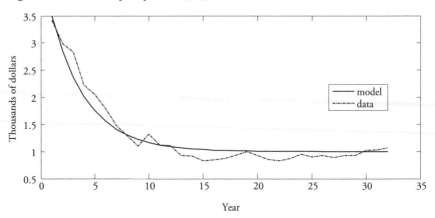

Source: Model simulation output; U.S. Bureau of the Census (1975).

Concluding Remarks

After the global financial crisis, the growth differential between advanced and emerging market economies is likely to become even larger. In other words, we can expect faster convergence. Capital flows toward emerging economies will be stronger. With the growth differential being larger, the earlier trend of the relative prices of food, commodities, and energy increasing is also likely to continue at a higher speed. This will continue to put upward pressure on headline inflation in emerging market economies. Under this economic environment, in order to maintain price stability and financial stability at the same time, EME central

Figure 8-14. *Disinflation Contribution from Innovation to Southern Income by Fraction of Northern Income*

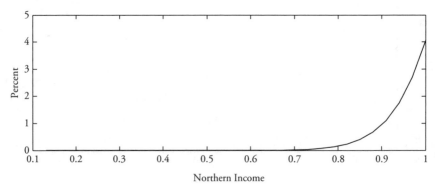

Source: Model simulation output.

Table 8-1. *Sensitivity to Parameter Values*

$\rho = 0.1$	$p_0 = 1$	$p_0 = 3$	$p_0 = 5$
$\gamma = 0.01$	0.0083	0.0185	0.0313
$\gamma = 0.05$	0.0250	0.0455	0.0625
$\gamma = 0.1$	0.0333	0.0556	0.0714
$\rho = 0.3$	$p_0 = 1$	$p_0 = 3$	$p_0 = 5$
$\gamma = 0.01$	0.0094	0.0224	0.0417
$\gamma = 0.05$	0.0375	0.0789	0.1250
$\gamma = 0.1$	0.0600	0.1154	0.1667
$\rho = 0.5$	$p_0 = 1$	$p_0 = 3$	$p_0 = 5$
$\gamma = 0.01$	0.0096	0.0234	0.0446
$\gamma = 0.05$	0.0417	0.0926	0.1563
$\gamma = 0.1$	0.0714	0.1471	0.2273

banks will have to employ other tools besides short-term policy interest rates. Macroprudential tools will be especially helpful both in controlling long-term financial instability risks accumulating and in achieving the necessary counter-cyclical policies in this volatile environment.

An important channel creating a significant gap in measured inflation between advanced and emerging economies is the new goods' bias. The bias has become more and more important through time, as the pace of innovation has increased and the price decline profile has become steeper. The North-South model reveals the impact of this bias and shows how the impact depends on the economic environment. To prevent any financial instability risks arising from this bias, EME authorities should be aware of the value of higher inflation targets and macroprudential tools.

References

Berkmen, Pelin, and others. 2009. "The Global Financial Crisis: Explaining Cross-Country Differences in the Output Impact." Working Paper WP/09/280. Washington: International Monetary Fund.

Calvo, Guillermo A., and Enrique G. Mendoza. 2000. "Rational Contagion and the Globalization of Securities Markets." *Journal of International Economics* 51: 79–113.

Central Bank of the Republic of Turkey. 2010. "Monetary Policy Exit Strategy." April.

Dornbusch, Rudiger. 1976. "Expectations and Exchange Rate Dynamics." *Journal of Political Economy* 84: 1161–76.

Kose, M. Ayhan, and Eswar S. Prasad. 2010. "Resilience of Emerging Market Economies to Economic and Financial Developments in Advanced Economies." Economic Paper 411. European Commission.

Lucas, Robert E. 2002. *Lectures on Economic Growth.* Harvard University Press.

Reinhart, Carmen M., and Vincent R. Reinhart. 1999. "On the Use of Reserve Requirements in Dealing with Capital Flow Problems." *International Journal of Finance and Economics* 4:27–54.

PART IV

Developing a Sound Global Regulatory Architecture

9

The Impact of Changes in the Global Financial Regulatory Landscape on Emerging Markets

TARISA WATANAGASE

The Global financial crisis in 2008 can be attributed to a number of factors, but the main root causes are twofold: inadequate supervision, including a large unregulated shadow-banking sector; and systemic risks originating in the financial imbalances of several economies and in the interconnectedness of financial institutions' balance sheets through leverage and the creation of opaque products. In response, the Basel Committee on Banking Supervision (BCBS) developed a financial regulatory framework to reform, improve, and strengthen the financial sector as well as to reduce systemic risks and enhance financial stability, taking into account the lessons learned from the crisis. The G-20 has also called for international financial institutions to work on a number of reforms to strengthen and stabilize the global financial system.

These proposals, collectively called Basel III, released in December 2010, are extensive and have many dimensions and components. The implementation of the capital requirement, a major component of Basel III, is due to start in January 2013, according to a phase-in timetable (see box 9-1). In addition, there are already some regulatory and legislative changes at national levels, such as the U.S. Dodd-Frank Wall Street Reform and Consumer Protection Act and the European Market Infrastructure Regulation, which will no doubt have implications beyond their borders. Because of the extensive coverage and implications of Basel III, it is expected to substantially change the global financial regulatory landscape.

In this chapter I discuss the relevance of Basel III to Asian emerging markets (AEMs) and review some of the proposed regulations of Basel III in order to

Box 9-1. *Basel III and Related Measures: Key Features and Year of Implementation*

Basel III

Capital

—Definition of capital raises both its quantity and quality

Quantity: minimum common equity tier-1 ratio = 4.5 percent; tier-1 ratio = 6 percent, total capital ratio = 8 percent: 2013–15

Quality: defines common equity as core capital and enhances inclusion criteria of additional tier-1 and tier-2: 2013

—Capital buffers: build up common equity above the minimum capital requirement (conservation 2.5 percent, countercyclical 0–2.5 percent): 2016–19

—Risk coverage: refines the calculation of risk-weighted assets for better prudence: 2013

—Leverage ratio: non-risk-based supplementary measure to constrain excessive leverage: 2018

Liquidity

—Liquidity risk measurement

Liquidity coverage ratio: banks to maintain adequate liquidity for a severe stress scenario for up to thirty days: 2015

Net stable funding ratio: banks to maintain sustainable maturity structure of assets and liabilities over a one-year horizon: 2018

Global systemically important banks

—G-SIBs to have higher loss-absorbency capacity, with an additional progressive common equity tier-1 requirement of 1–2.5 percent. Identification of G-SIBs to use quantitative indicators and qualitative elements: 2016

Related measures and other ongoing work

OTC derivative market reform

—All standardized OTC derivative contracts to be traded on exchanges or electronic trading platforms and cleared through central counterparties; OTC derivative contracts to be reported to trade repositories; non-centrally-cleared contracts to be subject to higher capital requirements: 2012

Procyclicality

—Capital buffers

Capital conservation buffer: build up buffer to increase banking sector resilience going into a downturn; countercyclical buffer: build up buffer for broader macroprudential goal of protecting the banking sector in periods of excess aggregate credit growth: 2016–19

—Forward-looking provisioning (IFRS 9)

International Accounting Standards Board, Financial Accounting Standards Board, and Basel Committee on Banking Supervision to consider moving from incurred-loss to expected-loss provisioning (provisioning on performing loans in good time before they turn nonperforming): 2015

Macroprudential policy tools and framework
—Financial Stability Board, International Monetary Fund, and Bank for International Settlements to do further work on macroprudential policy frameworks, including tools to mitigate the impact of excessive capital flows: ongoing.

Shadow banking, Financial Stability Board proposal
—Definition: system of credit intermediation that involves entities and activities outside the regular banking system, focusing particularly on the interconnectedness within the financial system that may cause systemic risk and regulatory arbitrage
—Three steps for monitoring the shadow-banking system: map overall shadow-banking system, identify concerns, assess systemic risk and regulatory arbitrage concerns: ongoing.
—Monitoring tools: set of harmonized metrics to capture additional information on banks' liquidity profiles: ongoing.

Source: Bank of Thailand, Financial Institutional Strategy Department and Prudential Policy Department.

evaluate their likely implication for—and their adequacy in enhancing—the stability of the Asian banking and financial system. This is followed by a discussion of the challenges faced by the regulators of AEMs, given their capacity and institutional constraints, in effectively managing their financial regulations. The chapter concludes with policy recommendations for AEMs to strengthen and enhance their financial systems. Where appropriate, my experience at the Bank of Thailand is drawn upon.

Relevance of Basel III to Asian Emerging Markets

Asian emerging markets had fairly resilient economies and financial markets when the 2008 global crisis broke out. Economies that experienced major challenges during the Asian crisis in particular had revamped their supervisory frameworks to be risk focused, requiring banks to put in place robust risk-management systems. Apart from the problems of a temporary liquidity squeeze and a dollar shortage in some economies in September and October 2008, most AEMs did not have major difficulties in their financial sectors. The impacts of the global crisis were felt indirectly via the trade channel, with exports and imports plummeting. This led to two quarters of economic slowdown or contraction but to a strong rebound thereafter. Therefore, one may have the impression that all these regulatory reforms are meant for the crisis-hit advanced economies and are not relevant to AEMs. In fact, there are at least three reasons that Basel III and other regulatory reforms are highly relevant to AEMs.

First, the world economy has long been integrated through trade, but more recently financial markets have become even more integrated due to technological and financial innovations. A major crisis in one corner of the world can have significant adverse impacts on the rest of the world, as was witnessed in the 2008 global crisis. Hence it would be in all countries' interest, including the AEMs', to ensure that Basel III can keep individual financial institutions safe and financial markets stable. AEMs' financial products, services, and markets are mostly less diverse and sophisticated than the advanced economies', with the financial sector playing the conventional role of financial intermediary, providing mostly plain vanilla products. Hence some Basel III regulations, such as those on securitization, may not be directly relevant to some AEMs. However, with continued financial market deepening, the risk profiles of AEMs' financial markets will change and become more complicated. A comprehensive regulatory framework to tackle different risks will no doubt further strengthen and stabilize AEMs' domestic financial systems going forward.

Second, all AEMs have foreign banks in their economies, and these can be fairly significant. Basel III will have direct implications on these foreign operations. In addition, although there has been some emerging market participation in the formulation of some components of Basel III, most proposed regulations are formulated and calibrated mainly based on advanced markets' contexts and data, which can be significantly different from the AEMs'. Hence, it is in the interest of AEMs to ensure that the regulations proposed by Basel III are also appropriate in the context of an emerging market.

Third, even though most AEMs are currently resilient, they can be susceptible to financial instability, partly because of the lack of depth of their financial markets and partly because of insufficient data for monitoring and policy analysis, among other things. Data on housing and real estate, a sector prone to financial imbalances, are more often than not grossly inadequate. Small AEMs, in particular, lack adequate instruments to deal with global volatilities and capital flows. The regulatory proposals of Basel III on countercyclical and macroprudential measures are, therefore, of particular interest to AEMs, as these promise to further enhance their economic and financial stability.

Adequacy of Basel III for Regulatory Reform

Is Basel III the answer to AEMs' concerns and requirements? Note that the increased minimum capital requirement, with more focus on tier 1 and on improved quality, enables banks to absorb losses better and improves the resilience of individual financial institutions to better withstand shocks (see box 9-1). Other requirements on capital include buffers to build up capital in good times for rainy days. Changes are also due to be made to the leverage ratio. Further changes affect liquidity, systemically important financial institutions (SIFIs), and market infrastructure. These include a clearing and settlement mechanism, better collection of data, and monitoring through exchanges. The aim is to reduce the interconnectedness and the systemic risk of the financial sector in addition to strengthening individual institutions. Regulations also apply to other financial institutions, not only banks. No doubt, Basel III is a significantly improved regulatory framework to deal with the root causes of the recent crisis, but five weaknesses remain.

First, like its predecessor, Basel II, Basel III focuses substantially more on rules and regulations than on supervision. More specifically, the focus is on pillar1, even though pillar 2 is more important. A brief recounting of pillar 2 of Basel II may be helpful. Pillar 2 is about a supervisory review for supervisors to ensure that banks perform their comprehensive assessment of risks and have adequate risk management with adequate oversight by the board. If a supervisor does not believe that the level of capital and risk management is commensurate with the bank's risks, he would demand corrective actions, which may include additional capital. In short, pillar 2 focuses on the risk management of banks and requires supervisors to take discretionary supervisory measures when necessary. Pillar 2 also spells out the supervisory review process for certain products and risks. In the case of securitization, for example, supervisors should review the extent of risk transfer, market innovation, and so on, and if the associated risks are deemed excessive, the supervisor should require a reduction of exposure or a capital increase or a combination of both. In spite of these well-spelled-out principles, supervision and risk management in some countries were weak before the global crisis, partly because of the opacity of products but also due to inadequate attention to risky behaviors and products (such as "no doc" loans and interest-payment-only mortgages) and excessive reliance by supervisors on not only the self-control and self-regulation of banks but also on market mechanisms—believing that banks with risky behaviors would be penalized by the market. Had supervision and risk management before 2008 been more vigorous—that is, more in line with what pillar 2 prescribes—weaknesses in the financial sectors associated with a lax credit underwriting standard, securitization of subprime mortgages, and excessive leverage could have been detected, and corrective actions might have lessened the extent of the global crisis, if not totally prevented it.

Based on my Bank of Thailand supervisory experience, I cannot stress too much the importance of supervision and risk management. After the 1997 Asian crisis, the Bank of Thailand revamped its supervisory framework to focus on risks, ensuring that banks have a good risk-management system in place and holding banks' management and their boards of directors accountable for their risk management. It took a few years before both the supervisory staff and the bank managers were comfortable with the switch from compliance to risk-based supervision, but risk management has since become a critical part of the banking business and bank supervision in Thailand. At the time of the 2008 global crisis, the Thai banking sector's investment in products related to collateralized debt obligation accounted for only about 0.1 percent of total assets, in spite of the fact that, one, there was no regulation against investing in such products and, two, because of the sluggish domestic economy, banks had abundant liquidity to make the investment if they wanted to. I had learned from a few bankers that they did not invest in these products because they looked like black boxes to them. No doubt lessons from the Asian crisis and the continued risk focus of both the supervisor and the banks fostered such a prudent attitude. In today's fast-changing world, with its new technologies and innovations, the nature and the source of risks are likely to shift rapidly, making it difficult to maintain regulations that are adequate for dealing with the changing risks. I therefore believe that risk-based supervision and risk management, not regulations, are the most important ingredients for a safe and sound financial sector.

Coming back to Basel III, pillar 2 is also about risk management and supervision—similar to that of Basel II but with additional principles based on what was learned from the last crisis. The BCBS has issued a consultative paper on the revision of the core principles for banking supervision to strengthen supervisory practices and risk management. The core principles also respond to several key trends and developments that emerged during the last few years of market turmoil, such as the need for greater intensity and resources to deal effectively with systemically important banks and the importance of applying a systemwide, macroeconomic perspective to the microprudential supervision of banks.[1] The proposed revised core principles are a significant improvement over the current set. However, my concern is that pillar 2, because of its lack of enforceability, may not be adopted (as happened to pillar 2 of Basel II).

I strongly believe that, for systemically important countries (that is, those with large financial sectors with a significant effect on other countries), it should be mandatory to take part in the World Bank–IMF joint assessment of the Financial Sector Assessment Program (FSAP) and the Reports on the Observance of Standards and Codes (ROSC). This will enable an international assessment of the adequacy of supervisory frameworks and also of the risks and resilience of these countries' financial sectors, according to international standards and codes such as the Basel core principles for supervision. The problem is, of course, that we cannot realistically expect the World Bank or the IMF to successfully push for such a requirement, given that most systemically important economies are major shareholders and voters in these institutions. This is where the BCBS can make a significant difference, in ensuring support from the global community for such a requirement or working out alternative mechanisms for enforcement. Enforcement mechanisms have been proposed, for example, by Barry Eichengreen and by

---

1. Basel Committee on Banking Supervision (2011b).

Stijn Claessens.[2] The former's proposal is to create a World Financial Organization (WFO), analogous to the World Trade Organization (WTO), which would establish principles for prudential supervision obligatory for all countries seeking freedom of access to foreign markets for domestically chartered financial institutions. Of importance is the fact that the WFO would authorize the imposition of sanctions against countries that fail to comply with international standards for the supervision and regulation of their financial markets and institutions. Other members would be within their rights to restrict the ability of banks and nonbank financial institutions chartered in the offending country to do business in their markets. In a similar proposal, Claessens would create an international charter for banks engaged in cross-border activity. Internationally active banks would be required to secure a charter from an international college of supervisors and be subject to its supervision. When members of the college determine that a bank is in violation of its charter, it could impose cease-and-desist orders, limit the operations of said institutions, and require remedial action. The BCBS can further pursue these proposals or propose its own, with the objective of enforcing the adoption of risk-based supervision and risk management along the lines of pillar 2 and the Basel core principles for banking supervision.

Second, preventing moral hazard by providing the right incentives is important in discouraging excessively risky behavior. In my view, pillar 2 of Basel III and the Basel core principles on banking supervision should include the principle for remuneration of bank management, which should reflect long-term performance or the risk-adjusted returns of the bank. In addition, bank managers who fail a bank through their reckless behavior must face the consequences. Under the Thai Banking Act, the top management and members of the board of directors of a failed bank are removed. Those suspected of fraudulent behavior or gross negligence are prosecuted and, if found guilty, face a jail term or a personal fine and are banned from becoming a member of a bank's top management or a bank board again. It clearly is a moral hazard issue if the top management can manage a bank in a reckless manner and not suffer any consequences, the way we have witnessed in the recent global crisis.

Third, on the issue of systemically important financial institutions, the methodology of identifying globally systemically important banks (G-SIBs) has been agreed upon.[3] The requirement is for G-SIBs to have additional loss-absorption capacity with additional capital and to meet a higher expectation under supervisors' data-aggregation capabilities. A preliminary group of twenty-nine G-SIBs has been identified. Work is ongoing to identify other financial institutions in this category and also to create a new international standard that would apply

---

2. Eichengreen (2008); Claessens (2008).
3. Basel Committee on Banking Supervision (2011a).

to national resolution regimes, resolution powers and tools, recovery, resolution plans, creditor hierarchies, and institution-specific cross-border cooperation agreements.[4]

By definition, G-SIBs are large and complex and global. Hence all work on cross-border issues—particularly an institution-specific resolution plan—will be valuable to G-SIBs' home and host supervisors alike, so as to work out an orderly resolution for a G-SIB. However, precisely because of G-SIBs' complex nature—with their operations spanning many jurisdictions, with different national resolution laws (which are usually part of a broader legal regime)—the new international standard as a reference for national resolution may not be easily adopted, not to mention national interests that may prevent such adoption. In this case, one may not have any other choice but to work out a resolution plan based on the national resolution regime in question, which can be inconsistent across jurisdictions. In addition, in cases where some provisions of the resolution laws have not been contested in court, one may have to wait for a court case to set the precedent of a court ruling. In reality, therefore, a resolution plan can be full of inconsistencies and shrouded in uncertainty. This can lead to excessive risk taking by investors and bank managers if they perceive that the resolution plan is not credible and that the authorities will not allow the bank to fail because of its systemic identity as a G-SIB. This is clearly a potential case of moral hazard.

Fourth, the leverage ratio, a non-risk-based ratio that includes off-balance-sheet exposures, has been proposed (and in fact implemented) to cap the leverage of both an individual financial institution and the leverage buildup of the entire financial sector, to help contain systemic risks. Although this ratio will be able to contain leverage as intended, there are two problems that I see with it. The first problem is that we have moved to a risk-based approach since Basel II because it is only logical for riskier services or products to be subject to higher charges. I find it difficult to understand the reason for resorting to a non-risk-based ratio, even though it is used as a backstop to supplement the risk-based capital requirement. This may look like a minor technical detail, but in fact it leads to the second problem, which can be serious. Because of the ratio's non-risk-based nature, all off-balance-sheet items are treated equally in the computation of required capital when they become on-balance-sheet items. However, when converting an off-balance-sheet item into an on-balance-sheet item, a conversion factor is used: following the Basel 1 tradition, the exposure of a derivative is only its notional amount, hence it has a smaller conversion factor, resulting in a smaller on-balance-sheet item, than a traditional financial product with relatively low risk, such as trade finance. The consequence is that it is more costly for banks to carry trade finance than a derivative product on their off-balance sheet, although

---

4. Financial Stability Board (2011).

it's clear that the latter has a higher risk. Therefore, the leverage ratio may unintentionally penalize AEMs, whose banks usually carry more trade finance than derivative products (as a result of high exports and imports in their economies) on their balance sheets. Even more worrisome is that banks may try to economize on their charges by promoting derivative products to replace traditional trade finance, resulting in higher risks for individual banks and banking sectors.

Fifth, countercyclical capital buffers, global liquidity standards, and supervisory monitoring of liquidity are good Basel III initiatives to contain systemic risk for financial stability. A report jointly released by the Financial Stability Board, the International Monetary Fund, and the Bank for International Settlements traces the progress in implementing macroprudential policy and highlights the scope for further progress, such as in the areas of systemic risk identification and policy calibration for optimal policy design.[5] The technical expertise on these issues is still evolving, and a comprehensive theoretical and analytical framework has yet to be worked out. Hence work on better understanding and using such a policy for financial stability purposes is ongoing. International work is also under way to strengthen financial market infrastructure and improve market practices. A consultative report on harmonized principles for financial market infrastructure (covering payment systems, central securities depositories, securities settlements systems, and central counterparties, including guidance on trade depositories) has also been issued. The adequacy of the Basel III proposal for macroprudential measures, therefore, remains to be assessed.

Here, however, I'd like to offer a comment on the countercyclical capital buffer. In my view, it is better for it to come under pillar 2 to allow the authorities room for discretion in imposing this requirement rather than having to adopt it strictly according to the rule once a threshold—say the ratio of credit growth to GDP growth—has been reached. We need to humbly admit that our current understanding of the linkages of the real economy and the financial sector is rather incomplete. Our technical capability in calibrating the lead-lag effect in policy transmission, the turning point of business cycles, and so on is even more limited. In addition, depending on policy combinations or regulatory contexts, the need for capital buffers can differ. For example, a rapid increase of credit expansion may not be as grave a concern and supervisory action may not be needed if conservative macroprudential measures (such as the loan-to-value ratio or other prudential limits) are in place. Alternatively, if the fiscal policy is expansionary and the monetary policy fails to rein in rapid credit expansion, then a capital buffer may be needed even before credit growth reaches the set threshold.

In conclusion, Basel III represents a much improved regulatory framework for strengthening financial institutions, taking into account additional sources

5. FSB, IMF, and BIS (2011).

of risk that were not apparent when Basel II was introduced. It is also expected to reduce systemic risks through various regulations. Unfortunately, in my view Basel III will not be sufficient to prevent the next financial crisis unless more effort and attention are geared toward risk-based supervision and management and their enforcement.

Implications and Challenges of Basel III for Asian Emerging Economies

The extensive regulatory changes expected from Basel III will no doubt have significant implications for all economies. I outline five of them from the perspective of AEMs.

First, with the additional capital requirements both for each institution and for the mitigation of systemic risk, the cost of complying with Basel III's new capital requirements, not to mention other regulatory costs, can be substantial. Currently, most AEMs' banking sectors remain robust, with capital bases mostly exceeding the minimum Basel requirement. AEMs' strong economic conditions also contribute to the buildup of capital in their financial institutions. So the regulatory costs of Basel III should not be too overwhelming for most AEMs. However, raising sufficient funding from the market can be a challenge for some AEMs, depending on the exact timing of the AEM's implementation of Basel III going forward and the stock market condition, which can be quite volatile.

More important, currently, work to extend the new regulatory reform measures to other financial institutions is still under way, and this will eventually impose additional regulatory costs on the entire spectrum of the financial sector. The aggregate direct regulatory costs for AEMs may be manageable, since most AEMs are bank-based economies, with the banking system accounting for the biggest market share in the financial sector. The additional burden from the rest of the financial sector may therefore be small. However, what could be a concern is that the aggregate regulatory costs on all financial sectors of some advanced economies could be substantial, forcing financial institutions to cut back their assets or exposure both domestically and globally, which may have negative consequences not only on their own economies but also on AEMs, through financial and trade integration. In fact, this is a concern for all economies, not just AEMs, and continued assessment and monitoring of total regulatory costs and their implication is necessary. Adjusting the implementation timetables of different standard setters and supervisors can be an option.

Second, many G-SIBs have a significant presence in AEMs. The BCBS's principle of home-host supervisory coordination and colleges has contributed to better information sharing and coordination; however, the problem of the significant host still remains. The host supervisor of a foreign bank with a significant presence in the host country may not be part of a supervisory college, if the bank's presence is deemed small among the SIB's global operations. This situation may result in the host having inadequate information on the bank. Given this, Basel III regulations on G-SIBs are welcome initiatives in mitigating systemic risk, and they are expected to contribute positively to the stability of the host country's financial sector. However, in the short run, depending on the domestic market share of G-SIBs and market competition, the regulatory cost of these banks could be passed on to host-country consumers.

From a host country's perspective, requiring foreign bank operations to be set up as a locally incorporated subsidiary instead of a branch is a better business model. It provides a level playing field for all financial institutions, since the foreign subsidiary will need to have a separate capital base from that of the head office to support its operations. Supervising a subsidiary is obviously more effective, with more information readily available. As discussed earlier, due to the complexity and uncertainty involved with the resolution plan of a G-SIB— which may create moral hazard and lead to excessive risk taking by bank investors and managers—it may be in the interest of the home supervisor to make the SIB smaller. From this perspective, requiring a foreign bank branch to operate as a subsidiary is also in line with the home-country supervisor's interest.

In addition, many AEMs have their own megabanks. Of Asia's biggest 500 banks, such emerging economies as the People's Republic of China has 103; India has 43 and Indonesia has 27, just to give a few examples.[6] Therefore, the issues of systemically important banks and too-big-to-fail banks are highly relevant to emerging markets as well. Since these banks have more extensive domestic networks than global networks, it will be useful to apply the BCBS's recommendations for G-SIBs to these domestic systemically important banks, especially those recommendations on capital and data requirements and orderly resolution plans. A separation of investment banking from commercial banking also mitigates risks in the banking sector. Indeed, this recommendation also applies to advanced economies.

Third, the mitigation of systemic risk through macroprudential measures represents major challenges to AEMs, starting with the issue of identification. Systemic risk is the risk of widespread disruptions in the provision of financial services that have serious negative consequences for the economy at large. Since it is a systemwide risk, we need to identify, analyze, and monitor a variety of metrics, such as the buildup of financial imbalances in both the real and the financial sectors plus market liquidity and risk appetite. These indicators, particularly financial imbalances, are difficult to measure and monitor. Nor is it easy to identify the driving forces behind imbalances. Financial indicators, indexes, or even early-warning data are mostly about individual risk or individual institution

6. *Asian Banker* (2010).

risk and may not flag financial instability of a systemic nature. Some of the indicators may even give conflicting signals.

In addition, there are also problems about what tools to use and what the quantitative impacts of the selected tool are. No doubt significant technical challenges remain, and building up our knowledge base and technical expertise is necessary to better understand the complexity of (and ways to mitigate) systemic risk. Moreover, the skill set and competency for early detection of systemic risk usually reside across many departments of a central bank, such as examination and supervision, economic research, and economic policy. It is important to have staffs from these departments meet regularly so they can assess potential financial instability. Such regular dialogues broaden any one person's perspective beyond his discipline and can identify conditions that, together, may lead to vulnerability. Most important, meetings such as these foster a common culture—not just a sharing of information but a sharing of viewpoints. Even though most of the time it is difficult to integrate the information into a formal model for a vigorous analysis of imbalances, the dialogues still offer an important basis for policy judgment.

Fourth, institutional constraints can be another major challenge in mitigating systemic risk, if the responsibilities of microprudential and macroprudential supervision do not reside in the same agency and coordination between responsible agencies is not well established. It is important to put in place a supportive infrastructure for maintaining a sound financial sector and financial stability, including clear mandates for microprudential and macroprudential supervisors and for an effective and efficient mechanism for close consultation, coordination, and sharing of information. This mechanism should be in place for both the top level and the staff level, so that the interests of all agencies are aligned and the necessary prudential measures can be implemented.

Fifth, the amount of data needed for the implementation of Basel III is substantial. However, significant gaps remain for AEMs, especially data for the identification and monitoring of systemic risks. According to an IMF survey, the number of indicators cited by respondents for systemic risk monitoring is sixty, ranging from indicators of bank capital (such as the capital adequacy ratio) and performance (such as return on assets) to indicators of liquidity (such as the ratio of liquid assets to total assets) and indebtedness (such as the ratio of household debt to GDP).[7] The indicators cover both the domestic aspects (such as inflation) and the international aspects (such as net private capital inflows) of the financial system and include macroeconomic variables (such as the credit-to-GDP ratio), microeconomic variables (such as number of bankruptcy proceedings initiated), and sectoral variables (such as the real estate price index). Individual banks' exist-

7. International Monetary Fund (2011).

ing data may also need to be reclassified or disaggregated for the computation of related requirements.

Policy Recommendations

Thailand and a few other AEMs learned firsthand, from the painful experience of the 1997 Asian crisis, about the importance of maintaining both microeconomic and macroeconomic stability and in fact since that time have revamped relevant policy frameworks. In this section I offer eight policy recommendations to AEMs for reaching both of these policy objectives.

One: Supervision must change from one that measures compliance to one that measures management of risk. This point is discussed earlier, so here I limit the discussion to the capacity building needed to support this shift in emphasis. Since the two approaches of supervision require very different technical capabilities and mind-sets, supervisors and banks must work toward building their capacity in the area of risk management. To this end, the Bank of Thailand set up a commissioning process that requires examiners to pass qualifying exams before they can be commissioned as examiners in charge. To take the qualifying exam requires three to five years of training, both on the job and in the classroom in the new Examiners' School. To help foster banks' understanding of risk and risk management, a limited number of seats in the Examiners' School are open to bank staff members. The BOT's examination manuals are made available on the BOT website so that banks understand what risk-based supervision means and how they can improve their risk management to meet the BOT's requirements and expectations.[8] The BOT's continued dialogues with bank management are also very useful in building mutual trust and in fostering greater understanding of risk and risk management.

There may also be desirable changes of roles when supervision is risk based. For example, banks must be the owners of their own risks. They must have their own systems of identifying, measuring, monitoring, and controlling their own risks (and not rely on supervisors or external auditors). In this they will be supported by an appropriate governance structure and board oversight. The examination of domestic bank branches is no longer the role of the supervisor but has been shifted to banks as part of their internal control system, which the supervisor ensures is in place.

Two: The threat of financial imbalances must be regularly monitored, since these can lead to financial instability if left unchecked. The BOT regularly monitors seven areas that are vulnerable to the buildup of financial imbalances:

---

8. I should add that, under compliance-based supervision, examination manuals were not disclosed to prevent banks from concealing noncompliance in the areas of focus of examiners, an approach adopted by most compliance-based supervisors.

the housing and property market, the capital market, and the indebtedness of the external, banking, government, household, and corporate sectors. This is by no means an exhaustive list, as is evidenced by IMF surveys of a wide array of indicators. More recently, stress tests have been actively used to gauge the potential vulnerability of the banking sector.

Three: Macroprudential measures can prevent the buildup of systemic risk. They can be powerful tools and have been widely used in emerging markets to contain overindebtedness and excessive credit expansion and to limit credit amplification mechanisms of systemic risk, among other objectives. The most commonly employed macroprudential tools are the loan-to-value ratio, the limit on net open currency positions and the debt-to-income ratio, a ceiling on credit or credit growth, a limit on maturity mismatches, a cap on foreign currency lending, and a levy on noncore funding.

The BOT has successfully used macroprudential tools on a number of occasions. In 2003, when there were early signs of heating in the high-end property market, a loan-to-value ratio for that particular market segment was introduced, and banks were asked to report their financing of property development projects with loans exceeding 100 million baht per project. Even such a simple reporting requirement was enough to send a message to banks and developers alike about the central bank's increasing concerns, and the high-end property market gradually cooled down. Similarly, when credit card loans started to expand rapidly, minimum requirements (such as monthly income and monthly payment) were introduced.

Another interesting measure introduced in 2006 was the requirement for banks to observe International Accounting Standard 39, on impaired assets and their provisioning. This partial adoption of the standard was two years ahead of the Thai accounting body's planned schedule. Banks were made to set aside more provisioning under the new standard instead of paying out handsome dividends from their profits, which had continued to increase in the preceding few years. This was a discretionary countercyclical measure to build up buffers in good times for the rainy days and was implemented well before Basel III will make capital buffers a requirement in pillar 1.

Four: AEMs must ensure that capital inflows do not lead to potential systemic risk. Managing these flows is a significant challenge. Even though other policies—monetary policy, exchange rate policy, capital management policy, and macroprudential policy—deal with capital flows, they are not always effective and may pose conflicts. With the relatively robust economies of most AEMs and some threats of inflation and imbalances in some AEMs, cutting the interest rate to reduce the interest rate differential to discourage capital flows may not be an option. Exchange rate and capital management also have their limitations. Intervention can lead to even more liquidity or have an effect on the central bank's balance sheet, depending on the extent of sterilization. If not properly guarded, inflows can also lead to financial excesses, and disruption can be even bigger when there is a reversal of the flows. Even capital controls are not likely to work unless they are draconian ones, given the massive global liquidity as a consequence of crisis-hit economies' ultra accommodative monetary policy and the significantly higher rates of return in AEMs due to their much stronger economies. The potential gain from AEM currencies' appreciating trend also draws capital to the region. The issue of capital flows is a global problem, and no single country will be able to have a sustainable solution to it. A global problem needs an international solution and international coordination. Deeper systematic studies on ways to deal with capital flows—including the appropriate sequencing of developing different financial markets to build resilience against excessive capital flows and a decisionmaking framework for capital controls when necessary—are being carried out.[9] For a long-term solution, we may need a new international monetary system, since the current one (with only one dominant global currency) runs the risk of having excess global liquidity supplied by the issuer of the global currency.[10] In the meantime, it is important that AEMs take steps, including macroprudential measures, to further strengthen their resilience and ensure that imbalances do not develop as a consequence of the inflows.

Five: Outside interference and threats to central bank independence, from having financial stability as a mandate, can be an issue. Unlike monetary policy, which affects the entire economy with its rate cuts or hikes, financial stability tools usually affect only certain economic sectors, where financial imbalances are judged to be building up. Hence central banks could face immense lobbying and resistance against such measures. Broader acceptable policy space and power, therefore, requires a strong policy framework and a matching governance structure to shield the central bank from interference and to support its independence. It is important that central banks, which are usually the macroprudential supervisors, are legally guaranteed to be independent. In the case of the BOT, monetary stability and financial stability, both microeconomic and macroeconomic, are entrusted by law to two different committees with clear mandates. The committees have more external than internal members, for checks and balance purposes, but are chaired by the governor. The independence of the committees and the governor is guaranteed by law, making external interference difficult. So far the governance structure has worked well.[11]

Two questions arise here. First, why then should a central bank take up the dual mandates of maintaining both price and financial stability, given the potential threat to its independence? Second, would the dual mandates pose a conflict for a central bank and further threaten its credibility and independence?

9. See World Economic Forum (2011).
10. For a discussion on this point, see Watanagase (2010).
11. For more details, see Watanagase (2011).

There are a few reasons that a central bank should take up the mandate of financial stability. First, price and financial stability are closely related. The lack of the latter eventually leads to booms and busts, which have significant implications for price stability and may, in turn, lead to loss of central bank credibility in maintaining price stability. In fact, even if financial stability is not an explicit mandate of a central bank, it would still want to ensure that, over time, financial stability is achieved to support sustainable price stability. Second, a central bank is likely to be the lender of last resort should a systemic situation arise, regardless of whether financial stability is its mandate or not. Obviously, placing the financial stability mandate into the central bank's own hand, while at the same time putting in place other mechanisms to safeguard its independence, would likely be a better alternative for maintaining monetary policy credibility over time and for closer surveillance so as to mitigate the risk of financial instability. Third, in maintaining price stability, a central bank monitors a wide array of macroeconomic indicators, such as market liquidity, credit growth, external and fiscal balances, all of which have important bearings on economic growth and inflation. Many of these indicators are also important for assessing financial stability. Hence there is a synergy between the two mandates. In addition, many central banks in AEMs are also microsupervisors and hence are able to leverage all microprudential and macroprudential data for financial stability purposes.

As for the potential trade-off or conflict between the two mandates, the traditional view is that in general price stability tends to promote financial stability. Low and stable inflation does not lead to distorted relative prices and therefore prevents resource misallocation, whereas high inflation, usually related to higher price volatilities, adds to the problem of predicting the rate of return on investments and to the problem of resource misallocation. High inflation is usually a result of excess liquidity and credit, which eventually lead to excessive real and financial investments—and to financial imbalances. So it is comforting for central banks that, in general, there is no conflict between the two mandates. However, experience has shown that financial imbalances can develop even with low and stable inflation, as in the case of the United States leading up to the 2008 crisis and in the case of Japan in the 1990s. So price stability is not a sufficient condition for financial stability. Conflicts seem to arise in a period of significant and unprecedented disinflation and may also be associated with a number of factors, such as the low pricing power of firms, positive supply-side developments, and well-anchored low inflation expectations. Very often there may be simultaneous financial deregulation, which adds opportunities as well as new risks to investment decisions. But even in this case, if a central bank sets its goal of price stability with a longer time horizon, the conflicts would disappear. With a view to the medium term, a central bank may allow short-term inflation to be lower than the short-term optimal rate by, say, tightening its monetary policy in order to have medium-term price stability.[12]

However, in reality it may not be desirable or practical to use monetary policy, when inflation is low and stable, to deal with financial imbalances, since the perceived policy inconsistency (tightening when inflation is low and stable) may affect the central bank's policy credibility. In addition, substantial tightening may be needed for the measure to have any meaningful impact on asset prices when bubbles are already building up, a measure that can be very disruptive to the general economy. This is where macroprudential tools can be more effective, as discussed earlier.

Six: Macroprudential measures must not be used as a substitute for the necessary adjustment of monetary policy to achieve financial stability. In the years before the global crisis, there were debates on leaning against the wind, using countercyclical measures to burst the bubble or cleaning up the mess after the bubble bursts. The verdict is now clear: cleaning up the mess is extremely difficult, given the limited policy options. A monetary policy that keeps the interest rate low for too long, even though it leads to abundant liquidity, provides incentives for high leverage, and sows the seeds of instability. If financial imbalance is building up because of such an accommodative monetary policy, changing the course of the monetary policy is the right approach.

Seven: A supportive market infrastructure contributes significantly to financial stability. Apart from improving the market infrastructure, such as adding a clearing and settlement mechanism, further developing and enhancing the domestic bond market is very useful for AEMs. Most AEMs lack a fully developed and diversified financial sector, one that offers an entire spectrum of financial assets with different risks and returns. With the exception of Malaysia, almost all AEMs have a small corporate bond market; their funding and investment are concentrated in the banking sector and the stock market, the latter of which may not be sufficiently regulated, making it prone to financial imbalances. A deeper bond market provides an important additional market for funding and investment and better risk diversification. The small Thai private bond market could not have become an alternative source of funding for the corporate sector after the Asian crisis, when the banking sector became very conservative in its credit underwriting, partly in reaction to the crisis and partly to conserve its capital. This led to a credit crunch, which contributed to the huge contraction of GDP.

Obviously, regulation and supervision must keep pace with the development of the bond market as well as other financial markets for them to contribute to financial stability. Having said that, I must quickly add that, with the current massive global liquidity, deciding whether or not a well-developed and

---

12. For an insightful discussion on central banks' dual mandates and their potential conflicts, see Issing (2003).

well-regulated bond market contributes positively to financial stability calls for a more complicated analysis. On the one hand, capital inflows are likely to increase if the bond market is an additional channel for investment, and outflows may be higher and more disruptive should there be a change in investors' risk appetite. On the other hand, responses to monetary policy measures should be more stabilizing, since the impacts on the stock and the bond markets are usually in the opposite direction. Hence funds may shift between different markets in the economy, reducing disruptive inflows and outflows.

Eight: What is most important in maintaining financial stability is the will to take away the punch bowl when the party gets interesting—that is, adopting monetary policy or macroprudential policy, which are unpopular measures. Without such a will, any simple excuses can lead to delayed actions or non-actions. Clear legal mandates, supportive governance structure, and market infrastructure—as discussed above—make it somewhat easier for the relevant authorities to make the tough decisions. In addition, communication has an important role. During normal times, the macroprudential supervisor or the central bank need to have frequent dialogues with politicians, bankers, and the general public to build acceptance that the boom and bust cycle is detrimental to economic well-being and that it would be in the best interest of all for the authorities to undertake unpopular measures when needed. It may sound highly idealistic and naïve to hope for such acceptance, but with the memories of the global crisis still vivid, now is the best time for such a strategy. The fact that most Asian economies have been able to safeguard financial stability with unpopular macroprudential measures may suggest that they were able to get the support of the masses, who still remember the pain of the 1997 crisis. This is the case with Thailand, where there have been campaigns for prudent risk management by both households and the business sector, the latter including both banks and other corporations. Prudent risk management means a willingness to trade short-term gains for long-term sustainability, a willingness that is much higher today than previously.

References

Asian Banker. 2010. Issue 101. October.

Basel Committee on Banking Supervision. 2011a. "Global Systemically Important Banks: Assessment Methodology and the Additional Loss Absorbency Requirement."

———. 2011b. "Revised Core Principles for Effective Banking Supervision."

Claessens, Stijn. 2008. "The New International Financial Architecture Requires Better Governance." In *What G20 Leaders Must Do to Stabilize Our Economy and Fix the Financial System,* edited by Barry Eichengreen and Richard Baldwin. VoxEU.

Eichengreen, Barry. 2008. "Not a New Bretton Woods but a New Bretton Woods Process." In *What G20 Leaders Must Do to Stabilize Our Economy and Fix the Financial System,* edited by Barry Eichengreen and Richard Baldwin. VoxEU.

Financial Stability Board. 2011. "Key Attributes of Effective Resolution Regimes for Financial
   Institutions."
FSB, IMF, and BIS. 2011. "Macroprudential Policy Tools and Frameworks." Joint progress
   report to the G-20.
International Monetary Fund. 2011. "Macroprudential Policy: An Organizing Framework."
   Background paper.
Issing, Otmar. 2003. "Monetary and Financial Stability: Is There a Trade-Off?" Speech. Con-
   ference on Monetary Stability, Financial Stability, and the Business Cycle, BIS, March.
Watanagase, Tarisa. 2010. "The International Monetary System." Speech. EMEAP-Eurosystem
   High-Level Seminar, Australia, February 10 (www.bot.or.th).
———. 2011. "Pursuing Monetary and Financial Stability: Bank of Thailand's Perspec-
   tives." Speech. Ninth SEACEN-BIS Executive Seminar, Phnom Penh, January 19 (tarisa-
   watanagase.blogspot.com).
World Economic Forum. 2011. "The Financial Development Report 2010."

10

International Financial Reforms: Capital Standards, Resolution Regimes, and Supervisory Colleges and Their Effect on Emerging Markets

DUNCAN ALFORD

While the 2007–08 financial crisis began in the United States, the crisis quickly spread globally, causing decreases in gross domestic product and employment levels around the world.[1] The crisis revealed numerous general weaknesses in the supervision and regulation of global banks and financial institutions. National governments and international bodies also recognized these weaknesses in the regulatory and supervisory system of global financial institutions and have begun to take steps to improve the system with the hope of avoiding, or at least mitigating, future financial crises.

Since the fall of 2008 when, the G-20 met in Washington, D.C., at the beginning of the financial crisis, the heads of state of the G-20 have proposed a flurry of reforms to the international financial system.[2] These proposals cover a wide range of issues and reflect a serious response to the severe financial crisis; however, many portions of the reforms have not yet been fully implemented. The principal proposals include the following:

The author wishes to thank the attendees at the Asian Development Bank Institute conference for their helpful comments. The author also wishes to thank Rachel Atkinson, Amir Nowroozzadeh, Taylor Smith, and Megan Brown for their assistance. All errors or omissions are the author's alone.

This chapter is based on research conducted through December 30, 2011. A working paper containing additional discussion and analysis and more detailed sources is located on SSRN (http://papers.ssrn.com/sol3/papers.cfm?abstract_id=2007979).

1. Edward Hadas, "Is the Crisis Over?" *New York Times,* April 22, 2009, p. B2.
2. Financial Stability Board (2011e).

—A significant increase in the amount of the capital requirement for international banks, along with a new liquidity ratio intended to strengthen bank resilience during a financial crisis, all part of the Basel III proposal.

—Intensified supervision of systemically important financial institutions (SIFIs). This proposal defines a SIFI and provides for additional loss-absorbency capital to be held by the SIFI because of the systemic risk posed if the institution fails. This intensified supervision will also provide for an improved recovery and resolution regime for SIFIs and the use of supervisory colleges to improve supervisory coordination found lacking during the recent financial crisis.

—Regulation of the shadow banking sector. This proposal will define shadow banking and propose supervision of this sector to respond to the concern that increased regulation and supervision of the traditional financial sectors (banking, insurance, and securities) will drive financial activity to unregulated sectors. These regulations are intended to address the systemic risk posed by the shadow-banking sector and any regulatory arbitrage resulting from recent financial reforms.

—Increased regulation and supervision of over-the counter (OTC) and commodity derivatives.

—Improved macroprudential frameworks and tools. Before the financial crisis, policymakers failed to detect (or they ignored) systemic risks, particularly macroeconomic risks.

—Convergence of international accounting standards. The International Accounting Standards Board and the Financial Accounting Standards Board provide two competing sets of standards, making the comparison of the finances of global banks difficult. The G-20 has urged both bodies to converge their standards to create one high-quality global accounting standard.

—Remuneration practices. This proposal places limits on the compensation practices of financial institutions in order to reduce systemic risk.

—Improved adherence to agreed international financial standards through the use of peer reviews of individual G-20 nations, including thematic peer reviews, and the use of supervisory colleges for important cross-border financial institutions.

This chapter focuses on three of the above proposed reforms: the improved capital requirements intended to reduce the risk of bank failure (Basel III), the improved recovery and resolution regimes for global banks, and the development of supervisory colleges of cross-border financial institutions to improve supervisory cooperation and convergence. In the final section of this chapter I address the implications of these regulatory reforms for Asian emerging markets.

In some ways, these three proposals can be seen as the bookends—and also the books—of a reformed regulatory and supervisory system. The capital standards are intended to minimize the risk of bank failure—the beginning bookend. A recovery and resolution regime is intended to provide an orderly solution in the event of a bank failure—the last bookend. Supervisory colleges are the books that allow for consistent and effective implementation of these bookend standards.

Before the recent financial crisis, numerous commentators had already concluded that capital levels held by banks were simply too low. The lack of capital intensified the effects of the financial crisis and caused national governments to bail out certain financial institutions in order to preserve financial stability. While supervisors, the financial industry, and academics debate the details of the proposed increase in capital requirements for banks, all such groups, including the financial industry, agree that some increase is necessary.[3]

The recent financial crisis highlighted the ineffective supervisory cooperation among national bank supervisors related to cross-border financial institutions. As a result, several international governmental organizations, national governments, and commentators have called for the use of supervisory colleges to supervise global financial institutions, in particular, those SIFIs that have been the recipients of government financial support during the crisis.[4] During the financial crisis, member states of the European Union (EU) committed aid to banks in the amount of approximately 30 percent of EU GDP and paid out amounts equivalent to 13 percent of EU GDP.[5] As President Nicolas Sarkozy and Prime Minister Gordon Brown noted in 2009, "Better regulation and supervision are the means by which the risk to the taxpayer can be reduced for the longer term."[6]

An international regime for the orderly winding up of insolvent banks is a necessary component for truly effective international regulation and supervisory coordination. Without such a regime, policymakers are left with two stark choices: failure of the financial institution, with the resulting economic disruption; or the use of taxpayer funds to recapitalize the financial institution. Several international bodies and commentators have proposed solutions for winding down insolvent financial institutions. This chapter also explores some of these proposals.

G-20 Summits and Financial Reforms

The G-20, asserting itself as the preeminent forum for international economic cooperation, has addressed the need for reform in the governance, regulation, and supervision of the international financial system.[7] The G-20 has called on its

3. International Institute of Finance (2011); Bray (2011).
4. International Monetary Fund (2009); Financial Services Authority (2009); Group of Thirty (2009); Group of Thirty (2008).
5. Van Rompuy (2011).
6. Gordon Brown and Nicolas Sarkozy, "For Global Finance, Global Regulation," *Wall Street Journal*, December 10, 2009, p. A25.
7. Group of Twenty (2009b).

members to implement Basel III, to contribute to the effectiveness of supervisory colleges, and to adopt a resolution regime for financial institutions.

Beginning with the Washington Summit in November 2008 to address the financial crisis, the G-20 has recommended the expanded use of colleges of supervisors to supervise SIFIs.[8] Their communiqué from that summit states that, by March 31, 2009, "Supervisors should collaborate to establish supervisory colleges for all major cross-border financial institutions, as part of the efforts to strengthen the surveillance of cross-border firms. Major global banks should meet regularly with their supervisory college for comprehensive discussions of the firm's activities and assessments of the risks it faces."[9]

During the London Summit, on April 2, 2009, the G-20 leaders established the Financial Stability Board (FSB), as successor to the Financial Stability Forum (FSF), with the goal of extending "regulation and oversight to all systemically important financial institutions, instruments and markets."[10] They emphasized the use and development of colleges of supervisors in supervising global banks. Furthermore, the FSB would expand its membership to include all G-20 countries, FSF members, Spain, and the European Commission, in recognition of the global nature of the financial system and the growing importance of emerging markets in the world economy.[11]

At the end of the G-20 Summit held in Toronto in June 2010, the heads of state recognized the importance of a resolution regime addressing systemic institutions and committed themselves "to design and implement a system where we have the powers and tools to restructure or resolve (wind down) all types of financial institutions in crisis, without taxpayers ultimately bearing the burden, and adopted principles that will guide implementation."[12] The heads of state stated their clear intention to reduce moral hazard by designing and implementing such a regime. Any resolution regime should provide for:

—Proper allocation of losses to reduce moral hazard and protect taxpayers

—Continuity of critical financial services, including uninterrupted service for insured depositors

---

8. The following countries constitute the G-20: Argentina, Australia, Brazil, Canada, People's Republic of China, France, Germany, India, Indonesia, Italy, Japan, Mexico, the Netherlands, the Republic of Korea, Russia, Saudi Arabia, South Africa, Turkey, the United Kingdom, and the United States. Group of Twenty (2010c). The G-20 represents 89 percent of global GDP and two-thirds of the world's population. Korea-FSB Financial Reform Conference (2010).

9. Group of Twenty (2008).

10. Group of Twenty (2009a).

11. Finance ministries and central banks from the following nations are members of the Financial Stability Board: Argentina; Australia; Brazil; Canada; People's Republic of China; France; Germany; Hong Kong, China; India; Indonesia; Italy; Japan; Mexico; the Netherlands; the Republic of Korea; Russia; Saudi Arabia; Singapore; South Africa; Spain; Switzerland; Turkey; the United Kingdom; and the United States (www.financialstabilityboard.org/members/links.htm).

12. Group of Twenty (2010b).

—Credibility of the resolution regime in the market

—Minimization of contagion

—Advanced planning for orderly resolution and transfer of contractual relationships

—Effective cooperation and information exchange domestically and among jurisdictions in the event of a failure of a cross-border institution.

At the Seoul Summit in November 2010, the G-20 heads of state continued their commitment to the reform of the international financial system. In their declaration, the leaders promised to deliver the "core elements of a new financial regulatory framework, including bank capital and liquidity standards, as well as measures to better regulate and effectively resolve systemically important financial institutions, complemented by more effective oversight and supervision."[13] The G-20 leaders "endorsed the policy framework, work processes, and timelines proposed by the FSB to reduce the moral hazard risks posed by systemically important financial institutions and address the too-big-to-fail problem." In particular, the G-20 agreed that global SIFIs "should be subject to a sustained process of mandatory international recovery and resolution planning" and that nations should implement the Basel Committee's cross-border resolution recommendations.

Basel III Capital Standards

During the financial crisis of 2007–08, the leaders of the G-20 tasked the Basel Committee on Banking Supervision (Basel Committee) to improve the capital standards of international banks, as the weakness of international capital standards (Basel II) was seen as a major cause of the crisis. In December 2010 the Basel Committee issued new, more stringent capital standards for banks, known as Basel III.[14] The heads of state of the G-20 had previously endorsed this proposal at the November 2010 Seoul Summit.

Minimum Capital Standard

The Basel Committee proposed that international banks hold total capital equivalent to 8 percent of risk-weighted assets, as opposed to the current level of 2 percent of risk-weighted assets. The definition of risk-weighted assets also changed. More stringent criteria were applied to types of assets, and the risk weights applied to certain assets increased. The intent of the revisions of the Basel capital framework was to capture all material risks of a financial institution. During the recent financial crisis, the Basel II framework failed to capture on-balance-sheet and off-balance-sheet risks and derivative-related exposures of

13. Group of Twenty (2010a).
14. Basel Committee on Banking Supervision (2010/2011).

financial institutions. Under the prior standard, Basel II, the definition of risk-weighted assets underestimated risk exposures, the definition of capital did not reflect the institution's ability to absorb losses, and the required minimum capital ratios were too low.[15] This failure and the resulting lack of capital intensified the financial crisis. Basel III requires more capital both in quality and in amount. The effect of the Basel III revisions to risk coverage is "to increase the capital charges associated with exposure to counterparties to OTC derivatives, repos and stock lending transactions, in each case which are not cleared through central counterparties and thus provide incentives to employ more standardized derivatives to be cleared centrally."[16]

Capital under Basel III consists of three components: common equity tier-1 capital, additional tier-1 capital, and tier-2 capital. Basel III emphasizes the importance of common equity as capital. The goal of the Basel Committee is to develop a *minimum* standard; national supervisors are free to apply more stringent capital requirements. The minimum level of common equity tier-1 capital will be 4.5 percent of risk-weighted assets, with total tier-1 capital being 6 percent and total capital, including tier-2 capital, being 8 percent after the phase-in period. International banks must meet these capital requirements by January 1, 2015.

In addition to this core capital standard, international banks must also meet a capital conservation buffer equivalent to 2.5 percent of risk-weighted assets. Also, at the discretion of national supervisors, banks may be required to hold an additional amount of capital as a countercyclical buffer equivalent to 2.5 percent of risk-weighted assets. Thus the total capital required for international banks could potentially increase from 2 percent of risk-weighted assets, under the previous standard, to 13 percent, under the new, more stringent Basel III standard.

Leverage Ratio and Liquidity Ratio

The Basel Committee also proposed a leverage ratio for international banks. This ratio is calculated as the amount of capital held by the bank divided by the amount of exposure of the bank. Exposure includes the value of bank assets and the value of derivatives and off-balance-sheet items. Again, the intent is to capture all risks, both on and off the balance sheet, for which the bank is liable. The ratio will be tested at a level of 3 percent from January 1, 2013, to January 1, 2017. The Basel Committee states that this ratio may change depending on the committee's evaluation of its effect on bank operations.

The Basel Committee also recommends a liquidity standard for international banks as part of the new Basel III standard—the first time the Basel Committee has addressed liquidity. The liquidity standard will be measured by two separate ratios: a liquidity coverage ratio and a net stable funding ratio. The liquidity

15. Shadow Financial Regulatory Committee (2011).
16. Morrison & Foerster (2010).

coverage ratio is the value of high-quality liquid assets over the total net cash flow of the bank for a thirty-day period. This ratio should be greater than or equal to one and should be reported monthly to the appropriate supervisor.

In contrast to the liquidity coverage ratio, the net stable funding ratio is intended to promote the resilience of the bank over the longer time period of one year. This ratio is the bank's available stable funding over its required stable funding. The required stable funding is an amount determined by the appropriate supervisor using assumptions regarding the liquidity risk profile of the bank. The available stable funding is the sum of a bank's capital, preferred stock with a maturity over one year, nonmaturing deposits, term deposits, and wholesale funding that is expected to remain with the bank in the event of a financial crisis. This net stable funding ratio should be greater than or equal to one and must be reported quarterly. The supervisor in the home jurisdiction typically enforces this ratio according to the home jurisdiction's standards. With respect to retail and small business deposits, the liquidity standards of the host jurisdiction are applied.

Supervisors must balance the tension between increasing bank capital to promote financial stability against the effect of decreased economic growth caused by a reduction in bank lending necessitated by the higher capital levels. The "Quantitative Impact Study," conducted by the Basel Committee as part of the development of Basel III, shows that 577 billion euros were needed to meet these new capital standards for a sample of international banks.[17] This same sample earned after-tax profits of 209 billion euros in 2009. Retained earnings alone may not be sufficient to fund these new capital standards.

Additional Capital Required for Global SIFIs

The Basel Committee has also proposed additional, more stringent, capital standards for global SIFIs. These banks are a subset of the international banks subject to Basel III generally because they pose systemic risks to the world economy and thus will receive more intense supervision. The Basel proposal is intended to create a framework for identifying these systemically important banks and not to create a fixed list of such institutions. The Basel Committee proposes an "indicator-based measurement approach," consisting of five indicators of equal weight. The five indicators are:

—Cross-jurisdictional activity, which will be measured by the amount of cross-jurisdictional claims and cross-jurisdictional liabilities, with the idea that the greater the cross-jurisdictional activity of the institution, the more difficult it will be to resolve the institution.

—Size, which will be measured by the total exposures of the bank used in the calculation of the leverage ratio under Basel III. The theory is that the larger the bank, the more likely that its failure would damage the global economy.

17. Basel Committee on Banking Supervision (2010b).

—Interconnectedness refers to the network of contractual obligations within which the bank operates and is measured by three subindicators: intrafinancial system assets, intrafinancial system liabilities, and the wholesale funding ratio.

—Substitutability refers to whether there are substitutes or alternatives for major lines of business or services of the bank and is measured by the amount of assets under custody, the amount of payments cleared and settled through payment systems, and the value of underwritten transactions in debt and equity markets.

—Complexity is measured by the notional value of OTC derivatives, the amount of level-3 assets (whose fair value cannot be determined by using observable measures), the trading book value, and the "available for sale" value. This criterion recognizes that the systemic impact of the failure of a bank would typically be more severe as the complexity of the bank increases.[18]

In November 2011 the FSB designated twenty-nine financial institutions to be systemic and therefore subject to the additional capital requirement (see appendix 10A).[19] These banks must hold an additional amount of capital, ranging from 1 percent to a potential 3.5 percent of risk-weighted assets, depending on the bank's rating. The higher the rating, the more systemically important the bank, the more capital that must be held. This loss absorbency capital is *in addition to* the other forms of capital required by Basel III.

This additional capital for global SIFIs must consist of common equity, tier-1 capital. The Basel Committee considered the inclusion of bail-in capital but decided not to include these instruments.[20] Rather, in its view, bail-in capital could be used to meet other types of capital required to be held by banks. The effect of this proposal is to increase the capital required to be held by global, systemically important banks from 2 percent of risk-weighted assets to potentially 16.5 percent, if all types of Basel III capital are imposed in addition to the loss absorbency capital for a global SIFI.

I address the implications of the reform of capital standards on emerging markets in the conclusion of this chapter.

Supervisory Colleges

One tool used to improve the international legal framework for financial supervision is the college of supervisors or supervisory colleges for cross-border financial institutions. These ad hoc groups are intended to improve the exchange of information among supervisors with the goal of ensuring safe and sound banking practices, reducing the possibility of governmental assistance to financial

18. Morrison & Foerster (2011).
19. Financial Stability Board (2011b).
20. Bail-in capital refers to debt that converts to equity upon the triggering of certain events.

institutions, and building confidence generally in the international financial system. The hope is that these colleges, which meet on a regular basis to discuss the supervision of a particular financial institution, will identify issues or problems early, then address them quickly, and thus reduce the risk of a bailout or a bank failure.

The G-20 and the European Union have been particularly active in developing these colleges and codifying best practices for their operation. However, colleges of supervisors are a limited, incomplete response to inadequate coordination of supervision of global financial institutions. International supervisory coordination is necessarily hindered because each national supervisor will strive to minimize its use of taxpayer resources to cover any losses from bank failures. At times of crisis, national supervisors tend to ring-fence assets and neglect (or ignore) efforts at supervisory coordination.

A convergence of the types and extent of powers of supervisory authorities is needed to improve coordination of supervision of cross-border financial institutions. Currently, the legal powers of supervisors vary widely among nations. When the supervisors participating in a college have similar legal powers and authority, the college can be more effective. Similarly, the skills and capacity of supervisors varies widely, particularly when one compares the typical developed nation to the typical emerging market. Likewise, the supervisory approach can vary among nations; for example, some countries prefer on-site supervision, while others rely on off-site surveillance. Past experience with supervisory colleges illustrates that they are not a complete solution to the issue of effective supervision of global banks.

Supervisory colleges were not first created as a result of the 2007–08 financial crisis. Initially, financial supervisors formed these groups to monitor financial institutions with cross-border operations. For example, in the late 1980s a college of supervisors, including authorities from the United Kingdom, Luxembourg, and other European nations, supervised the Bank of Credit and Commerce International (BCCI), a bank with operations in several dozen countries. However, this college proved ineffective, and the bank was ultimately liquidated because of internal fraudulent activities.[21]

To compensate for the weak supervision of the BCCI, bank supervisors from the Cayman Islands; France; Hong Kong, China; Luxembourg; Spain; Switzerland; the United Arab Emirates; and the United Kingdom created a college of supervisors in 1987 to coordinate their supervisory efforts. In the end, this scheme proved unworkable and allowed supervisors to shift responsibility for any BCCI transgression among themselves. No single supervisor had any incentive to supervise BCCI properly, and the supervisors did not cooperate adequately among

---

21. See generally Alford (1992).

themselves in sharing information on BCCI operations. In a 2004 speech, Callum McCarthy, then head of the Financial Services Authority in the United Kingdom, concluded that "in some cases the resources [of a supervisor] are simply not up to the task of acting as a home regulator for a large group," and in the case of BCCI, "the resources then available in Luxembourg," the home supervisor, were not sufficient.[22]

European Union and Colleges of Supervisors

The EU has been particularly active in utilizing colleges to supervise financial institutions operating in multiple member states. Their experience can be instructive for other financial supervisors, including those from emerging markets, despite the differences in development of their respective economies.

The European Banking Authority (EBA) and its predecessor, the Committee of European Banking Supervisors (CEBS), have as their objective "to foster supervisory convergence across the Community."[23] In furtherance of this objective, the CEBS was active in supporting the development of supervisory colleges of cross-border banks within the European Union and has stated that "the establishment of supervisory colleges and their functioning . . . is a cornerstone of the new institutional framework."[24]

The recent financial crisis focused renewed attention on colleges of supervisors as one of several tools to reduce risk within the international financial system. In January 2009 the CEBS updated its guidance on supervisory colleges and provided more specific detail on the operations and best practices of the colleges of supervisors. In its "Colleges of Supervisors—10 Common Principles," CEBS and its sister agency, the Committee of European Insurance and Occupational Pension Supervisors, provide that a college of supervisors shall supervise any cross-border insurance group, banking group, or financial conglomerate.[25] The colleges—flexible, permanent forums for cooperation and coordination among financial supervisory authorities—shall have agreements in place describing the cooperation between the supervisors and the practical organization of the supervisory activities of the financial institution. For banking groups, the consolidating supervisor as defined in the Capital Requirements Directive (CRD) shall initiate the cooperation process. The colleges shall also promote the harmonization of supervisory approaches, coordinate all major supervisory decisions, plan and coordinate supervisory on-site inspections, and share the findings from such visits with other members of the college.

---

22. McCarthy (2004).

23. Committee of European Banking Supervisors (2009). See also Alford (2006).

24. Committee of European Banking Supervisors (2010).

25. Committee of European Banking Supervisors/Committee of European Insurance and Occupational Pension Supervisors (2009).

The EU regulation creating the European Banking Authority grants the EBA the authority to mediate disputes between the national supervisory authorities.[26] The regulation states that if the national supervisors cannot reach an agreement after a conciliation period, the EBA "may . . . take a decision requiring them to take specific action or to refrain from action in order to settle the matter, with binding effects for the competent authorities concerned, in order to ensure compliance with Union law."[27] This power is intended to promote convergence of supervisory practice and builds upon the mediation powers previously granted to the CEBS.

The EU has taken additional steps to buttress colleges as a supervisory tool. In several directives, the EU institutionalized greater cooperation among supervisors supervising cross-border banks. In the adoption of the Basel II directive dealing with capital requirements of credit institutions, the European Union created specific rules dealing with cooperation among supervisors of cross-border banks operating in the EU.[28] In this directive, chapter 4 (articles 124-44) lays out rules determining which supervisor, also known as the lead supervisor, exercises consolidated supervision over the cross-border bank.[29] Articles 125 and 126 set forth detailed rules identifying the lead supervisor, depending on the structure of the credit institution and its relationship to any parent financial holding company. Membership in the college shall include supervisors from all EU member states where the credit institution has a subsidiary. Under article 126(3), the supervisors may waive these rules, appoint a lead supervisor selected among themselves to supervise the credit institution, and notify the commission of such appointment. In addition, article 131 of the CRD requires that the supervisors "shall have written coordination, cooperation agreements in place."[30] Within the EU, these colleges carry out the tasks set forth in the CRD, generally limited to regulating capital requirements of financial institutions. In practice, colleges of supervisors may expand their purview to include other supervisory matters.

Until the enactment of the EBA regulation, one weakness of the college of supervisors within the EU was the lack of a mandatory mediation process if the supervisors could not agree on an action with respect to the supervision of the financial institution. As seen in the recent financial crisis, this lack of mediation allowed supervisors to act on their own and not in coordination with their peers. For example, in the fall 2008 rescue of Fortis—the financial group with operations in Belgium, the Netherlands, and Luxembourg—the national

26. Regulation 1093/2010, L 331, 12. See appendix 10D.
27. See article 20(3).
28. Directive 2006/49, L 177, 201; 2006/48/, L 17, 1; 2006/49, L 177, 201; 2006/48, L 177, 1. See appendix 10D.
29. Directive 2006/48, articles 125–32, as amended by Directive 2009/111, L 30, 97. See appendix 10D.
30. Directive 2006/48, article 131. See appendix 10D.

supervisors struggled to coordinate their actions.[31] At first, the Benelux governments purchased 49 percent of the equity of Fortis. Then a few days later, the Dutch government seized the Dutch operations of Fortis, and the Belgian and Luxembourgian operations were sold to BNP Paribas.[32] These events illustrate a lack of effective supervisory cooperation, particularly during times of crisis. Even among supervisors who have a long practice of cooperation—namely, the Benelux authorities—cooperation can break down in times of crisis as national interests come to the fore. Recognizing the weaknesses in the supervisory system highlighted by the financial crisis, the EU responded with legislative proposals to reform the EU system.

European Union's Reform of Financial Supervision

On February 23, 2009, a high-level group of advisers, chaired by Jacques de Larosière, former governor of the Banque de France, issued its report on the reform of the EU system of financial supervision, also known as the Larosière Report.[33] Appointed by José Barroso, the president of the European Commission, in the fall of 2008 the High-Level Expert Group was charged with a broad mandate "to make proposals to strengthen European supervisory arrangements covering all financial sectors, with the objective to establish a more efficient, integrated and sustainable European system of supervision."[34] While a complete analysis of this report is beyond the scope of this chapter, it does note the report's recommendations that are related to supervisory cooperation within the EU. Recommendation 18 in the Larosière Report advises that "colleges of supervisors would be set up for all major cross-border institutions."[35] For cross-border institutions, the colleges of supervisors introduced by the revised CRD and the solvency II directive should take the lead in supervision.

The report also states that the "relatively restrictive use of supervisory colleges should be expanded immediately." By the end of 2009, supervisory colleges should be established for all major cross-border firms within the EU, estimated to be at least fifty financial institutions. Level-3 committees would participate in this process by defining the supervisory practices and arrangements for the functioning of the colleges of supervisors and would themselves participate in the

---

31. Nikki Tait and Jennifer Hughes, "Trichet Calls for Supervision of All Institutions," *Financial Times,* February 24, 2008.

32. Ulrich Volz, "Europe Needs a United Approach to the Credit Crunch," *Wall Street Journal,* October 7, 2008, p. A27.

33. Larosière and others (2009). This group held eleven public meetings and consulted widely to develop its thirty-one recommendations to improve financial services regulation within the EU. For a time line of the current effort to reform the EU legal framework for financial supervision, see appendix 10C.

34. High-Level Expert Group (2008).

35. For this and the following, see Larosière and others (2009, pp. 47. 48, 51).

supervisory colleges.[36] The clear intent is to expand the mandate of the CEBS to be more inclusive of supervisory players and to broaden the tasks of colleges beyond those stated in the CRD. The report recommends transforming level-3 committees into three supervisory authorities, one for each financial sector: banking, securities, and insurance—the European Banking Authority (the EBA), the European Securities Markets Authority (the ESMA), and the European Insurance and Occupational Pensions Authority (the EIOPA).

After over a year of negotiation, the EU Council and the European Parliament in September 2010 agreed on final versions of legislation reforming the EU's financial regulatory system. I focus on the EBA regulation that transformed the CEBS into a European supervisory authority, the European Banking Authority.[37]

The EBA has the authority to submit both regulatory technical standards and implementing technical standards to the European Commission for approval.[38] Once a standard has been submitted, the commission can reject or request amendments to the standard. However, the commission cannot change the text of the standards without coordinating with the EBA. While this legislation does not provide regulation-making authority equivalent to that of national supervisory agencies, it does provide the EBA with significant influence in creating the standards. The regulation explicitly provides that the EU Council or the European Parliament can revoke this delegation of power to issue technical standards.

Member states throughout the negotiations were concerned about the power of the EBA to issue decisions directly applicable to financial institutions. Some member states and national supervisors, particularly in the United Kingdom, were concerned that the EBA would circumvent the authority of national supervisors. The final regulation does allow the EBA, under certain limited conditions, to issue decisions directly applicable to financial institutions.

The EBA also has the power to settle disagreements between national supervisors of cross-border financial institutions. The regulation requires the EBA to attempt at first to mediate any dispute. If the national supervisors cannot reach an agreement, then the EBA by a majority vote of its board of managers issues a decision settling the matter. The EBA decision supersedes any earlier decision issued by the national supervisor. This dispute-settlement power coupled with the supremacy of the EBA decision over national supervisors will enable the EBA to create "a sound, effective and consistent level of regulation and supervision"

36. Level-3 committees are the Committee of European Banking Supervisors (CEBS), the Committee of European Securities Regulators (CESR), and the Committee of European Insurance and Occupational Pension Supervisors (CEIOPS). These committees were set up under the Lamfalussy process to advise the commission and its committees on implementing measures need to effectuate financial regulation.

37. Regulations 1093/2010; 1094/2010; 1095/2010. See appendix 10D.

38. Regulation 1093/2010, pp. 24–25. See appendix 10D.

within the EU—one of the goals of this regulation. However, this power to settle disputes is limited by the safeguard provision providing that no such decision "impinges in any way on the fiscal responsibilities of Member States."[39]

The regulation provides for the EBA to be closely involved in the operation of colleges of supervisors. The EBA is "able to participate in the activities of colleges of supervisors, including on-site examinations."[40] The final regulation enumerates specific tasks of the EBA related to colleges of supervisors.[41] For instance, the EBA may develop draft regulatory and implementing technical standards related to the operation of colleges of supervisors. Finally, the EBA shall "have a legally binding mediation role to resolve disputes between competent authorities."[42]

The EBA's authority to issue decisions resolving a dispute among national supervisors or in the event of a financial emergency is subject to a broad safeguard. The EBA shall not issue a decision that "impinges in any way on the fiscal responsibilities of the Member State."[43] If a member state believes that an EBA decision does impinge on its fiscal responsibilities, it can appeal to the Council of the European Union to review the decision. Depending on the type of decision, the council by its action or inaction can render the decision ineffective. Additional language was added stating that any abuse of the safeguard, particularly where there is no material fiscal impact, "shall be prohibited as incompatible with the internal market." This broadly worded safeguard provision significantly weakens the EBA's authority. However, this article does not apply to decisions issued by the EBA and endorsed by the European Commission related to the breach of EU law. If the action of a national supervisor breaches EU law, the safeguard provision and its delaying procedure do not apply.

The EBA is not optimally independent for a regulatory agency. National supervisors who are subject to its decisions serve on the EBA board. The grounds for dismissal of the head of the EBA are not specified. A representative of the European Commission serves on the board in a nonvoting capacity but nevertheless "raises the issue of potential political interference on the [EBA's] policy decisions."[44]

Colleges of supervisors are crucial for harmonized supervision within the EU. Proper supervision is not possible "unless the [national] supervisors responsible for monitoring the subsidiaries (and even branches) of those groups are fully

---

39. Regulation 1093/2010, article 38. See appendix 10D.

40. Regulation 1093/2010, article 21.

41. The EBA is expected to collect all relevant information needed for the effective operation of the colleges and to institute EU-wide stress tests of financial institutions. The EBA can request further deliberations by colleges, may require the consolidating supervisor to schedule a meeting of the college, and can add items to the agenda of the college.

42. Regulation 1093/2010, article 21, p. 4.

43. For this and the following, see Regulation 1093/2010, article 38, pp. 1–5.

44. Masciandoro, Neito, and Quintyn (2011).

involved in the supervision exercised by the 'home supervisor' over the parent company."[45] There are two potential dangers with colleges: one, inconsistent decisions between colleges and, two, failure to take any action in the event of disagreement within a college. The ESAs will reduce inconsistency by attending the colleges as a coordinator and identifying and communicating best practices among colleges. The EBA's powers to issue regulatory and implementing technical standards regarding the operation of supervisory colleges, to mediate disputes among supervisors in a college, to issue binding decisions to a national supervisor, and to issue a decision directly to a financial institution if the supervisor fails to comply with the decision will strengthen the EBA's ability to develop more uniformity in banking supervision within the EU. However, all such decisions are subject to the broad safeguard provision.

The previous explanation of the developments within the EU illustrates the difficulty in integrating the supervision of cross-border financial institutions. Even within the EU, where there is a legal framework to enact reform, harmonizing financial regulation and supervision has been difficult and is still incomplete after several decades of effort. The EBA is not a true supranational regulatory agency. Member states can appeal its decisions, including those issuing technical standards, to the European Council. The EBA's expanded mediation role is an improvement over past practice, but it is not a definitive solution. All decisions are subject to the broad safeguard provision, which was designed to protect national sovereignty.

Any international agreement to harmonize the regulation and supervision of financial institutions will be even more difficult to achieve because there is no legal framework on which to rely (as exists in the EU). The incentive to maintain national sovereignty is even greater in the international arena without a vehicle similar to the EU treaty structure supporting the economic integration of Europe and an "ever closer union among the peoples of Europe."[46] However, European supervisory authorities, such as the EBA, created by the EU "offer important lessons for efforts to create a comparable body outside the European Union."[47]

Basel Committee on Supervisory Colleges

In October 2010 the Basel Committee issued eight general principles on the operation of colleges of supervisors.[48] One principle states that supervisory colleges are not a substitute for effective national supervision of financial institutions. Another states that supervisory colleges are not decisionmaking bodies but rather "provide a framework to enhance effective supervision of international banking

---

45. Larosière and others (2009, p. 5).
46. European Union (2010).
47. Pan (2010).
48. Basel Committee on Banking Supervision (2010a).

groups."[49] Further, supervisory colleges provide a useful forum in which to share information regarding the overall risk assessment of a banking group and in which to discuss and plan the supervisory assessment of a financial group. Ultimately, the regular interaction and exchange of information among supervisors within a college should enhance mutual trust and understanding among the supervisors.

The principles do not prescribe a particular structure of a supervisory college; rather the college structure should be flexible and proportionate to the size and complexity of the financial institution. The principles do recognize that the home supervisor who leads the college should designate members of a core college and a general college. The home supervisor should have regular, continuous communication with members of the core college, who represent the jurisdictions in which significant operations of the financial institution exist. Members of the general college represent jurisdictions in which the financial institution has less significant operations. The college should hold regular physical meetings among the supervisors; the core college should meet at least once annually. The Basel Committee recognizes that the operation of supervisory colleges and crisis management groups are distinct but complementary activities. The implications for emerging markets of the development of supervisory colleges are explored in the conclusion to this chapter.

Resolution and Insolvency Regimes

At the urging of the G-20, both the FSB and the Basel Committee have proposed the creation of a resolution regime for SIFIs. During the recent financial crisis, the lack of such a regime necessitated the bailout of financial institutions by national governments in order to preserve financial stability and prevent an even more severe economic downturn. The creation of a resolution regime, particularly in a cross-border context, has proven difficult, and despite the urging of the G-20 and considerable effort by various international bodies and academics, few concrete actions have been taken thus far.

In creating a bank resolution regime, the different objectives of a corporate insolvency regime and a bank insolvency regime must be recognized. Corporate insolvency laws attempt to reach "a fair and predictable treatment of creditors and the maximization of assets to satisfy creditors' claims."[50] On the other hand, the bank insolvency regime must "ensure the protection of (insured) depositors and the continuity of banking and payment services" and minimize the contagion of a bank failure. As long as these goals are attained, a bank should be allowed to fail in order to avoid moral hazard.

---

49. Basel Committee on Banking Supervision (2010a, p. 1).
50. Basel Committee Cross-Border Resolution Group (2010, p. 9).

Commentators present three theoretical approaches for the resolution of financial institutions: universalism, territoriality, and modified universalism.[51] Under the universalist approach, SIFIs are subject to a single resolution process. Home country laws with respect to bankruptcy and resolution would apply to all assets of the SIFI, wherever it is located. This approach would require some sort of ex ante burden-sharing agreement among the relevant national authorities. From the supervisor's point of view, the ideal structure of a SIFI under this approach would be a single entity. Under this approach, national regulatory authority, particularly the authority of the host supervisor, is not preserved.

Under the territoriality approach, there would be no sharing of assets between supervisors in different countries in the event of a SIFI failure. The ideal SIFI structure for this approach would be stand-alone subsidiaries within each country of operation. This approach encourages the ring-fencing of assets during a crisis. In other words, no transfer of assets across jurisdictions is allowed. This approach fails to attain efficient cross-border financial integration, as each subsidiary is separately capitalized and intragroup transfers are restricted.

Under the modified universalist approach, the home country addresses the overall resolution of the SIFI, while the host country is responsible for the resolution of the local host operation. This approach is similar to the bankruptcy procedure, with a main proceeding and ancillary proceedings in other jurisdictions. Under this system, the mutual recognition and broad harmonization of supervisory and resolution regimes would be helpful. Under this approach, some national regulatory authority is ceded by the host jurisdiction to the home jurisdiction.

Historically, the territoriality approach has prevailed. The territoriality approach ignores international coordination and the realities of globalization. The universal approach is not currently feasible because there is no political consensus or will to create a global financial regulator or resolution authority. Even in the EU, where financial integration has progressed significantly and there is an overarching legal framework for financial integration, the creation of a true pan-European regulator or resolution authority has not occurred.

European Union Proposal for a Resolution Framework

In October 2009 the European Commission proposed the creation of a resolution framework for European cross-border banks (see appendix 10B for the important documents). Noting that the "recent crisis has exposed the EU's lack of an effective crisis management [framework] for cross-border financial institutions," the commission sought comments on an EU harmonized resolution and insolvency regime for cross-border financial institutions.[52]

---

51. Claessens, Herring, and Schoenmaker (2010).
52. European Commission (2010).

Current EU laws regarding the resolution of EU financial institutions are minimal. The Directive on the Reorganization and Winding Up of Credit Institutions (the Winding Up Directive) takes a modified universal approach to the resolution of EU cross-border institutions and provides that courts located in the same jurisdiction as the home supervisor govern the resolution of the parent institution and any branches.[53] However, this directive does not apply to financial institutions that operate as subsidiaries in member states. Many European financial institutions operate as subsidiaries in their cross-border operations, and thus national laws, with significant variations, govern the resolution of the subsidiaries of an insolvent parent financial institution. The Winding Up Directive principally focuses on determining which national court has jurisdiction over the proceedings in a particular case and intends to ensure that there is only one set of insolvency proceedings for a distressed financial institution; it does not provide a complete, EU-wide system for resolving in an orderly manner the claims against a failing credit institution. The directive does not apply to non-EU incorporated institutions and makes no attempt to harmonize national insolvency legislation.[54]

History reveals that, in a financial crisis, national law predominates. Given the variations in national insolvency laws, the resolution of cross-border institutions becomes difficult and inefficient. Without a pan-European resolution regime, member states tend to ring-fence national assets. For example, the actions taken regarding Fortis in 2008 illustrate the strong incentive to ring-fence assets even among bank supervisors with a significant history of cooperation.[55] As the commission notes, "If insolvency law is national, domestic authorities have a legitimate as well as strong political interest to ring-fence the national assets of an ailing bank in order to protect national deposits and maximize the assets available to the creditors of the national entity."[56]

After receiving and considering public comments, the European Commission, in "An EU Framework for Cross-Border Crisis Management in the Banking Sector," sets forth in general terms the content of legislation related to crisis management within the EU financial sector. The framework intends that financial institutions be allowed to fail without risk to financial stability and without cost to taxpayers. This crisis management framework is based on the following seven principles:

—Put prevention and preparation first.
—Provide credible resolution tools.
—Enable fast and decisive action.
—Reduce moral hazard.

53. Directive 2001/24; Basel Committee on Banking Supervision, Cross-Border Bank Resolution Group (2010, p. 23). For list of directives, see appendix 10D.
54. European Commission (2009, p. 9).
55. Goodhart and Schoenmaker (2009).
56. For this and following, see European Commission (2009, pp. 3–4, 8).

—Contribute to a smooth resolution of cross-border groups.

—Ensure legal certainty.

—Limit the distortions of competition.

The commission's framework is composed of three steps: a legislative proposal for a harmonized regime for crisis prevention and bank recovery and resolution, the further harmonization of bank insolvency regimes within the EU, and the creation of an integrated resolution regime that could include a single European resolution authority. To accomplish this objective, the commission is developing three classes of measures: "preparatory and preventative measures; early supervisory intervention; and resolution tools and powers."[57] Some member states possess these tools now; for some of them, these tools will be new. Each member state will be required to designate a resolution authority to exercise these powers. The resolution authority should be an administrative body rather than a judicial body. In most cases, an existing authority, such as the central bank, the finance ministry, or a deposit guarantee scheme, can be designated the resolution authority.

To meet its stated goals, the European Commission proposes a new type of entity: a resolution college. The resolution college will build upon the existing colleges of supervisors by including the resolution authorities for cross-border groups. The commission recognizes that ideally there would be a single pan-European authority that "would deliver a rapid, decisive and equitable resolution process for European financial groups, and better reflect the pan-EU nature of banking markets."[58] However, the commission recognizes that it would be difficult politically to create such an integrated system. The resolution colleges are a more moderate and realistic approach to bank resolution. The EBA would serve as an observer for the resolution colleges, much as it does for the colleges of supervisors.

In order for a resolution regime to be credible, there must be resolution funds available. The commission recognizes that much more work is needed to create a credible funding mechanism and that a framework must include a mechanism to finance any resolution, with the cost being primarily borne by the shareholders and creditors of the financial institution. The commission recommends some sort of ex ante funding by financial institutions for any resolution regime. The European Commission is currently reviewing comments from a consultation on the creation of a resolution framework for financial institutions within the EU.

Basel Committee Cross-Border Resolution Group

Other international standard-setting bodies have also issued guidelines related to crisis management. The Basel Committee on Banking Supervision (through its

---

57. European Commission (2011, p. 4).
58. European Commission (2011, p. 12).

Cross-Border Resolution Group) also issued a report that "seeks to complement the work of the FSB by providing practical detailed approaches to implement the FSB's 'Principles for Cross-Border Cooperation on Crisis Management' related to the resolution of cross-border banks."[59] Similar to the European Commission, the Basel Committee took a middle-ground approach, recognizing that the status quo was not acceptable and that an international agreement on the resolution of cross-border banks was "both unlikely and unenforceable as the practical implications of burden sharing give rise to considerable challenges."[60]

The report makes ten recommendations related to improving the coordination of the resolution of cross-border financial institutions. It recommends that national supervisory authorities have the necessary tools for the orderly resolution of a cross-border institution. Each nation should have a national framework providing for the resolution of financial groups. Over time, supervisory authorities should seek the convergence of these resolution tools to allow for better coordination of a resolution and should consider procedures that would "facilitate the mutual recognition of crisis management and resolution proceedings." Contingency plans of SIFIs should address "a period of financial distress" and should be a regular part of the supervisory process. Key home and host supervisors of SIFIs should "agree, consistent with national law and policy, on arrangements that ensure the timely production and sharing of needed information." The drafters recognize that a territorial approach by supervisors predominates because of "the absence of a multinational framework for sharing fiscal burdens for [financial] crises or insolvencies" and "the fact that legal systems and the fiscal responsibility are national."

Key Attributes of Effective Resolution Regimes for Financial Institutions

Building on its earlier July 2011 report and in preparation for the G-20 Cannes Summit in November 2011, the FSB issued "Key Attributes of Effective Resolution Regimes for Financial Institutions," setting forth its minimum standard for a resolution regime applicable to global SIFIs.[61] The FSB's objective in issuing this new international standard is "to make feasible the resolution of financial institutions without severe systemic disruption and without exposing taxpayers to loss."[62] The key attributes are twelve essential features for a resolution regime. If a financial institution is systemically significant, it must be subject to a resolution regime. Each nation must designate a resolution

59. Basel Committee on Banking Supervision, Cross-Border Resolution Group (2010). See also Financial Stability Forum (2009).

60. For this and the following, see Basel Committee on Banking Supervision, Cross-Border Resolution Group (2010, pp. 1, 2, 19).

61. Financial Stability Board (2011a, 2011c). The leaders of the G-20 approved the key attributes at the November 2011 summit in Cannes. Group of Twenty (2011, para. 13).

62. For this and the following, see Financial Stability Board (2011b, pp. 3, 11, 13).

authority. If there are several possible authorities, the nation must designate a lead authority. The resolution authority must have operational independence and the ability to enter into agreements with resolution authorities from other jurisdictions. The resolution authority must have a broad range of powers, including the ability to replace senior management of the SIFI, to terminate contracts, to override shareholder rights, to transfer or sell assets, to create bridge banks, and to create an asset management vehicle. Any setoff or netting rights must be clear and transparent. The resolution regime must respect the hierarchy of creditors' claims with some flexibility on the part of the authority in order to contain the systemic impact of the resolution of the financial institution.

Creditors should have "a right to compensation where they do not receive at a minimum what they would have received in a liquidation of the firm." However, judicial action should not impede the implementation of the resolution. Creditors should seek compensation, rather than injunctive relief. Resolution should not rely on public ownership or public bailout funds. The resolution authority should have the ability to cooperate with resolution authorities from foreign jurisdictions, and the authority's statutory mandate should "strongly encourage the authority wherever possible to achieve a cooperative solution with foreign resolution authorities." National insolvency law should not discriminate against creditors based on their nationality. Home and key host authorities should maintain and participate in crisis management groups for each SIFI. Crisis management groups should enter into institution-specific cross-border cooperation agreements.[63]

The home resolution authority in cooperation with other members of the crisis management group should conduct regular resolvability assessments of the financial institution. "Robust and credible recovery and resolution plans" should be in place, with the home resolution authority leading the development of the resolution plan and updating the plan annually.[64] Finally, there should be no legal, administrative, or political impediments to exchanging information with foreign resolution authorities. The SIFI must maintain management information systems capable of producing needed financial information to supervisors on a timely basis.

"Key Attributes" offers an international standard for resolution regimes in the event of the failure of a SIFI.[65] This new standard reinforces the role of the home resolution authority and attempts to provide incentives for national authorities to cooperate in planning and conducting the resolution of a SIFI.

---

63. Financial Stability Board (2011b); annex I describes the essential elements of such an agreement.
64. Financial Stability Board (2011b, p. 16).
65. Financial Stability Board (2011d).

Recovery and Resolution Plans—"Living Wills" for Financial Institutions

Supervisors are requiring financial institutions to develop living wills as part of the planning for a financial crisis. In the United States, the Dodd-Frank Act requires systemically significant financial companies to report a plan "for rapid and orderly resolution in the event of material financial distress or failure."[66] U.S. regulators and Congress have thus adopted living wills as a tool to avoid bank failures. The Federal Reserve and the FDIC recently promulgated regulations stating the details that financial institutions must disclose in these plans.[67]

Financial conglomerates have hundreds—sometimes thousands—of subsidiaries, creating very complex institutions.[68] This complexity is a reflection of regulatory arbitrage, and any orderly wind-down is hampered by the "lack of international agreement on cross-border resolution."[69] Large financial institutions should have a wind-down plan that will assure their regulators and college of supervisors that the institutions can be wound down without unacceptable contagion effects. Such plans will "make the primary supervisor and the college of supervisors aware of what they need to do if a SIFI approaches bankruptcy."

An outstanding issue is whether regulators will require a financial institution to restructure its operations and related corporate entities in advance, to allow for a more orderly wind-down proceeding. In any event, regulators must have special resolution authority in order to avoid a last-minute government bailout. The resolution authority must support market discipline allowing for "wiping out shareholders, changing management, and paying off creditors (promptly) at estimated recovery cost (not at par)."

A living will is a recovery and resolution plan for a financial institution.[70] Typically the bank will draft the initial plan to be reviewed and challenged by the supervisors. The core supervisory college—the home supervisory and key host supervisors—typically conduct this review. The living will should cover all operations of the bank; therefore, there should be one plan rather than separate national plans. The development of living wills may lead to the simplification of complex legal structures of global financial institutions.

Living wills ideally should include a burden-sharing plan among the institution's supervisors. Each country's burden will be aligned to the benefit that the country would receive in the event of financial distress—that is, the economic

66. Dodd-Frank (2011). See also Zaring (2010).

67. "FDIC Adopts 'Living Wills' Regulations" (2011). Financial regulatory agencies in the United States have recently issued regulations regarding recovery and resolution plans that must be filed by banks operating in the United States.

68. For instance, Lehman Brothers had "a presence in some 50 countries and comprised almost 3000 legal entities before the crisis." Constancio (2011).

69. For this and the following, see Goldstein (2011, pp. 13, 14).

70. Avgouleas, Goodhart, and Schoenmaker (2010).

value of the "maintenance of financial stability."[71] The core supervisory college would prepare the burden-sharing agreement. Because each country would have a financial obligation pursuant to the burden-sharing agreement, "it has an incentive to make sure that supervision is properly done to minimize the possibility of failure." However, living wills will not be as effective as intended without a harmonized insolvency procedure for financial institutions across nations, which does not currently exist.

In assessing the current status of cross-border resolution recommendations, the Basel Committee notes that, overall, recent reforms show a "clear trend towards the introduction of special resolution regimes (SRRs) and tools aimed at 'public interest' objectives," though such reforms are being implemented by jurisdictions at a varied pace.[72] These reforms address the gap in national resolution regimes, which lack "certain essential powers, including the power to terminate unnecessary contracts, continue needed contracts, sell assets and transfer liabilities." The lack of these powers risks increasing the cost and difficulty of resolution.

Despite countries having implemented necessary domestic resolution changes, "uncertainty remains as regards the mechanisms and processes to implement and ensure recognition of resolution measures in a cross-border context." A small number of jurisdictions have "cross-border agreements that specifically deal with cooperation and coordination in managing and resolving a financial crisis." These agreements generally consist of bilateral or multilateral memoranda of understanding that promote heightened cooperation; however, they are usually nonbinding and are not institution-specific.

Conclusion

Before analyzing each of the three reforms discussed, it should be pointed out that there are limitations on the ability of emerging markets to implement any reform of, or change in, financial regulation and supervision. Before the November 2010 G-20 summit in Seoul, the Republic of Korea and the FSB held a conference highlighting the concerns of emerging markets with the ongoing financial system reforms.[73] Speakers at this conference noted that emerging markets are particularly vulnerable to external shocks to their economy, are susceptible to changes in capital inflows and outflows during times of crisis, and have few tools to smooth out the flow of capital.[74] Asian markets learned this lesson during the 1997–98 financial crisis.

---

71. For this and the following, see Avgouleas, Goodhart, and Schoenmaker (2010, pp. 6, 8).

72. For this and the following, see Basel Committee on Banking Supervision (2011b, pp. 2, 4).

73. Korea-FSB Financial Reform Conference (2010).

74. Emerging market financial systems were designed to mobilize domestic savings to foster economic growth and with no conception of a future global, interconnected financial market. Sheng (2009).

Emerging markets generally lack the supervisory capacity to implement many of the proposed reforms. Existing supervisors in emerging markets generally are few in number, lack sufficient resources, and lack the supervisory knowledge and experience comparable to that available in developed nations. For any reforms to be effectively implemented, additional training and resources must be devoted to the emerging market's supervisory capacity.

Emerging markets are at different stages of development; this fact is rarely acknowledged in reform proposals. Many potential customers in emerging markets are outside of the formal banking sector. For instance, in Kenya only 23 percent of customers participated in the formal banking sector in 2009. The banking sector in emerging markets tends to be a large share of the credit market generally, as opposed to the securities markets, which tend to be less important and less sophisticated. Customer behavior and the structure of the banking system can differ significantly from those in the developed countries. Because of the significant differences in the development of emerging markets and industrialized nations, proposed reforms should allow for the exercise of national discretion by emerging markets and for a phase-in of these reforms, depending on the level of development of the emerging market.

Basel III—Implications for Emerging Markets

A general concern with the Basel Committee has been the dominance of supervisors from the Western developed world in the creation of its standards. Historically, the membership of the Basel Committee has been relatively small and closed, consisting of supervisors from certain OECD member countries.[75] During the development of the Basel III proposal, the membership of the committee doubled, to twenty-seven member nations, with the intent of aligning its membership with that of the G-20, which includes the larger emerging markets.[76] Despite this increase in membership, there is a concern that Basel III represents the interests of banks in the developed world more so than those in emerging markets.

Few emerging market banks are global SIFIs, and therefore few are subject to the additional loss absorbency capital requirement and other reforms focused on SIFIs. In the FSB's recent list of systemically important financial institutions, only one financial institution headquartered in an emerging market was included—the Bank of China. Furthermore, emerging market supervisors have typically required higher levels of capital in the banks they supervise than those required under Basel III. Therefore, the initial effect of Basel III on emerging market banks will likely be moderate.

75. The Organization for Economic Cooperation and Development is based in Paris and its membership consists principally of developed nations. Members of the OECD are listed at www.oecd.org.

76. Rehm (2011). Emerging market members of the Basel Committee include China, Turkey, South Africa, Brazil, and India.

However, the world economy is dynamic; in the near future, no doubt some emerging market banks will grow and become global SIFIs. According to a recent analysis, emerging markets represent 54 percent of world GDP, 50 percent of world trade, and approximately 25 percent of financial assets.[77] Recent trends indicate that emerging markets will continue to gain an increasing share of all three measures. In addition, global banks have significant operations in emerging markets. For example, the Spanish bank Santander operates in numerous countries in Europe and Central and South America, and approximately 44 percent of its earnings come from emerging markets.[78] Similarly, HSBC operates around the globe, with nearly half of its earnings generated in emerging markets.[79] While Basel III may have little immediate effect on banks headquartered in emerging markets, the higher capital requirements will affect global banks that can dominate the banking system of certain emerging markets. In order to fund the higher capital requirement, the parent company may charge higher interest rates for credit in all its operations, wherever located. Host jurisdictions, often emerging markets, will benefit little from this higher level of capital held by the parent bank, although host operations may have funded a portion of this capital through higher interest rates charged to borrowers.

Emerging markets may suffer the indirect economic effect of decreased capital inflows resulting from Basel III. Under Basel III, SIFIs will hold a higher level of capital and may limit their investments in smaller financial markets, which for now tend to be emerging markets. Thus emerging market supervisors have focused on and should monitor the implementation of Basel III and the additional loss absorbency capital for global SIFIs. If present economic growth trends continue, some of their supervised banks will relatively soon become global SIFIs and, therefore, subject to more intense supervision.

Supervisory Colleges—Implications for Emerging Markets

Similar to Basel III, international efforts to establish supervisory colleges have also focused on global SIFIs. Within a supervisory college, the home supervisor generally takes the lead in college activities. The host supervisor within a college has a limited role, particularly where foreign banks operate in their jurisdiction through a branch rather than as a subsidiary.

Supervisory colleges as currently envisioned "endorse the leadership of the home-country regulator" and do not address conflicts between the home and host regulator.[80] Home-country supervisors are frequently based in developed

---

77. "Why the Tail Wags the Dog," *The Economist,* August 6, 2011.
78. Santander (2011).
79. HSBC (2011).
80. Erik Berglof and Katharina Pistor, "European Financial Regulation's Wrong Turn," *New Times,* September 29, 2009.

nations and may have little understanding of emerging markets. Because global bank operations in emerging markets tend to be relatively small, supervisors from emerging markets are likely not included in the core college, consisting of the supervisors from the jurisdiction where the SIFIs' most significant operations are located. Rather, supervisors from emerging markets are typically relegated to the general college.

Home-country control is the core principle of international supervisory cooperation.[81] The EU reinforces this principle with the use of the EU passport for banks, allowing a bank licensed in one EU jurisdiction to operate as a branch throughout the EU. This system of home-country rule assumes that most financial risk would emerge from a host jurisdiction and be transferred to home jurisdictions. The assumption is that host jurisdictions are typically emerging markets and that home jurisdictions are developed nations. Most of the financial institution's activities are centered in the home jurisdiction, namely, a developed economy. In interconnected global financial markets, these historical assumptions no longer hold. The 2007–08 financial crisis illustrates how the risk of contagion can come from any jurisdiction in an interdependent world.

Host countries in which foreign-owned banks control the banking system have little leverage over home supervisors supervising those banks. For example, in Eastern Europe, large, foreign-owned banks control a significant share (over 45 percent) of the banking assets in Slovenia, Poland, and Estonia, among others. The host jurisdiction may represent a small portion of the global bank's activities, and the home supervisor is less concerned with the host's portion of the global bank's operations, because a failure there would likely have a minor effect on the institution as a whole. The home supervisor is focused on the global bank as an entity and encourages diversification within the bank to minimize the risk of failure. The host supervisor is primarily concerned with the stability of the financial system in the host jurisdiction and how the bank licensed in the home jurisdiction could affect that stability.

The host supervisor lacks information on the entire operation of the bank, while the home supervisor lacks information on or understanding of the impact that a failure of the bank will have in the host jurisdiction. The home supervisor has little incentive to change its behavior, as it does not bear the costs of failure within the host jurisdiction. In the past, the costs incurred in a host jurisdiction were typically borne by a multilateral financial institution, such as the International Monetary Fund, which places conditions on the host jurisdiction in exchange for financial assistance.

Incentives for supervisors to share information are weak. A key challenge arising in the operation of supervisory colleges is the legal constraint on sharing

81. Pistor (2010).

confidential information about financial institutions among the supervisors. Thus far, statements regarding cooperation among supervisors, including sharing information, during a financial crisis are not enforceable. During a crisis, supervisory cooperation deteriorates quickly because of "the complex distribution of tasks between home and host-country authorities, the lack of *ex ante* burden-sharing agreements, and the limited power of host authorities to protect markets."[82] Full cooperation among supervisors will be hindered because of the absence of a cross-border insolvency procedure for financial institutions. Since an orderly way to resolve claims against a cross-border financial institution does not currently exist, supervisors necessarily focus on protecting their national interests—the rights of residents within their jurisdiction who may have claims against a failing financial institution.

This effort to create supervisory colleges has not yet extended to regional SIFIs. As regional banks grow in size, regional supervisory colleges should be established similar to those in the EU and for global SIFIs. As financial institutions become more active regionally, colleges should be "developed in a parallel fashion."[83]

Supervisory colleges are strengthened when members have similar legal powers and are independent of political influence. Often, this is not the case. Recognizing that both supervisory intensity and supervisory effectiveness were lacking during the financial crisis, the FSB in the fall of 2010 recommended strengthening supervision and revising the Basel "Core Principles for Effective Banking Supervision."[84] Supervisors must have adequate resources, an appropriate mandate, and true independence. Approximately one-third of the 130 nations reviewed under the IMF–World Bank Financial Sector Assessment Program do not have a truly independent bank supervisor. Similarly, resources devoted to bank supervision vary by country: the number of supervisors assigned to a SIFI range from fourteen officials per SIFI in one country to over a hundred supervisory officials per SIFI in another.

Because host supervisors generally have little influence within a college, supervisors from emerging markets with similar interests may want to combine efforts to influence a supervisory college. Countries at similar stages of economic development and with similar policy interests—such as vulnerability to capital flows—may wish to combine efforts and speak with one voice in a particular college to influence outcomes regarding a financial institution. Of course, such combining is easier said than done, as national interests and policies come into play. Home supervisors typically call college meetings and invite attendees, so emerging market supervisors may first need to combine their efforts to ensure

82. Financial Stability Board (2011d).

83. Arner and Park (2010, p. 12).

84. Financial Stability Board (2010). In December 2011 the Basel Committee issued a revised version of the core principles. See Basel Committee on Banking Supervision (2011a).

they are included in the core college. Once they have secured a presence or a representative voice in the core college, emerging market supervisors can then raise their concerns regarding the effect of global SIFIs on the financial stability in their jurisdictions.

Resolution Regimes—Implications for Emerging Markets

Unlike Basel III and the development of supervisory colleges, there has been little discussion of the effect on emerging markets of the third reform discussed—resolution regime proposals. Such proposals discussing the resolution of cross-border financial institutions typically include two components: the recovery of the financial institution and the resolution, or winding down, of the institution. In a recovery plan whose goal is to maintain the bank (or at least a portion of it) as a going concern, the smaller operations of a global bank, typically those in an emerging market, may be wound down first. The bank operations in the emerging market may be significant to that market but would be small in comparison to the bank's global operations. In an effort to save the bank as a going concern, smaller operations may be closed first, or capital support from the parent company to smaller operations may be withheld.

The home supervisor and the related college of supervisors typically approve the resolution plan for a global bank. As seen in the discussion of supervisory colleges, host supervisors tend to have little leverage over the home supervisor or within the college. As a result, the host supervisor, frequently from emerging markets, will likely have little influence on the contents of the resolution plan.

The resolution regime proposals thus far tend to encourage banks to operate as subsidiaries in foreign markets. Because global cooperation is in practice difficult, some nations have insisted on more local self-sufficiency of bank operations within their borders, by requiring the creation of subsidiary structures for national operations. For instance, Malaysia requires foreign banks to operate as subsidiaries within its borders. While the subsidiary structure may have the added benefit of facilitating the resolution of cross-border banks, this structure may be costly for some banks, as it will prevent the use of certain business models and may require higher levels of capital and liquidity than an integrated bank would need. While operating as a subsidiary allows for separate capitalization and for the ring-fencing of assets in the event of financial distress, the subsidiary structure may not be economically efficient. Over the long term, the subsidiary structure may discourage operations in emerging markets, because the parent corporation may not wish to commit this level of capital to emerging markets and hinder the transfer of capital within the parent's global operations.

A new concordat between home and host countries with respect to crisis management is needed.[85] Supplanting the Basel Concordat that focused on

---

85. Claessens, Herring, and Schoenmaker (2010, p. 99).

home-host supervisory coordination, this new concordat would set standards allowing for the resolution of cross-border banks. Under the new concordat, financial institutions would be able to enter a market only if effective resolution arrangements existed in both the home and host countries. "Key Attributes," issued by the FSB, may be the beginning of this new concordat.

Until a resolution regime for cross-border financial institutions is effectively implemented, national governments are unlikely to relinquish their sovereignty over the resolution of claims against an insolvent financial institution. As seen in the creation of the European Banking Authority, the United Kingdom insisted on placing a brake on EBA decisions because of the possibility of a member state expending national government funds to comply with an EU decision, counter to the member state's own public policy choice. While colleges of supervisors may improve the surveillance function over cross-border financial institutions by improving the flow of prudential information, truly full supervisory cooperation will not occur until a credible, international regime for the resolution of financial institutions is designed and implemented.

Appendixes

Appendix 10A. *Twenty-Nine Systemically Important Financial Institutions Subject to Additional Loss-Absorbency Capital*

Bank of America	JPMorgan Chase
Bank of China	Lloyds Banking Group
Bank of New York Mellon	Mitsubishi UFJ FG
Banque Populaire CdE	Mizuho FG
Barclays	Morgan Stanley
BNP Paribas	Nordea
Citigroup	Royal Bank of Scotland
Commerzbank	Santander
Credit Suisse	Société Générale
Deutsche Bank	State Street
Dexia	Sumitomo Mitsui FG
Goldman Sachs	UBS
Group Crédit Agricole	Unicredit Group
HSBC	Wells Fargo
ING Bank	

Source: Financial Stability Board (2011b).

Appendix 10B. *International Bank Resolution Framework Documents, 2001–11*

Directive 2001/24/EC on the Reorganization and Winding Up of Credit Institutions	April 2001
FSF Principles for Cross-Border Cooperation on Crisis Management	April 2009
Report and Recommendations of the Cross-Border Bank Resolution Group, issued by the Basel Committee	September 2009
An EU Framework for Cross-Border Crisis Management in the Banking Sector	October 2009
An EU Framework for Crisis Management in the Financial Sector	October 2010
Technical Details of a Possible EU Framework for Bank Recovery and Resolution	January 2011
Financial Stability Board, Effective Resolution of Systemically Important Financial Institutions	July 2011
Financial Stability Board, Key Attributes of Effective Resolution Regimes for Financial Institutions	November 2011

Appendix 10C. *European Union, Financial Supervision Legal Framework, 2008–11*

October 29, 2008	Barroso appoints Larosière group	José Barroso, "From Financial Crisis to Recovery: A European Framework for Action," speech, Extraordinary Commission, October 29, 2008, Brussels (http://europa.eu/rapid/pressReleases Action.do?reference=SPEECH/08/566&format =HTML&aged=)
February 25, 2008	Larosière Report is published	Jacques Larosière and others, "The High-Level Group on Financial Supervision in the EU" (http://ec.europa.eu/internal_market/finances/docs/de_larosiere_report_en.pdf)
March 4, 2009	European Commission issues a document based on the Larosière Report	Communication from the European Commission for the Spring European Council: Driving European Recovery (http://eur-lex.europa.eu/LexUriServ/LexUriServ.do?uri=COM:2009:0114:FIN:EN:PDF)
June 19, 2009	European Council approves the European System of Financial Supervisors and the Economic and Social Research Council	Brussels European Council document: Presidency Conclusions (www.consilium.europa.eu/ueDocs/cms_Data/docs/pressdata/en/ec/108622.pdf)
September 16, 2009	European Union publishes amendments to capital requirements directive	From the *Official Journal of the European Union:* Directive 2009/111/EC of the European Parliament and of the Council (http://eur-lex.europa.eu/LexUriServ/LexUriServ.do?uri=OJ:L:2009:302:0097:0119:EN:PDF)

(continued)

Appendix 10C. *European Union, Financial Supervision Legal Framework, 2008–11 (continued)*

September 23, 2009	European Commission proposes regulations creating three European supervisory authorities	Communications from the European Commission: proposal for a regulation of the European Parliament and of the Council establishing a European banking authority; proposal for a regulation of the European Parliament and of the Council establishing a European insurance and occupational pensions authority (http://eur-lex.europa.eu/LexUriServ/LexUriServ.do?uri=COM:2009:0502:FIN:EN:PDF); proposal for regulation of the European Parliament and of the Council establishing a European securities and markets authority (http://eur-lex.europa.eu/LexUriServ/LexUriServ.do?uri=OJ:L:2009:151:0019:0021:EN:PDF)
November 2010	EU regulations create the three European supervisory authorities	From the *Official Journal of the European Union:* Regulation 1093/2010 establishing the European banking authority regulation (http://eur-lex.europa.eu/LexUriServ/LexUriServ.do?uri=OJ:L:2010:331:0012:0047:EN:PDF); Regulation 1094/2010 establishing the European insurance and occupation pension supervisory authority (http://eur-lex.europa.eu/LexUriServ/LexUriServ.do?uri=OJ:L:2010:331:0048:0083:EN:PDF); Regulation 1095/2010 establishing the European securities and markets authority (http://eur-lex.europa.eu/LexUriServ/LexUriServ.do?uri=OJ:L:2010:331:0084:0119:EN:PDF)
November 2010	EU regulation creates a new macroprudential supervisory framework	From the *Official Journal of the European Union:* Regulation 1092/2010 on European Union macroprudential oversight of the financial crisis and establishing a European systemic risk board (http://eur-lex.europa.eu/LexUriServ/LexUriServ.do?uri=OJ:L:2010:331:0001:0011:EN:PDF)
July 2011	European Commission proposes a directive and a regulation regarding capital requirements (Basel III)	Communications from the European Commission: proposal for a directive on access to the activity of credit institutions and the prudential supervision of credit institutions and investment firms and amending Directive 2002/87/EC of the European Parliament and of the Council on the supplementary supervision of credit institutions, insurance undertakings, and investment firms in a financial conglomerate (http://eur-lex.europa.eu/LexUriServ/LexUriServ.do?uri=COM:2011:0453:FIN:EN:PDF); proposal for a regulation on prudential requirements for credit institutions and insurance firms (http://eur-lex.europa.eu/LexUriServ/LexUriServ.do?uri=COM:2011:0452:FIN:EN:PDF)

Appendix 10D. *European Union, Significant Laws Governing Financial Institutions*

Directive 2001/24/EC of the European Parliament and of the Council of 4 April 2001 on the Reorganization and Winding Up of Credit Institutions (http://eur-lex.europa.eu/ LexUriServ/LexUriServ.do?uri=OJ:L:2001:125:0015:0023:EN:PDF0)

Directive 2006/48/EC of the European Parliament and of the Council relating to the taking up and pursuit of the business of credit institutions, art. 125–32 (http://eur-lex.europa.eu/ LexUriServ/LexUriServ.do?uri=OJ:L:2006:177:0001:0001:EN:PDF)

Directive 2006/49/EC of the European Parliament and of the Council of 14 June 2006 on the capital adequacy of investment firms and credit institutions (http://eur-lex.europa.eu/ LexUriServ/LexUriServ.do?uri=OJ:L:2006:177:0201:01:EN:HTML)

Directive 2009/111/EC of the European Parliament and of the Council of 16 September 2009 amending Directives 2006/48/EC, 2006/49/EC and 2007/64/EC as regards banks affiliated to central institutions, certain own funds items, large exposures, supervisory arrangements, and crisis management (http://eur-lex.europa.eu/LexUriServ/LexUriServ. do?uri=OJ:L:2009:302:0097:01:EN:HTML)

Regulation (EU) 1092/2010 of the European Parliament and of the Council of 24 November 2010, Establishing a European Systemic Risk Board (http://eur-lex.europa.eu/LexUriServ/ LexUriServ.do?uri=OJ:L:2010:331:0001:0011:EN:PDF)

Regulation (EU) 1093/2010 of the European Parliament and of the Council of 24 November 2010, Establishing a European Supervisory Authority (European Banking Authority), Amending Decision 716/2009/EC and repealing Commission Decision 2009/78/EC (http://eur-lex.europa.eu/LexUriServ/LexUriServ.do?uri=OJ:L:2010:331:0012:0047:EN: PDF)

Regulation (EU) 1094/2010 of the European Parliament and of the Council of 24 November 2010, Establishing a European Supervisory Authority (European Insurance and Occupational Pensions Authority) (http://eur-lex.europa.eu/LexUriServ/LexUriServ.do?ur i=OJ:L:2010:331:0048:0083:EN:PDF)

Regulation (EU) 1095/2010 of the European Parliament and of the Council of 24 November 2010, Establishing a European Supervisory Authority (European Securities and Markets Authority) (http://eur-lex.europa.eu/LexUriServ/LexUriServ.do?uri=OJ:L:2010:3 31:0084:0119:EN:PDF)

References

Alford, Duncan. 1992. "1992 Basle Committee Minimum Standards: International Regulatory Response to the Failure of BCCI." *George Washington Journal of International Law and Economics* 241: 26.

———. 2006. "The Lamfalussy Process and EU Bank Regulation: Another Step on the Road to Pan-European Regulation?" *Annual Review of Banking and Financial Law* 389: 25.

Arner, Douglas W., and Cyn-Young Park. 2010. "Global Financial Regulatory Reforms: Implications for Developing Asia." Working Paper 57. Manila: Asian Development Bank (http://aric.adb.org/pdf/workingpaper/Arner_Park_2010_Global_Financial_Regulatory_ Reforms.pdf).

Avgouleas, Emilion, Charles Goodhart, and Dirk Schoenmaker. 2010. "Living Wills as a Catalyst for Action" (http://fic.wharton.upenn.edu/fic/papers/10/10-09.pdf).

Basel Committee on Banking Supervision. 2010a. "Good Practice Principles on Supervisory Colleges" (www.bis.org/publ/bcbs170.pdf).

————. 2010b. "Quantitative Impact Study" (www.bis.org/publ/bcbs186.htm).

————. 2010/2011. "Basel III: A Global Regulatory Framework for More Resilient Banks and Banking Systems" (www.bis.org/publ/bcbs189.htm).

————. 2011a. "Core Principles for Effective Banking Supervision: Consultative Document."

————. 2011b. "Resolution Policies and Frameworks: Progress So Far." Executive Summary.

Basel Committee on Banking Supervision, Cross-Border Resolution Group. 2010. "Report and Recommendations" (www.bis.org/publ/bcbs169.pdf).

Bray, Michael. 2011. "Financial Regulatory Reform: Avoiding the Trap of Overregulating Banks" (www.cliffordchance.com).

Claessens, Stijn, Richard J. Herring, and Dirk Schoenmaker. 2010. "A Safer World Financial System: Improving the Resolution of Systemic Institutions." Geneva Report on the World Economy 12. Brookings.

Committee of European Banking Supervisors. 2009. Commission decision of January 23, 2009 establishing the Committee of European Bank Supervisors. O.J. (L 25) 23, para. 12.

————. 2010. Annual Report (http://eba.europa.eu/Publications/Other-Publications/Annual-Report.aspx).

Committee of European Banking Supervisors/Committee of European Insurance and Occupational Pension Supervisors. 2009. "College of Supervisors—10 Common Principles." CEBS 2008 124 (www.c-ebs.org/getdoc/aeecaf1a-81b5-476a-95dd-599c5e967697/Clean-V3-formatted-CEBS-2008-124-CEIOPS-SEC-08-54-.aspx).

Constancio, Vitor. 2011. "A European Solution for Crisis Management and Bank Resolution" (www.bis.org/review/r111117c.pdf).

Dodd-Frank. 2011. Wall Street Reform and Consumer Protection Act. 12 U.S.C. § 5325(d)(1).

European Commission. 2009. Communication from the Commission to the European Parliament, the Council, the European Economic and Social Committee, the European Court of Justice and the European Central Bank. "An EU Framework for Cross-Border Crisis Management in the Banking Sector" (http://eur-lex.europa.eu/LexUriServ/LexUriServ.do?uri=COM:2009:0561:FIN:EN:PDF).

————. 2010. "Communication from the Commission to the European Parliament, the Council, the European Economic and Social Committee, the Committee of the Regions and the European Central Bank: An EU Framework for Crisis Management in the Financial Sector" (http://ec.europa.eu/internal_market/bank/docs/crisis-management/framework/com2010_579_en.pdf).

————. 2011. DG Internal Market and Services. "Technical Details of a Possible EU Framework for Bank Recovery and Resolution."

European Union. 2010. Preamble to the Treaty on the European Union. O.J. (C 83) 3, 15.

"FDIC Adopts 'Living Wills' Regulations." 2011. CCH Federal Banking Law Reports 2435 (September 15). 12 C.F.R. pt. 243 (2012); 12 C.F.R. pt. 381 (2012).

Financial Services Authority. 2009. "Turner Review: A Regulatory Response to the Global Banking Crisis" (www.fsa.gov.uk/pubs/other/turner_review.pdf).

Financial Stability Board. 2010. "Intensity and Effectiveness of SIFI Supervision" (www.financialstabilityboard.org/publications/r_101101.pdf).

————. 2011a. "Effective Resolution of Systemically Important Financial Institutions" (www.financialstabilityboard.org/publications/r_110719.pdf).

————. 2011b. "FSB Announces Policy Measures to Address Systemically Important Financial Institutions (SIFIs) and Names Initial Group of Global SIFIs" (www.financialstabilityboard.org/press/pr_111104cc.pdf).

————. 2011c. "Key Attributes of Effective Resolution Regimes for Financial Institutions."

————. 2011d. "Overview of Progress in the Implementation of the G20 Recommendation for Strengthening Financial Stability" (www.financialstabilityboard.org/publications/r_111104gg.pdf).

————. 2011e. "Progress in the Implementation of the G-20 Recommendations for Strengthening Financial Stability."

Financial Stability Forum. 2009. "FSF Principles for Cross-Border Cooperation on Crisis Management" (www.financialstabilityboard.org/publications/r_0904c.pdf).

Goldstein, Morris. 2011. "Integrating Reform of Financial Regulation with Reform of the International Monetary System." Washington: Peterson Institute for International Economics (www.iie.com/publications/wp/wp11-5.pdf).

Goodhart, Charles, and Dirk Schoenmaker. 2009. "The de Larosiere Report: Two Down, Two to Go." Financial Times Forum, March 13 (http://blogs.ft.com/economistsforum/2009/03/the-de-larosiere-report-two-down-two-to-go/#axzz1yjbDGYw9).

Group of Thirty. 2008. "The Structure of Financial Supervision: Approaches and Challenges in a Global Marketplace 48" (www.deloitte.com/assets/Dcom-UnitedStates/Local%20Assets/Documents/us_fsi_banking_G30%20Final%20Report%2010-3-08.pdf).

————. 2009. "Financial Reform: A Framework for Financial Stability" (www.group30.org).

Group of Twenty. 2008. "Declaration Summit on Financial Markets and the World Economy."

————. 2009a. "Declaration on Strengthening the Financial System." London Summit.

————. 2009b. "Leaders' Statement, Preamble." Pittsburgh Summit.

————. 2010a. "Leaders' Declaration." Seoul Summit. November 11.

————. 2010b. "Toronto Summit Declaration." June 26.

————. 2010c. "What Is the G-20?" (www.g20.org).

————. 2011. Leaders' summit. "Final Communiqué."

High-Level Expert Group. 2008. "High-Level Expert Group on EU Financial Supervision to Hold First Meeting on 12 November." Press release 1P/08/1679 (http://europa.eu/rapid/pressReleasesAction.do?reference=IP/08/1679&format=HTML&aged=0&language=EN&guiLanguage=en).

HSBC. 2011. "First Half 2011 Interim Results." New York.

International Institute of Finance. 2011. "The Cumulative Impact on the Global Economy of Changes in the Financial Regulatory Framework."

International Monetary Fund. 2009. "Initial Lessons of the Crisis for the Global Architecture and the IMF" (www.imf.org/external/np/pp/eng/2009/021809.pdf).

Korea-FSB Financial Reform Conference. 2010. "An Emerging Market Perspective" (www.g20.org/Documents2010/09/Korea-FSB%20Financial%20Reform%20Conference%20booklet.pdf).

Larosière, Jacques, and others. 2009. "The High-Level Group on Financial Supervision in the EU" (http://ec.europa.eu/internal_market/finances/docs/de_larosiere_report_en.pdf).

Masciandoro, Donato, Maria J. Neito, and Marc Quintyn. 2011. "The European Banking Authority: Are Its Governance Arrangements Consistent with Its Objectives." Vox, February 7.

McCarthy, Callum. 2004. "How Should International Financial Service Companies Be Regulated?" (www.fsa.gov.uk/Pages/Library/Communication/Speeches/2004/SP196.shtml).

Morrison & Foerster. 2010. "Basel III: The (Nearly) Full Picture." San Francisco (www.mofo.com/files/Uploads/Images/101223-Basel-III-The-Nearly-Full-Picture.pdf).

————. 2011. "Defining Global Systemically Important Banks and Additional Loss Absorbency Requirements." San Francisco.

Pan, Eric. 2010. "Four Challenges to Financial Regulatory Reform." *Villanova Law Review* 55: 771.

Pistor, Katharina. 2010. "Host's Dilemma: Rethinking EU Banking Regulation in Light of the Global Crisis." Working Paper 286/2010. European Corporate Governance Institute.

Rehm, Barbara A. 2011. "Basel III Point Man Answers Critics of the Capital Rules." *American Banker* 176, no. 170.

Santander. 2011. "2011 Financial Report, First Half."

Shadow Financial Regulatory Committee. 2011. "Statement 207." February 14.

Sheng, Andrew. 2009. *From Asian to Global Financial Crisis: An Asian Regulator's View of Unfettered Finance in the 1990s and 2000s 360.* Cambridge University Press.

Van Rompuy, Herman. 2011. "Reshaping Europe's Economy: The Role of the Financial Sector." February 9 (www.consilium.europa.eu/uedocs/cms_data/docs/pressdata/en/ec/119231.pdf).

Zaring, David. 2010. "A Lack of Resolution." *Emory Law Journal* 60.

Contributors

VIRAL V. ACHARYA
C. V. Starr Professor of Economics,
Department of Finance, New York
University Stern School of Business

DUNCAN ALFORD
Associate Dean, Director of the
Law Library, and Professor of Law,
University of South Carolina
School of Law

FRANCISCO CEBALLOS
Research Analyst, International
Food Policy Research Institute

TATIANA DIDIER
Research Economist, Office of the
Chief Economist for Latin America
and the Caribbean, World Bank

SUBIR GOKARN
Deputy Governor, Reserve Bank
of India

MASAHIRO KAWAI
Dean and CEO, Asian
Development Bank Institute

KIYOHIKO G. NISHIMURA
Deputy Governor, Bank of Japan

CYN-YOUNG PARK
Assistant Chief Economist and
Director of the Economic Analysis
and Operations Support Division in
the Economics Research Department,
Asian Development Bank

ESWAR S. PRASAD
Nandlal P. Tolani Senior Professor
of Trade Policy and Professor of Eco-
nomics, Cornell University;
Senior Fellow and New Century
Chair in International Economics,
Brookings Institution

SERGIO L. SCHMUKLER
Lead Economist, Development
Research Group, World Bank

YOSHINORI SHIMIZU
Professor Emeritus and Senior
Research Professor, Graduate School
of Commerce and Management,
Hitotsubashi University

TARISA WATANAGASE
Former Governor, Bank of Thailand

MEHMET YÖRÜKOĞLU
Deputy Governor, Central Bank
of the Republic of Turkey

Index

ABMI (Asian Bond Market Initiative), 102, 103
Accounting standards, 103, 246
Acharya, Viral V., 13
Advanced economies, 191–221; bond markets in, 124, 130; debt markets in, 119; financial diversification in, 112, 117; financial offshoring in, 113; financial sector growth in, 80, 81; and global financial crisis, 141, 145, 146, 158, 167, 192; and growth and inflation differentials compared with emerging economies, 207–18; and new goods' bias, 209–12; nonbank financial companies in, 97. *See also specific countries*
AEMs. *See* Asian emerging markets
Alford, Duncan, 8
Arbitrage, 15, 28–29, 40, 42, 48, 67
ASEAN+3 Economic Review and Policy Dialogue, 9, 101, 103, 104
ASEAN+ Macroeconomic Research Office (AMRO), 102, 104
Ashikaga Bank (Japan), 59, 60
Asian Bond Fund Initiative, 102

Asian Bond Market Initiative (ABMI), 102, 103
Asian emerging markets (AEMs), 77–109, 225–43; access to banking systems in, 82, 83, 85–86; achieving global balance in, 85–88; balancing regulation and innovation in, 106–07; banking soundness indicators in, 80; and Basel III standards, 227–37; bond markets in, 99–100, 103, 124–28, 129, 130; capital markets in, 102–03; challenges for, 234–37; composition and size of, 80–82, 90–96, 100, 101; demographic data in, 176, 177; diversity and stability in, 88–89, 92–93, 97, 99–104; economic growth and development in, 105–06; financial crisis in (1997–98), 79, 82, 101; financial diversification in, 117, 118; financial sector growth in, 68, 69, 79–85; and global financial crisis, 79, 107, 175, 227; overview, 77–79, 225, 227; pension systems in, 97–98; policy recommendations and implications for, 104–07, 237–42; promoting

Asian Development Bank Institute

The Asian Development Bank Institute is a subsidiary of ADB that functions as its think tank and focuses on knowledge creation and information dissemination for development in the Asia and Pacific region. Based in Tokyo, it helps ADB's developing member economies build knowledge, capacity, and skills to reduce poverty and support other areas that contribute to long-term growth and competitiveness in the region. This is done through policy-oriented research, seminars and workshops designed to disseminate thinking about best practices, and a range of other capacity building and training initiatives.

Brookings Institution

The Brookings Institution is a private nonprofit organization devoted to research, education, and publication on important issues of domestic and foreign policy. Its principal purpose is to bring the highest quality independent research and analysis to bear on current and emerging policy problems. The Institution was founded on December 8, 1927, to merge the activities of the Institute for Government Research, founded in 1916, the Institute of Economics, founded in 1922, and the Robert Brookings Graduate School of Economics and Government, founded in 1924. Interpretations or conclusions in Brookings publications should be understood to be solely those of the authors.